UNION VOICES

SUNY Series in the Anthropology of Work
June C. Nash, Editor

UNION VOICES

LABOR'S RESPONSES TO CRISIS

Edited by
Glenn Adler
and
Doris Suarez

State University of New York Press

331.880973
U582

Published by
State University of New York Press, Albany

For information, address State University of New York
Press, State University Plaza, Albany, N.Y. 12246

Production by Diane Ganeles
Marketing by Fran Keneston

Library of Congress Cataloging-in-Publication Data

Union voices : labor's responses to crisis / edited by Glenn Adler and
    Doris Suarez.
        p.   cm. — (SUNY series in the anthropology of work)
    Includes index.
    ISBN 0-7914-1247-4. — ISBN 0-7914-1248-2 (pbk.)
    1. Trade-unions—United States. I. Adler, Glenn, 1958–   .
II. Suarez, Doris, 1960–   . III. Series.
HD6508.U43   1993
331.88'0973—dc20   91-38444
                                                              CIP

10 9 8 7 6 5 4 3 2 1

TP

Contents

Foreword

The Center for Labor-Management Policy Studies of the City University of New York Graduate School and University Center was established in early 1988 at a critical juncture in the history of labor and management relations. Organized labor in the United States has entered a new era of economic constraints and political uncertainties unrivaled in its history. Immense problems face an increasingly globalized domestic economy with labor beset by the climate of doubt these changes engender.

These changes include the rapid deterioration of American economic superiority; the crippling effects in some industries of foreign competition fueled by the migration abroad of manufacturing; a climate of deregulation that has been pushed to extremes; a service economy that has exploded on the American scene; and unprecedented growth of two-wage earner families and a record proportion of women in the labor force.

These shifts and changes call for fresh ideas, new definitions, and new models and paradigms. To meet this challenge the Center sponsors the Samuel Gompers Union Leadership Awards. This yearly grant program is designed to assist union officers, staff members and rank-and-file workers in the development of new approaches for labor unions. The unionists whose research is included in this volume originally presented their work at all-day conferences in October 1989 and 1990.

Victor Gotbaum

Acknowledgments

The editors are grateful to Victor Gotbaum for his support and for having the insight to establish the Samuel Gompers Leadership Award Program. We also wish to acknowledge James Parrott, Assistant to the President, International Ladies' Garment Workers' Union, who put forward the idea which stimulated the Gompers Program. The student fellows and staff at the Center for Labor-Management Policy Studies, Patricia Belcon, Stavros Gavroglou, Richard Greenwald, Michael Kapsa, Seung-kyung Kim, Jonathan Kranz, Steve Sleigh, Fabian Steinberg, Saki Miyashiro, Kay Powell, and Sumner Rosen gave us encouragement and valuable comments.

We also wish to thank Professor June C. Nash who backed the manuscript and brought it before SUNY Press. Without her efforts the book would not have been published. It is indeed an honor for the volume to be published in her *Anthropology of Work* series.

Doris Suarez wishes to express gratitude to her parents and sister, Debra, for their lifelong confidence and encouragement. Most importantly, she thanks her parents for their intellectual direction and far-reaching insight. Thanks also to Ben for his inspiration and help in this undertaking.

Glenn Adler wishes to thank René Matthews for her patience and fortitude which helped him in this, as in so many other projects, and for her unfailing wisdom and keen editorial judgment.

The book is dedicated to Richard Styskal, former Deputy Director of the Center and Professor of Political Science at the Graduate School of the City University of New York, who was tragically killed in an automobile accident in August 1990. Richard Styskal, together with Victor Gotbaum, built the Center into an active, productive forum for labor studies, and was instrumental in setting up the Gompers Program. He enthusiastically promoted our efforts in this project. Above all, he was an involved mentor to the fellows at the Center, giving us intellectual guidance and friendship.

Introduction: Union Voices

Glenn Adler and Doris Suarez

I. Introduction

The American labor movement faces serious challenges in the decade ahead which threaten the standing of trade unions as a vital force among American workers. Unions are on the defensive in a rapidly changing political and economic environment. Since the 1960s, industrial manufacturing, the historic base of unionism, has been radically transformed under the pressure of a new international division of labor. New forms of global competition, corporate restructuring, and technological innovation have undermined the traditional position of blue collar workers while employment has expanded in the largely unorganized service sector. Coupled with the anti-labor policies and prejudices of the past two national administrations, these conditions have contributed to a rollback of union strength and influence, reflected in steeply declining membership, and the erosion of workers' rights and living standards. At the same time, however, these problems contain within them the potential for new strategies to revitalize the labor movement and move forward.

The contours of the crisis of labor and directions for the future have been vigorously debated within the labor movement and the academic community. The available literature, however, is dominated by contributions from universities and policy statements from top union officials. Published perspectives from within the ranks of labor are less common. Yet shopfloor workers and local and national staff are daily confronted by the challenges to labor and are the source of many creative responses within the movement.

The eight articles in this volume were written by labor activists reflecting on their direct experiences. They produce original research on topics of immediate interest to their own situations

1

which nonetheless engages the broader concerns of the labor movement. Overall, the authors analyze today's workplace and workers, and trade union responses in this new milieu. The starting point in these essays is the changing domestic and international economy, and the directions these changes take under the control of management. Some chapters focus on the workplace and examine union initiatives to respond to different production methods and demands. The other chapters identify and discuss major social and political problems facing workers and their unions as a consequence of this changing economic environment.

The papers cluster around three central and interlocking themes which confront all workers and unions. Part One examines changing technology and work organization, especially its effect on health and safety, and worker displacement. Part Two analyzes the impact of the changing economy on workforce composition and the problem of responding to the needs of new work constituencies, especially among women and new immigrant groups. And, in Part Three, the question of developing new union practices, especially to promote alliances between unions and other social movements, nationally and internationally, is explored. In addition, the papers are linked together by the authors' reflections on their unions' efforts, successful and otherwise, to address the serious problems facing them. Some were closely involved in creative programs meant to arrest union decline, and report—with great sadness—on defeats. Others draw on their experience to outline new and possibly better responses for their unions.

If labor is to remain a vital force among American workers, it will be due in part to the efforts and ideas of such individuals. They are the voices of a generation of unionists who will play an important role in deciding the direction of the labor movement into the next century.

II. Labor's Crisis: Toward a New Social Contract?

Those looking for new developments in the American trade union movement can take little comfort from the statistics on union strength. Union membership has declined virtually every year since its peak in 1954 when 34% of the non-farm workforce was organized in trade unions. Today less than 17% of American workers are members of unions, and the absolute number of members continues to decline, from 17,717,000 in 1983 to 16,975,000 in

1986.[1] Furthermore, union success rates in certification elections declined from 74.6% in 1947 to less than 50% in 1975, to 46.4% in 1984. Finally, decertification elections occur with far greater frequency, and during the 1980s unions lost more than 75% of these contests.[2]

It is a truism that union power has been declining for much of the post-war period; the only debate concerns when and why the slide started. Tomlins, for example, as well as Moody, trace the roots of the decline to the terms of the New Deal compromise which brought labor's formal incorporation in 1935 under the National Labor Relations Act. Goldfield, however, locates the decline in management's counteroffensive since the 1950s, launched in response to labor's early dramatic victories under the official system, as reflected in strike settlements and certification elections.[3]

All writers agree that the challenges facing trade unions stem from a longer-term transformation in the global economy which has dramatically affected all advanced industrial societies. The change is rooted in the development and application of new technologies in the core countries, which altered the labor process in traditional manufacturing sectors, while creating whole new information-based industries.[4] Blue collar employment in the main manufacturing industries dropped dramatically during the 1970s, with the most significant decline coming in steel, auto and rubber, and mining. At the same time, employment in non-manufacturing sectors has grown the fastest, especially employment in the service sector which "accounted for most of the dramatic U.S. job growth over the past 20 years and for virtually all net new job growth in the past 10 years."[5] For example, salespersons, waiters and waitresses, health-care workers, and clerical workers are currently among the fastest growing jobs and this expansion is projected into the 1990s; in fact, today three out of four people work for a service industry employer.

The impact of these changes on skill levels and wage rates has been a subject for considerable debate. The most optimistic accounts forecast a rapid rise in skill levels as more highly trained, well-educated workers are needed to operate the new technologies. Several authors suggest that the logic of capitalist production does not inevitably lead to mass production, a division of labor and deskilling of workers' tasks. New technological developments (universal machines, i.e., flexible specialization), can generate small-scale craft-based forms of production: skills are enhanced, wage rates are increased, worker control and equality on the shopfloor is strengthened, and the general trend of labor-management relations is cooperative. The argument suggests the basis for the decline of existing organizations representing labor and capital, and the possibility of a new, more vital "yeoman democracy," bringing improvement in the conditions of working life.[6]

More pessimistic interpretations, influenced largely by the work of Braverman, see a further deskilling of workers, with an increased consolidation within management of information and control over work. Such approaches emphasize the negative consequences of technological change and restructuring: regional affects of deindustrialization, the elimination of skills, job displacement, and the breakdown of the social contract between labor and management.[7] These authors also discuss the deterioration of conditions at work caused by the reorganization of production processes. Specifically, they see management's control over new technology as providing the capacity for new forms of speedup, and increased mental and physical stress on workers. In addition, technological advance has also created conditions for the return of work forms commonly associated with early industrial capitalism: the rise of part-time work, home work, and sweatshop labor in unregulated small establishments.[8]

Each of these views accepts that these outcomes are not a reflex of new technology per se, but reflect social relations of production, including management decisionmaking, organization of work, and the extent of worker participation and resistance. Indeed, comparative studies, across countries and industrial sectors, show great diversity in the extent of managerial unilateralism or cooperation. They also describe variation in worker participation, job security, and the enhancement of rights. Cornfield, for example, in a comparison of 14 sectoral case studies identifies the macroeconomic conditions facing each sector and extent of prior unionization as important variables influencing the attractiveness of unilateralism by management or the possibilities of workers to exert power over changing conditions in the workplace.[9]

And yet U.S. unions have fared particularly poorly in the face of such challenges, both in their ability to protect members at risk and to take advantage of opportunities to expand. The steep declines in membership among the AFL-CIO industrial giants are well known: the Steelworkers lost more than half their members between 1973 and 1983, while UAW membership fell by more than one-third between 1969 and 1983.[10] Certainly other unions, notably those organizing in the public sector, posted impressive membership gains over the same period, yet overall the union movement lost ground. While the number of wage and salary workers in services increased from 18,400,000 to 21,036,000 between 1983 and 1986, the number of union members in this sector actually *fell* from 1,410,000 to 1,329,000! The wholesale and retail trade also suffered a decline in membership, despite an increase in employment of nearly 2 million workers. Whereas nearly one-quarter of manufacturing workers are union members, only 7.2% of wholesale and retail workers, and only 6.3% of service workers are union members.[11]

These statistics are even more sobering when seen in international comparison. From the late 1960s to the early 1980s "the proportion of union members in the labor force increased significantly in Canada, Denmark, Sweden, and Italy . . . and remained relatively stable in Switzerland and Germany."[12] Furthermore, European trade unions have had far greater success organizing in sectors which their American counterparts have found uncongenial. European bank workers, for example, are heavily unionized, whereas "the financial sector in the United States is distinguishable by its almost total lack of a union presence. In the U.S. banking sector, barely half a dozen banks are unionized, including only one large bank."[13] If the international tide has been running against labor, European unions have been better able to shore up, if not strengthen their membership, while protecting workers' rights. In the United States there has been no shortage of worker grievances, but unions have been unable to organize them effectively or even to defend previous gains among already organized workers.

In the post-war period, it is through labor unions and coalitions with social democratic parties that workers have secured economic and political gains, and influenced the condition of their lives. The social contract under Keynesian welfare statist structures rewarded both capital and labor, and however limited, gave workers historic real wage increases, social benefits, and a legal, institutional base for participation in government. Being a union member continues to reap benefits where it counts for many workers: average weekly earnings for unionized full-time workers in 1986 was $444 as compared to $325 for non-unionized full-time workers. Also, compare, for instance, median usual weekly earnings for most occupations between union members and those not represented by unions. In 1986 workers in service occupations earned $356 per week compared to $201 earned by their non-union counterparts, and manufacturing workers earned $58 more per week than non-unionized workers. Women and blacks also receive tangible rewards from union membership: non-union women earned $274 per week as against $368 for female trade unionists; and black unionists earned $387, $132 more per week than non-unionized black workers.[14]

The current crisis of labor goes well beyond the application of new technologies and the reorganization of the workplace, but concerns the undermining of the accord and the construction of a new order determined more unilaterally by capital and conservative state coalitions.[15] One of the key aspects of the unravelling of the accord has been the dismantling of national systems of labor law, what amounts to "the deregulation of labor relations."[16] Similarly, labor movements have experienced, with important national exceptions, declining power in electoral coalitions, influence in legislative decisionmaking, and leverage within national bureaucracies.[17]

This is not the first time that the future viability of unions has come into question. David Montgomery's first volume in his study of the American labor movement suggests its advance does not follow a straight trajectory, but that declines and revivals are normal features in the long development of workers' movements. "Their movement has grown only sporadically and through fierce struggles," Montgomery writes, "[and has] been interrupted time and again just when it seemed to reach flood tide, overwhelmed its foes only to see them revive in new and more formidable shapes, and been forced to reassess what it thought it had already accomplished and begin again."[18]

The dismantling of the old labor-capital accord provides labor with important opportunities to define a new relationship, in the words of Jacobi et al., "a new structural, functional, institutional order."[19] Seizing these opportunities demands structural transformations within labor itself as well as creative organizing strategies, and new alliances with progressive social groups.

There is no shortage of workers to organize, but the difficulties of organizing such workers demands strategies and tactics sensitive to the needs and characteristics of a wage labor force made up increasingly of women, people of color, and new immigrant groups. Similarly, the decline of factory-based manufacturing demands approaches to organizing in new environments: offices, educational institutions, sweatshops, and family homes. Many of these needs go beyond the traditional subject matter of collective bargaining to include issues such as health problems arising from the new technology, day care, maternal leave and flexible hours, sexual and racial harassment and discrimination, and immigration status. These concerns suggest the possible lines of alliance between unions and women's, environmental, civil rights, and immigrant groups, and the infusion of new ideas, energy, and strength that could flow from closer cooperation. Such unity might also provide a base for broader political movements capable of wielding electoral weight and influencing local and national legislatures and bureaucracies.

These possibilities point to the need for changes in union organization and leadership structures essential to a renewed commitment to unionism as a force for economic and social justice, domestically and internationally. How do unions reconcile differences between groups in such a heterogeneous workforce? What structures of representation need to be developed to incorporate such constituencies within unions, to bring their leaders into top positions, and to ensure that once brought in, their interests are given expression? In short, how can they gain power and influence in unions? Internal democracy gains value not only as a moral argument, but as a strategy necessary for binding together the working class to respond to capital and the state.[20]

Finally, the new social contract should include a recasting of international labor solidarity. To survive in a modern era characterized by the internationalization of production, markets, and labor, American unions need to emphasize cooperation with labor in other countries. The need for unions to forge links with their counterparts in other countries goes beyond a moral mandate, to form part of a practical strategy for preserving workers' positions at home. For labor to protect workers' rights and benefits in the United States, it must insist that the wages, benefits, and health of workers abroad are not undermined by the activities of multinational corporations.[21]

III. Union Voices

Thus far in this review, the descriptions of labor's crisis and suggestions for paths forward have relied mostly on academic treatments, and no matter how substantial the contributions, they nonetheless remain the work of outsiders writing from the sidelines. But organizers, officials, and members who live with these conditions on a daily basis are in an ideal position to develop solutions. Yet, their perspectives rarely inform the debates on analysis of the crisis and strategies for labor.

Their voices can indeed be heard in a number of collections where writers rely on the extensive testimony of workers directly experiencing working life.[22] The essays in this collection, however, are not oral histories of workers, though some of the writers include stories from fellow workers and their own personal experiences. Rather these are analytical chapters, research papers, written by workers and union staff members reflecting on their own problems and practice.

Tom L. Robbins worked in the meatpacking industry where he contracted Carpal Tunnel Syndrome on the job, and Jonathan Rosen was the safety officer on the labor-management safety committee he writes about. His position enabled him to interview workers who recalled safety conditions at A. O. Smith Automotive Products Company in the early days: "When I first got hired in 1951, out in the streets you could tell the person who worked at Smith. He or she had one finger missing or two." Raymond Scannell visited the "workplaces of the future" at bakery and tobacco factories as a member of his union's Task Force on Technological Change. May Ying Chen, an Asian-American, has been a leader in addressing Asian labor issues for HERE and the ILGWU. Susan Strauss is a machinist at the General Electric Company and an active member of her local's Women's Committee, a driving force for women's issues in the union and company. Susan Eaton uses her experiences as a woman trade unionist to formulate a program for developing women leaders. She relates instances of an anti-feminist union culture in which male coworkers boasted of their weekly visits to airport strip joints and where sexual harassment was a problem. Kim Fellner has been a union staffer for over 15 years and was the speechwriter for Ed Asner, former president of the Screen Actors' Guild. She gives a firsthand account of the AFL-CIO reaction to Asner's opposition of its policies in Central America. Don Stillman was the UAW's 'point man' for the "Campaign for Justice for Moses Mayekiso." He was a central planner of the strategy of the international campaign and he traveled to South Africa to meet with Mayekiso and his lawyers.

These union activists represent the potential for the revival of the labor movement: they directly confront the conditions of crisis and are essential participants in experiments toward establishing the new social contract. Rank-and-file innovations have always played a crucial role in union advances through adversity. In Montgomery's words, workers' daily experience and the solidarity nurtured by that experience has been "the taproot of [labor's] resilience. . . . When working-class activists sought a path out of the depression of the 1930s, they . . . reopened controversy over what had been considered accomplished, and began to organize anew on the basis of the ways America's heterogeneous working people actually experienced industrial life."[23] That same taproot needs to be drawn on in the current period.

The perspectives these unionists bring to their research encompass a wide range of contemporary union activities. Part One focuses on technological change and the reorganization of the production process in manufacturing. The papers present contrasting union responses to problems generated by industrial restructuring, especially health and safety, and job displacement. **Tom L. Robbins** deals with union responses to health and safety in a situation where unions have no control over restructuring. He studies the spread of Carpal Tunnel Syndrome in the Iowa meatpacking industry, describes growing health problems among meatcutters whose unions were largely broken and are now subjected to management's unilateral introduction of speedup and deskilling, and he suggests a limited legal program for protecting such workers.[24] **Jonathan D. Rosen** analyzes his union's health and safety activities in a Wisconsin truck frame plant, as a case study of joint labor-management relations which allowed workers some participation. But the union's effectiveness was limited by its exclusion from fundamental decisionmaking on issues of plant relocation and downsizing which eventually undermined workers' job security. Finally, **Raymond F. Scannell** describes his union's efforts to develop a new strategy for influencing the introduction of new technologies in the bakery, confectionery and tobacco industries. On the one hand, he rejects total resistance to technological change, and on the other, cooperative labor-management programs, proposing instead a policy of "adversary participation" in which workers engage management with the goal of increasing their power over the workplace.

The papers in Part Two are also concerned with the impact of the changing economy: the current state of industry has contributed to the erosion of economic and affirmative action gains made by women and minorities in the 1970s and early 1980s, thereby undermining their progress. They focus, however, on the changes the new economy has wrought on the composition of the workforce, specifically, the employment of women and new immigrant groups in the industrial and service sectors. Each takes as its point of departure the problems the labor movement has organizing such workers and promoting their interests within the unions. **May Ying Chen**'s contribution examines strategies for organizing the unorganized, focusing on new Asian immigrant workers in the New York metropolitan area. This problem has been exacerbated in the 1980s because New York City's unionized manufacturers have gone out of business or contracted out work abroad at the same time as the introduction of non-union work into Chinatown's shops is on the rise. **Susan R. Strauss**' chapter examines the failure of affirmative action policies, developed by her union and management at the General Electric plant, to open up higher skilled jobs to women and minorities. Shrinking production levels at GE and the general retreat from affirmative action in national politics has decimated training programs and undermined job advancement for women workers. In response to the feminization of the workplace, Strauss argues, unions must develop more sophisticated programs to promote equality on the job. The point is further developed by **Susan C. Eaton** who analyzes why women are underrepresented in leadership positions in unions and develops strategies to increase their representation. Eaton argues that greater involvement of women in labor's hierarchy will enhance the economic position of this growing sector of the workforce. "Women need unions and unions need women leaders for each to build a more just future."

The problems described in the previous sections and the strategies advocated suggest the need for changes in the way unions work. Part Three focuses on the problems within unions' internal structure and politics, and points to the need for progressive agendas emphasizing solidarity with other social movements at home and abroad. In the current decade, the 1989 U.S. - Canada Free Trade Agreement, the creation of a European common market in 1992, and the proposed U.S. - Mexico Free Trade Agreement indicate a further advancement of the globalization and integration of the economy. These international agreements threaten to establish new patterns of trade and new competition between workers across borders, thereby weakening workers' rights and living standards. Unions must develop worldwide networks to work towards new international labor standards in defense of workers' interests. **Kim Fellner**'s essay on the fate of sixties activists in the union movement stresses the stultifying effect of union bureaucracy and political culture on organizing. She contemplates the AFL-CIO's foreign policy and how it works against promoting international solidarity and workers' rights. And, she asserts the need for changes in union practice to promote an internal union culture which can nurture creative responses to the problems outlined in the other contributions. Finally, **Don Stillman**'s assessment of an international union solidarity campaign suggests a model for constructive global political links which assist unions abroad while simultaneously developing the political consciousness of workers at home. These bonds will help to establish rights and protections that are mutually beneficial for unions here and abroad.

Notes

1. U.S. Bureau of the Census, *Statistical Abstract of the United States: 1988*, 108th ed. (Washington, D.C.: U.S. Government Printing Office, 1987), Table 667, Union Members by Selected Characteristics, 402.

2. Seymour Martin Lipset, "Preface," in Lipset, ed., *Unions in Transition: Entering the Second Century* (San Francisco: Institute for Contemporary Studies Press, 1986), xvi. Lipset notes that not only have unions been losing more elections, but elections are themselves occurring far less frequently, declining from around 9,000 in 1973 to close to 3,500 in 1983–84. The ratio of certification to decertification elections was 4:1 in 1984, compared to 30:1 in 1960.

3. Christopher L. Tomlins, *The State and the Unions: Labor Relations, Law, and the Organized Labor Movement in America, 1880–1960* (Cambridge: Cambridge University Press, 1986); and Kim Moody, *An Injury to All: The Decline of American Unionism* (London: Verso, 1988). Michael Goldfield, *The Decline of Organized Labor in the United States* (Chicago: University of Chicago Press, 1987).

4. Michael J. Piore and Charles Sabel, *The Second Industrial Divide: Possibilities for Prosperity* (New York: Basic Books, 1984), 248–250.

5. Karen Nussbaum and John Sweeney, *Solutions for the New Work Force: Policies for a New Social Contract* (Washington, D.C.: Seven Locks Press, 1989), 194, see also 19 and 187–198. U.S. Bureau of the Census, *Statistical Abstract of the United States: 1988*, Table 631, Employment By Selected Industry, 380. See also U.S. Department of Labor, Bureau of Labor Statistics, "*Monthly Labor Review*," vol. 112, no. 12 (December 1989), Table 20, Annual Data: Employment Levels by Industry, 83.

6. Michael J. Piore and Charles F. Sabel, *The Second Industrial Divide*; Harry C. Katz and Charles Sabel, "Industrial Relations and Industrial Adjustment in the Car Industry," *Industrial Relations*, vol. 24 (1985): 295–315.

7. Harry Braverman, *Labor and Monopoly Capital: The Degradation of Work in the Twentieth Century* (New York: Monthly Review Press,

1974); Harley Shaiken, *Work Transformed: Automation and Labor in the Computer Age* (New York: Holt, Rinehart, 1985); and Shaiken et al., "The Work Process Under More Flexible Production," *Industrial Relations*, vol. 25 (1986): 167–183; Barry Bluestone and Bennett Harrison, *The Deindustrialization of America: Plant Closing, Community Abandonment, and the Dismantling of Basic Industry* (New York: Basic Books, 1982); Richard Hyman, "Flexible Specialization: Miracle or Myth?" in Richard Hyman and Wolfgang Streeck, eds., *New Technology and Industrial Relations* (Oxford: Blackwell, 1988). From the same collection see Peter Armstrong, "Labour and Monopoly Capital," for a review of criticisms of Braverman and a defense of his deskilling argument.

8. Eli Ginzberg, Thierry Noyelle, and Thomas Stanback, Jr., "Work Force Trends," in *Technology and Employment* (London: Westview Press, 1986). See also Nussbaum and Sweeney, 56–61.

9. Daniel B. Cornfield, ed., *Workers, Managers, and Technological Change: Emerging Patterns of Labor Relations* (New York: Plenum, 1987).

10. Leo Troy, "The Rise and Fall of American Trade Unions: The Labor Movement From FDR to RR," in Seymour Martin Lipset, ed., *Unions in Transition*, 92.

11. *Statistical Abstract of the United States: 1988*, Table 667, 402.

12. Seymour Martin Lipset, "Comparing Canadian and American Unions," *Society* (January–February 1987): 61–2. Also see Goldfield, *The Decline of Organized Labor*, Table 3, 16.

13. Over 90% of the bank and insurance employees in Sweden are unionized, while in Germany unionization rates in financial firms oscillate between 15 and 25%. Olivier Bertrand and Thierry Noyelle, *Human Resources and Corporate Strategy: Technological Change in Banks and Insurance Companies* (Paris: OECD, 1988), 52–54. For a comparison of union membership in the leading Western industrial countries see Goldfield, 1987, Table 3, 16.

14. *Statistical Abstract of the United States: 1988*, Table 667, 402. See also Richard B. Freeman and James L. Medoff, *What Do Unions Do?* (New York: Basic Books, 1984).

15. Otto Jacobi, et al., "Between Erosion and Transformation: Industrial Relations Systems Under the Impact of Technological Change," in Otto Jacobi, Bob Jessop, Hans Kastendiek, and Marino Regini, *Technological Change, Rationalisation and Industrial Relations* (New York: St. Martin's Press, 1986), 11–12.

16. See Robert H. Zieger, *American Workers, American Unions, 1920–1985* (Baltimore: Johns Hopkins University Press, 1986), 195–196.

17. "In the late 1970s and early 1980s . . . the collapse of labor's legislative power facilitated the adoption of a set of economic policies highly

beneficial to the corporate sector and to the affluent. . . . Without a strong labor movement, there is no broad-based institution in American society equipped to represent the interests of those in the working and lower-middle classes in the formulation of economic policy." Thomas Byrne Edsall, *The New Politics of Inequality* (New York: Norton, 1984), 176–177. H. Brand, "The Decline of Workers' Incomes, the Weakening of Labor's Position," *Dissent*, vol. 32, no. 3 (1985): 286–298, discusses the impact of the U.S. political environment, especially the government's economic policies, as a key factor in the retreat of the labor movement. See also Goldfield, who examines political explanations for labor's decline, including "new legal policies and laws which make it more difficult for unions to organize," "Labor in American Politics—Its Current Weaknesses," *Journal of Politics*, vol. 48, no. 1 (February 1986): 3–29.

18. David Montgomery, *The Fall of the House of Labor: the Workplace, the State, and American Labor Activism, 1865–1925* (Cambridge: Cambridge University Press, 1987), 7–8.

19. Jacobi, et al.

20. Otto Jacobi, "New Technological Paradigms, Long Waves and Trade Unions," in Hyman and Streeck, eds., *New Technology and Industrial Relations*, 199–200. Failure to make such changes "would mean the end of a trade union movement which is capable of intervention and social participation . . . a merely particularistic interest representation means the loss of the status which had been achieved in the post–war era."

21. Roger Southall, "At Issue: Third World Trade Unions in the Changing International Division of Labor," in Southall, ed., *Trade Unions and the New Industrialisation in the Third World* (Pittsburgh: University of Pittsburgh Press, 1988), 24–26; also, in the same volume, Nigel Haworth and Harvie Ramsey, "Workers of the World Untied: International Capital and Some Dilemmas in Industrial Democracy," 306–331.

22. See Richard Feldman and Michael Betzold, *End of the Line: Autoworkers and the American Dream* (New York: Wiedenfeld and Nicolson, 1988); and the classic collections by Alice Lynd and Staughton Lynd, *Rank and File: Personal Histories by Working-Class Organizers* (New York: Monthly Review Press, 1988), and Studs Terkel, *Working* (New York: Pantheon 1974).

23. Montgomery, *The Fall of the House of Labor*, 8.

24. Davis provides graphic evidence of midwestern packers' tactics of corporate reorganization to break unions and slash wages. "Morell, a branch of United Brands, extorted large concessions from its workers and then subcontracted slaughtering to Greyhound, which owned Armour, who sold it to Con Agra, which promptly deunionized it. Meanwhile, Wilson took direct advantage of the bankruptcy laws by invoking 'Chapter

Eleven,' closing down, and reopening the next day with wages cut by forty percent and restrictive workrules eliminated. The union's appeals to the Reaganized NLRB fell on deaf ears." Mike Davis, *Prisoners of the American Dream: Politics and Economy in the History of the U.S. Working Class* (London: Verso, 1986), 144.

Part One

Economic Change, New Technology, and Union Responses

Economic restructuring and the changes it brings in the labor process are the starting point of Tom L. Robbins' and Jonathan Rosen's examinations of safety and health in the workplace, as well as Raymond Scannell's description of the ongoing effort by his union to protect its workers facing work reorganization. Robbins' paper focuses on Carpal Tunnel Syndrome [CTS] and other repetitive motion disorders, a growing health problem, not only in assembly line industries, but also in the new computerized office settings. Robbins' research provides graphic evidence of the impact of CTS on Iowa meatcutters, and he traces its increased incidence to changes in the labor process, including speed-up and deskilling.

In Robbins' account, the Amalgamated Meatcutters and Butcher Workmen of North America and the United Packing Workers of America had by the 1940s successfully organized the majority of meatcutters in the midwest. They enjoyed high wages, better working conditions, and health and other benefits as a result of uniform standards arrived at through pattern bargaining throughout the industry. By the 1970s the system was breaking down. Some union shops closed down, while other employers sought to circumvent the union "'master rate' package," by hiving off new state-of-the-art, non-union independent plants. Among numerous examples, Iowa Beef Packers purchased a former unionized plant, and after remodeling, reopened it as a non-union facility. Efforts to organize these new plants have been sidetracked under the anti-union political stance and labor regulations of the past two Republican administrations. The meatcutters have found it very difficult to sustain national wage, health, and fringe benefit standards in the climate of deregulation and the breakdown in pattern bargaining.

In addition to cutting wage and benefit costs, these employers also undertook a massive reorganization of the labor process. Whereas a single meatcutter previously dissected an entire ham on a stationary table, the new plants featured assembly line techniques. Under the new "pace-boning" system, the meat now passes by on conveyor belts. Meatcutters stand in a single place, working on a

moving product, and "now make only a few identical cuts to several thousand hams daily, rather than the varied cuts necessary in
the whole ham process."

Unions have been unable to influence job classifications, production levels, line speed, or the design of work stations. The result, according to Robbins, is a dramatically increased rate of repetitive trauma disorders, "in direct proportion to the productivity
increases." Indeed, in some plants the injury rate is greater than
100%. The experience of deskilling and health risk in these new
plants represents another side of economic restructuring.

The absence of labor representation in the industry leaves
workers with little influence over health and safety. One consequence is company-designed health programs, where physicians
are in the employ of management. Under these circumstances, Robbins asserts, physicians pursue treatments which deal with immediate relief to keep the worker on the job, while the actual health
of the worker is given secondary consideration. In repetitive trauma
disorders, especially CTS, workers will be treated with drugs to
dull the pain, or surgery, which merely allow the worker to continue doing the job which caused the problem in the first place.
Workers are often forced to seek such treatment, through threats
of demotion and firing, or as a result of disciplinary action because
they are performing at reduced capacity. Sometimes pressure comes
from other workers who are forced to pick up the slack to meet
production goals. "Surgery may seem welcome to the most reluctant patient," when faced with these conditions. The conditions in
the modern plants of the midwestern meatpacking industry are
thus part of the dark side of flexible specialization and deregulation.

According to Robbins, the scientific literature on repetitive
trauma disorders suggests that the most effective treatment is
stopping the activity that caused the problem. In the workplace,
such a prescription entails wide-reaching reorganization of the labor process, including reskilling, job redesign, and slowdown. In
his conclusion, Robbins presents a strategy designed to provide relief to injured workers on the job. Above all, his proposal calls for
increased use of OSHA powers to enforce existing federal health
and safety laws, use of the courts to protect worker rights, and the
need for in-plant education and monitoring procedures. Without
worker control, not just in health and safety, but in the conditions
of their own employment, workers have little guarantee against
pain, disfigurement, and permanent disability.

Robbins writes about deteriorating health and safety in an industry where unions are forced to seek remedies outside the workplace because of their declining influence within these redesigned factories. Jonathan Rosen examines a single company where the union has been able, through economic restructuring, to enhance its influence—for a time. Rosen's paper analyzes the joint labor-management safety committees at the giant Milwaukee-based A. O. Smith Automotive Products Company.

In the early 1980s, A. O. Smith faced rapidly deteriorating market conditions as Japanese producers gained a large share of the domestic automobile and truck market. To survive in such a climate, A. O. Smith, following the lead of other automobile and components companies, decided to adopt new production strategies, "converting from a management driven system of shopfloor organization to one of team production." Management recognized that it could take advantage of the ability and knowledge of workers on the shopfloor to identify problems in the production process, while realizing cost savings by eliminating middle management and supervisory positions.

Health and safety was an area where these new developments had some impact. The union saw that management's new attitude created space to make progress on an issue of great concern to workers. Management saw a way to save money by reducing worker compensation costs—running to an estimated $11 million in 1986 alone—and improving productivity by cutting time lost to injuries and illness.

For workers, health and safety was literally a life and death issue. A. O. Smith experienced high accident rates—typical of the industry—including amputations, broken bones, and strains and sprains. Company responses to the problem were inadequate: quality circles, begun in 1982, were launched unilaterally without union participation. In 1985, however, the company and the unions began a program that involved real employee participation in which workers were given training to identify problems and a joint labor-management structure to formulate and introduce solutions.

Despite changes in work rules, elimination of large numbers of foremen, training, and establishment of joint weekly meetings, workers found that day-to-day problems were still dealt with in the traditional manner by management. In response, the union leadership began to press for shopfloor teams. At the same time, joint plant safety committees were formed, in which union members could have full-time participation as comanagers of health and safety.

The committees introduced technical education for workers,

stewards, and safety observers, including seminars on OSHA rights, began aggressive investigations of instances of CTS, and suggested treatment and job redesign, wrote a union safety observer's manual, and developed a Hazard Communications Update. But the efforts of the committee were ultimately disrupted by the very economic crisis which had stimulated management to search for new solutions in the first place. The committees were undermined by massive layoffs and reorganizations, and thus were never realized in the manner envisioned when they were proposed in late 1987. By the end of 1988, two of the nine committees had folded. Safety inspections were infrequent, or nonexistent, and safety training had not fully begun.

The most important obstacle to the development of an effective health and safety program has been the investment strategy of the company itself. A. O. Smith has been rapidly shedding workers: in the past fifteen years employment declined by more than 50%, and as Rosen was writing in 1989, over 1,000 workers were on layoff. At the same time A. O. Smith was "downsizing" the Milwaukee plant, it was opening smaller, state-of-the-art satellite factories in Indiana, Illinois, and Maryland.

In part, the strategy was shaped by the shifting demands of the big automobile producers for component suppliers to site themselves closer to assembly plants, themselves located in areas where unions are traditionally weak. Despite its interests in joint labor-management health initiatives, A. O. Smith's larger strategy for survival resembles that of the Iowa meatpackers: phasing out its main unionized production facility while developing non-union satellite plants with lower pay rates and fewer benefits. Significantly, the unions were never able to achieve the same labor-management participation on job security issues. Despite their attraction to new forms of workplace relations, management refused to provide employment guarantees which could build dedication in the workforce and stabilize manpower. Instead, it preferred to treat job security as its own prerogative.

Rosen's conclusions are extremely bleak. Job insecurity is causing morale problems which in turn "perpetuate the inefficiencies, quality problems, and incidents of injuries." Workers are thinking about life after A. O. Smith, and "among many, a bitterness has begun to set in." It may be that A. O. Smith was simply lagging behind the type of restructuring perfected in the Iowa meatpacking industry in the 1970s. If so, Robbins' chapter suggests what may lie in store for A. O. Smith workers, especially those in the new non-union plants.

Robbins' and Rosen's accounts of the labor wasteland left by union-busting firms in Iowa and the joint labor-management schemes at A. O. Smith underscore the limits to worker control over health and safety policy, deskilling, wage cuts, and job loss where workers have minimal influence over investment and production decisions. Raymond Scannell's work goes one step further showing how his union, the Bakery, Confectionery, and Tobacco Workers' International Union (BC&T), has crafted an approach to the changing character of manufacturing which attempts to wrest real decisionmaking power over the new automated workplace. He maintains that the revitalization and even survival of the union movement depends on its ability to develop policies to influence the design, introduction, and operation of new technologies.

The pressures facing the industry are similar to those which have reshaped meatpacking and auto. The number of companies and manufacturing plants has declined and ownership has been reorganized through mergers. Many companies have relocated in response to new competitive pressures brought on by changes in the national economy, and new locales have been selected to promote deunionization goals. In many sections of the industry new technology and work practices have been introduced, sometimes piecemeal within existing factories, sometimes wholesale in non-unionized greenfield plants. In many workplaces, practices differ from the job control and employment security rules codified in contract language negotiated industry-wide. But without concerted union responses, management has a freer hand to attack past practices, demand union concessions, and restructure work on its own terms.

Scannell argues that the culprit is not the technology itself, but the way in which it is designed and introduced, and unions should endeavor to make these into bargaining issues. He reviews the intellectual debate among academics on the nature of the restructured factory and how restructuring alters the traditional character of labor-management relations. He examines the relevance of this debate for the real work experiences of BC&T workers and other industrial workers. According to Scannell, cooperative strategies have failed. For example, "jointness" in the auto industry has not prevented job loss and decline in the auto unions. Unions can neither ignore the changes in technology nor can they enter into quality circles or labor-management schemes, which often replace a more visible bureaucratic control with a difficult-to-resist "intimate authoritarianism," extending managerial control, dividing workers, speeding up work, and busting unions.

Scannell borrows insights from European experiences, where he claims unions demand the opportunity to participate in decisionmaking without abandoning their traditional adversarial position in defense of their members' interests. He also recalls the historical situation of craft workers who were highly skilled and had control over the work process. He thus advocates "adversary participation," where unions refuse to be "'partners' cooperating in the ratification of management decisions," but instead view "the decision process as a new arena in which to struggle for worker rights and an alternative vision of the workplace and production process."

The position Scannell describes is the result of a long-term policy review within his union, which is attempting to develop a coherent strategy for coping with the changes in the industry. New technologies and the globalization of the economy have undermined the social contract between labor and management which worked best during the fifties and sixties to stabilize the workplace and provide workers with economic benefits. According to Scannell, adversary participation redefines labor's role to include fighting for workplace control. The strategy recognizes that there is a clash of interests between management and workers, and proposes that unions use the collective bargaining system to achieve some authority over the production process. The BC&T embraced the approach in 1990, and has begun pursuing the strategy in its negotiations where it has fought for contract language to establish a right to participate and bargain on issues of technological design and introduction. The goal is to set up pattern bargaining on these issues and, eventually, a model for the establishment of national and international standards.

Leaving *The Jungle*:
A Union Response to Questionable Medical Treatment in Repetitive Trauma Disorders

Tom L. Robbins*

I. Introduction

Twenty million workers in the United States are employed on assembly line jobs. The incidence of repetitive trauma disorders (RTDs) has been on the increase in the 1980s, and some industries have seen a dramatic rise in such disorders. The meatpacking industry is among the worst.

The recent introduction of "pace-boning"—the combination of assembly line techniques and deskilling—has brought about a rapid increase in these disorders in meatcutting operations. Among the most prevalent is Carpal Tunnel Syndrome (CTS), a potentially disabling injury of the hand and wrist.

In workers' compensation cases in Iowa, the choice of medical care is up to the employer. Some are prone to choose physicians who aim to keep the affected employees on the job, rather than allowing sufficient time for healing. Most workers, with little medical background, are at the mercy of the physician's judgment. Workers are then faced with little opportunity to prevent surgery, which may leave them jobless and with future employment opportunities severely limited by their medical history.

The rash of plant closings and other disruptions in the industry have left workers fearful for their jobs. Economic factors in the midwest deepen that fear. As a result, workers exercise OSHA

---

*Special thanks to Drs. William Blair, David Schwartz, and Laurence Fuortas; also to physical therapist Tom Cook, all associated with the University of Iowa. My most grateful appreciation to Roberta Till-Retz and all of the staff at the University of Iowa Center for Labor Education.

complaints, stoppages, and other potentially disruptive measures only as a last resort.

This chapter is designed to provide the worker and his or her labor union with a strategy to provide injured workers with relief from the injury-producing job. The strategy emphasizes three main points. First, medical evidence convincingly documents factors causing RTDs. Second, satisfactory treatment cannot be achieved in highly repetitive occupations without activity modification. Finally, the physician bears a responsibility to provide reasonable medical options to the patient.

It is hoped that this program, coupled with other viable strategies, will provide union leaders with the means to achieve a more effective dialogue with the employer, and give the employer incentives to develop programs to eliminate the epidemic. It is further hoped that the information provided here will help workers in other industries cope with similar circumstances.

II. Background

1. The Meatpacking Industry: Past and Present

As Upton Sinclair wrote many years ago, working in a packing plant has always been unpleasant. Dangerous, dirty, and unhealthy working conditions have been the norm.

Large corporations have dominated the industry since the turn of the century. Shortly after 1900, workers began to organize themselves under the banner of the Amalgamated Meatcutters and Butcher Workmen of North America, which was eventually crushed by the packers in the early twenties. In the thirties, with the suffering brought about by the Great Depression, coupled with the spirit of the New Deal and its accompanying labor legislation, workers again began to organize. This time the United Packing Workers of America (UPWA) was in the forefront. The Amalgamated had survived the debacle of the twenties by organizing retail meatcutters, and it too, organized some plants.

By the end of World War II, nearly every major packer in the industry was organized under nearly identical wage and fringe programs. Virtually every contract in the industry ended in the fall of every third year. Negotiations with all the major packers in Chicago were handled jointly by the Amalgamated and UPWA, and wages and fringes remained uniform throughout the industry until around 1970.

Thus, from the late forties through the early seventies, the unions were continually able to provide better wages and working conditions for the worker. Wages at today's purchasing power would often reach the $40,000-$50,000 level. A "master rate" package had been negotiated providing nearly identical wages and fringe benefits throughout the industry. More important, perhaps, the working conditions were rapidly improving through contract language, improved grievance procedures and even a more benevolent management attitude.

In 1963, Currier Holman and Andy Anderson opened a small beef plant in Denison, Iowa, known as Iowa Beef Packers (later IBP Inc.). It went largely unnoticed. In 1967 they opened a large beef slaughtering and processing plant in Dakota City, Nebraska. Within a few short years their empire included some 10 beef packing plants.

Amalgamated and UPWA, the two meatcutters' unions, had merged by the time IBP opened its flagship plant in Dakota City, Iowa, and were successful in organizing there, but three later IBP plants remained largely non-union. Soon other low-wage independents with modern efficient plants were making it difficult for the major packers to compete in the beef segment of the industry.

By the late seventies many of the major unionized packers abandoned their beef operations under competitive pressure from the low-wage, non-union independents. Others spun off non-union independent corporations to circumvent the master rate. The pork segment was beginning to be assailed with threats of plant closings and actual closings. The Amalgamated merged again in 1978, this time with the Retail Clerks, to form the United Food and Commercial Workers (UFCW). The master rates and conditions were still intact for a large sector, but others had caved in through a variety of packer schemes. Subsequent events unfolded in a manner destined to ravage the workers, their wages, and rights and benefits. A few examples illustrate the trend.

In 1981 the UFCW offered to freeze wages at the master rate plants (primarily pork) at $10.69 to allow organizing efforts to bring the lower-wage plants closer to the master rate. IBP opened its first pork facility in Storm Lake, Iowa, with a starting rate of $6 an hour with few fringes. The die was cast. Wilson Foods filed for bankruptcy in April 1983, imposing a $6.50 rate; the workers struck and recovered to $8 and some fringes. With few exceptions, those employers who hadn't already broken the wage pattern soon did in one way or another.

IBP subsequently opened two more Iowa pork facilities, in Columbus Junction and Council Bluffs. The former Oscar Meyer plant in Perry, Iowa, was purchased by IBP, remodeled and reopened in mid-1989 as a packer (sow) slaughtering facility. All are presently non-union. IBP is also planning a state-of-the-art plant in Waterloo.

Hormel closed its Ottumwa, Iowa plant, which was reopened by Excel at $5.50 per hour and subsequently organized with an $8 rate. Long and bitter strikes with IBP and Morrell further eroded the union's spirit.

The Reagan Administration's tough stance against labor, such as the firing of the Air Controllers (PATCO), and unfavorable NLRB decisions, coupled with hard-nosed attitudes by the packers, have made organizing new plants difficult in some instances and impossible in others. Hope for significant short-range gains is bleak. In a little over a decade, once proud and well-paid workers have been reduced to near poverty.

As local unions were reduced in size or eliminated, resources for those remaining became strained. Both money and manpower were significantly affected, and the local unions' focus was directed more to survival, and less to member service. As might be imagined, during such a period, safety and non-survival issues were given secondary consideration. Production increased to unprecedented levels, and with no contract protections, packers were free to speed the lines at will. Other devices were implemented to circumvent time-study standards.

2. Pace-Boning

One prominent device is the pace-boning line. In traditional ham-boning, workers pulled the ham from the conveyer to an attached cutting board and proceeded to remove the bone following specific seams. The entire piece was marketed as a boneless ham, sometimes with interior fat removed. A single ham could be dissected into ten or more pieces. The worker usually worked to a standard and would be required to produce a given number of pieces hourly. Proficient ham boners could perform a day's labor in perhaps six to seven hours, a pace that allowed time for necessary breaks, rest, and completion before the end of their shift.

Under the new pace-boning system, the ham is no longer removed from the conveyer, but is dissected while moving on the line. The old job standards no longer apply. Employers are free to establish new standards that provide an increase in man-hour productivity of between 30% and 50%.

Rather than being allowed to gain on the new standards as they could under the old piece rate, workers are now forced to stand in one place and work on a moving product, without the freedom of movement they had previously enjoyed. Even more significant from an RTD risk standpoint is that they now make only a few identical cuts to several thousand hams daily, rather than the varied cuts necessary in the whole ham process. Particularly at risk are those performing highly repetitive, highly stressed jobs, some of which produce multiple injuries annually. At least some of the increase in injuries can be blamed on the fact that these individual strokes are performed thousands of times daily.

Union leaders report that RTD injury rates have increased in direct proportion to the productivity increases. Efforts by unions to push management to reduce the injury rate have proven essentially ineffective. Suggested remedies have included job rotation (from one repetitive job to another), exercise programs, work height adjustments, and modified knife design.

3. Incidence Rates of Repetitive Trauma Disorders

It is difficult to ascertain the actual numbers of incidences of RTDs, as various states classify Carpal Tunnel Syndrome in various categories, and employer-reporting methods may vary widely. Ohio figures, however, show a three-fold increase from 1980–1984 of all RTDs.[1] In an Illinois meatpacking plant, the incidence of CTS surgery increased from two in 1971, to 68 in 1983. A total of 14.8% of the plant's employees had undergone surgery by 1983.[2] Other reports suggest increasing rates both in the United States and abroad.

Iowa's Division of Labor does not keep separate statistics on either work-related RTDs or CTS. It does keep track by grouping several maladies together under two categories: inflammation of joints,[3] and diseases of the nerves and peripheral ganglia, which includes CTS and Bell's Palsy. Cases are categorized according to information in the employers' first report of injury. Beginning in 1977 there were 400 cases reported in the first category, increasing to 877 cases in 1987. The second category, which includes CTS, rose from 12 cases in 1977 to 585 cases in 1987, an increase of over 2,000%. Since physicians often diagnose early CTS as tendinitis, or other infirmities in the first category, it is likely that the actual figures for CTS are even more dramatic.

Employers are required by federal law to keep OSHA 200 logs, which are a compilation of all accidents or injuries that occur on an employer's premises in a given year. However, employers bent on under-reporting injury statistics resort to many devices. Company nurses will treat the patients with wrist wraps and non-prescription medication or hot wax treatment, rather than referring them to a physician. Other employers will report an injury only if the patient insists on filing an accident report. Even when surgery occurs, patients undergo the operation on a Friday and return to work on Monday or Tuesday on light duty, and thus do not lose the required three work days that would compel logging the event as a lost-time incident. Nonetheless, examining the log from one plant with a pace-boning operation may indicate the potential gravity of RTDs in Iowa and in other states with large numbers of similar operations.

The following data have been obtained from the UFCW-organized Wilson facility in Cherokee, Iowa. As a processing-only plant it does not have the slaughtering operations which normally account for the high injury levels in the industry. The workforce is approximately 80% male and 20% female, which is typical for the state and industry. The turnover rate is moderate and would be much less than that of a new or non-union operation such as IBP, where nearly half the workforce is replaced in a given year. There are no obvious reasons why the Cherokee plant should have higher injury or illness rates than other operations.

Wilson County (Cherokee, Iowa) Injury and Illness Statistics, 1988

Type (Injury or Illness)	Lost Time Incidents	Non-Lost Time Incidents	No. of Days Lost
Plant Figures: 1988 (470 Workers)			
Injuries	49	327	1,924
Illnesses	36	174	1,483
Totals	85	501	3,407
Pace-Boning Section: 1988 (122 Positions)			
Injuries	20	103	989
Illnesses	26	89	960
Totals	46	192	1,949

The total number of injuries and illnesses plant-wide was 586, for an annual incidence rate of 124.7%. The figure approaches four times the rate generally reported for the meatpacking industry as a whole, which has the worst record of any industry in the nation. Thus, a Cherokee worker has little opportunity to survive one year without incident.[4]

Pace-boning had an incidence rate of 195%. This department also had 26 of a plant total of 36, or 72.2%, of the illnesses (which includes all RTDs). The expected illness rate, based on chance, would be near 25%. Pace-boners had a much higher rate of illnesses than the reminder of the plant workers. If one assumes over-staffing in pace-boning by 18 additional employees, the 122 positions in the department expands to a total of 140. Of the 330 workers in the remainder of the plant, only 10 had a lost-time illness, while pace-boners had an incidence rate of 26 for 140, leaving 114 unaffected. Pace-boners were far more likely to lose time as a result of a work-related illness than were their co-employees in the other departments.

III. RTDs: Medical Factors

1. Symptoms

Repetitive trauma disorders have long been recognized as being related to a patient's activities.[5] Terms such as cumulative trauma disorders, repetitive trauma disorders, repetitive strain disorders, and overuse syndrome are all terms used interchangeably to describe similar medical conditions. Perhaps most common among these various maladies are tendinitis and tenosynovitis, which can affect various parts of the body. There is little reason for the individual worker to be able to differentiate between the various infirmities, as their causes and treatment are often quite similar. They are generally caused from repeated overuse, and can be conservatively treated so that surgery is usually avoided.

Carpal Tunnel Syndrome, however, is noteworthy in several important respects. First, it is probably the most common RTD, and there is a great deal of medical literature available. Second, unlike most RTDs, CTS often ends in surgery. Finally, disability from both the ailment and subsequent surgery is a common and significant result.

When viewing the wrist with the palm facing upwards, the carpal arch, or tunnel, consists of a "U" shaped area surrounded by bones. A ligament runs across (transverse) the opening, effectively providing a cover for the "U", and forming a channel of limited volume. The median nerve runs through the tunnel, as do the sheathed tendons which control the operation of the hand and fingers. When the volume of the channel is exceeded, pressures are exerted on the median nerve, which affects the thumb side (thenar) of the hand causing loss of feeling (sensory) and weakness (motor).[6]

A typical patient will awaken in the middle of the night, or early morning hours with a numbness and pain in the thumb and first three fingers, sometimes extending up to the elbow, shoulder, or even into the cervical spine (neck). It is usually described as a tingling sensation. Unless patients have some experience with the disorder through the employer, their union, or acquaintances, they may lay the problem to the hand "falling asleep." Medical treatment is usually sought only after repeated instances.

As the malady continues, the patient will notice more frequent and severe numbness and weakness. Patients commonly complain of being unable to open a car door, remove a pan from the stove, or lift a child. As the disease progresses, the thenar muscle[7] will waste away, and patients will begin to complain of pain, rather than numbness.[8]

2. History

Compared to other common medical problems, CTS has only recently been identified.[9] The symptoms were noted as early as 1880 by James Putnam, a Boston neurologist, who suggested lack of circulation as the cause.[10] Dr. J. R. Hunt of Columbia University identified an entrapment of the median nerve as the culprit in thenar muscle atrophy, but failed to identify the numbness as part of the disease and, as a result, may have delayed identification of CTS for many years.[11]

For the first 40 years of this century, numbness of the hands was usually diagnosed as a disorder resulting from compression of the median nerve at the cervical spine, caused by an extra cervical rib. Though usually unsuccessful, surgery was often performed to remove the offending rib.

M. W. Woltman, a Mayo Clinic neurologist, believed the problem was caused by pressure on the median nerve at the wrist.[12] In 1946 surgery was being performed at the Mayo Clinic, and as late as 1950, only 12 patients had been surgically treated with a carpal tunnel release (CTR).[13] It was not until George Phelan published his first series of articles in the 1950s that CTS began to be routinely identified and treated with CTR. Recent diagnostic procedures have further enabled surgeons to diagnose the ailment more accurately.[14]

3. Causes

There are dozens of causative factors that enter the CTS equation which may include personal medical history factors such as diabetes, cervical spine arthritis, menopause, and pregnancy.[15] Most studies now indicate that the above factors may predispose certain individuals to CTS, but only when the patient is engaged in a stressful occupation.

It is now generally conceded that RTDs and CTS are work-related impairments. One study in an Illinois meatpacking plant found an incidence rate of 14.8% compared to the incidence in the general population of 1%.[16] Masear et al. (1986), Armstrong et al. (1987), and others have associated rest or the lack of it with RTDs. Thomas Armstrong considers a job with a short cycle time, or one with more than 50% of the time utilized in similar type movement as having too short a recovery time to prevent injury. Masear found a direct correlation between overtime worked and the incidence of CTS, and that patients often report a lessening of symptoms over weekends or even overnight. Rest, it appears, will tend to diminish incidence rates whether the rest occurs during the work cycle, during the workday, or during the week. Conversely insufficient rest, during at least one of these periods, appears to result in increased incidence rates.

The University of Michigan has been at the forefront in determining the relationship between occupation and CTS and other RTDs affecting the upper extremities. Studies by Armstrong, an ergonomist, inexorably link CTS with repetitiveness, force, posture, hand position (wrist flexion), and finger position.[17]

One recent study in a hardware manufacturing plant suggests that the stress of keeping up a rapid work pace may be a factor to be considered.[18] Hand-held vibrating tools can also cause CTS, as well as another disabling condition of the hand known as vibration white finger syndrome (VWFS). Both have similar symptoms such as tingling and numbness of the fingers, but the worker with VWFS will be more affected by the cold, as VWFS is a circulatory disease, as opposed to CTS, which affects the nerves.[19]

IV. Treatment: The Worker's Dilemma

Many employers in the meat industry have developed objectionable methods of dealing with injured workers. These may range from forcing workers to come in early for wrist wraps and splints, to frequent physical therapy visits (on the worker's time) with over-scheduled therapists, to placing light-duty workers in the most undesirable jobs and locations, and finally, to firing for fabricated reasons.

Treatment often consists of prescribing non-steroidal anti-inflammatory drugs (NSAIDs), which tend to reduce inflammation and pain. The patient will notice a nearly immediate reduction in symptoms. While this is desirable, particularly if the condition continues to improve, monitoring the symptoms becomes more difficult. The analgesic properties make the patient more comfortable, but mask the symptoms sufficiently to give the impression of improvement though the underlying condition may be worsening. NSAIDs also mask symptoms of other maladies which may occur during the treatment period. All drugs in this class also tend to cause stomach irritation, which can result in perforated or bleeding ulcers in long-term usage.

Other options may be offered, such as vitamin B-6, physical therapy, whirlpool baths, and others. Some, such as hot wax treatment, are generally considered to be worthless, while others may have some value when used in combination. None have been shown to be effective in treatment so long as the patient continues the activities that caused the problem. Nonetheless, the CTS-affected worker typically continues to work while being treated in such a conservative (non-surgical) manner.

Unless unusually astute, the worker-patient will have little opportunity to affect treatment offered by the employer or physician. With CTS as widespread as it is, workers in many locations are familiar with the treatment of their fellow workers. Often they will witness the progress of CTS in someone else, to the point where surgery is performed. As the pattern repeats itself, workers often become resigned to the inevitability of surgery. Often workers will not even seek treatment of the problem until the discomfort level becomes high enough to require pain relief from NSAIDs.

Workers have another reason to delay treatment and to reach for a quick fix when the pain becomes too great. Production supervisors' performance is usually judged by quantity produced, with little regard for the day-to-day problems that arise. Production goals cannot be met if consideration is given to workers performing at less than full capacity. Workers who cannot perform are disciplined, regardless of the state of their health, and fellow workers are often required to pick up the slack. In either case, the injured worker will be targeted by either the foreman or coworkers, or both, for uncomplimentary remarks and other unpleasant attention. Months of this kind of treatment causes a feeling of helplessness, frustration, and depression. Financial pressures from an inability to work overtime hours, inability to participate in physically active hobbies, and unrelenting pain all contribute to the isolation. By now surgery may seem welcome to even the most reluctant patient.

But even successful surgery will often leave the patient uncomfortable for sometimes months or years. Complaints of numbness, pain, and tingling are frequent. Those who continued working until the day of surgery may now have developed CTS in the other hand, and favoring the injured hand may have caused chronic shoulder or elbow disorders. The success rates reported may be misleading if the condition of the entire patient is considered.[20] Since weakening occurs in nearly all patients, the individual may or may not be able to continue in stressful work.

Despite any relief brought through surgery, the workers' condition will not improve unless the cause of the RTD is addressed: the job itself. Discussing a patient who had just undergone surgery, Dr. Dean Louis of Ann Arbor, Michigan, writes that,

> At this point there is usually relief of all symptoms, and after a period of recovery from the operation itself, the worker may then return to work. However, because of the prerogatives of seniority and the limited variety of work activities available in most plants, the worker may then find himself back on the same job. Invariably with this re-exposure, the symptoms will return, and this puts the worker in the middle of a real conundrum. The symptoms developed on the job. He has tried conservative means. It has been suggested that an operation would alleviate his problem, and although it did so temporarily, on return to the job, his symptoms returned. Frequently, at this point, the worker is out of work because he cannot maintain his productivity on his usual job . . .[21]

Those with surgeries considered less than successful are left to face an uncertain future. The probability of continued pain and numbness is great. Permanent disability is almost unavoidable and job change is likely to be necessary. Ultimately these results place a heavy burden on family life, and workers' compensation benefits rarely begin to offset the full economic and social impact of the injury.

V. An Alternative: The Sports Medicine Approach

When searching medical journals for treatment of RTDs, one is struck by how little is written regarding conservative treatment in an occupational context. By contrast, there is a wealth of information available in journals oriented toward sports medicine. The sports medicine approach grows out of a rapidly expanding field of expertise, which might provide valuable lessons for occupational therapy. Athletes suffer from many types of RTDs which can impair their performance or even end a career. As sports injuries have identical causes to those at work, namely overuse, similar treatment should yield similar results. Furthermore, medical professionals have developed their treatments in a field where the pressure to have a star athlete return to competition may be far greater than the pressure on a worker to return to the job.

Dr. James Puffer, of UCLA's School of Medicine and head physician for the 1988 U.S. Olympic team, and his colleague James E. Zachazewski stress several principles guiding the treating physician. First, the assessment of pain is the guiding cornerstone. The authors insist that:

> the patient's subjective complaint of pain is the only true guide that the physician and physical therapist can follow in determining the patient's progress. Flexibility, strength and function are all limited by pain. As pain subsides, these will all improve. Common sense and respect for the individual's complaint of pain should always prevail when designing the rehabilitation program.[22]

The proper classification of pain level is necessary so that an appropriate treatment can be developed, and effective assessment demands close communication between the patient and therapist. Second, vigorous physical therapy is vital as strengthening leads to quicker recovery and fewer reoccurrences. Finally, progress will be slow, particularly if the intervention occurs at a late stage of the injury's progress.

Among the conservative approaches suggested are activity restrictions, taping and support, heat (before activity), ice massages (after activity), friction massage, electrical stimulation, and stretching and strengthening exercises. Anti-inflammatories may greatly relieve symptoms, but the patient should be informed that they do not remove the underlying causes. If NSAIDs are ineffective, corticosteroids may be administered, but Puffer and Zachazewski recommend caution in using steroidal injections.

Sports medicine specialists emphasize early identification of the problem, appropriate treatment, patience, and constant communication with the patient to monitor progress. Above all, they stress that treatment of RTDs cannot happen overnight.

VI. The Physician's Responsibilities

Regardless of the source of his fee, the physician's first responsibility should be the well-being of his patient. The Hippocratic Oath's first requirement of the physician is *Primum non nocere*, "First, do no harm."

Workers have noted, however, that the type of care differs considerably when their private doctor also happens to be the company physician. When treated for non work-related infirmities the patients' wishes are treated with deference, but when the injury is work-related, patients often complain of the physician not listening to them or considering the type of treatment they desire. Dissatisfaction levels toward company physicians run quite high. Medical records often do not reflect the patient's account of the conversation between the parties. Commonly, the physician reports improvement while the patient reports just the opposite.

Dr. James H. Dobyns of the Mayo Clinic provides an insight into the appropriate medical management of workers' compensation injuries. He first describes the trials and tribulations, all too familiar to the injured worker, such as confusion about workers' compensation laws, vague messages from the employer to the physician, employer threats of withholding benefits, and other employer-initiated harassment. Dobyns, however, emphasizes the responsibility of the physician to the patient, rather than the employer. While he does not directly address the issue of conservative treatment, his comments regarding a patient's return to work conditions illustrate his approach:

> in some instances, truly 'light-duty' jobs, appropriate to the problem are available; in other instances such jobs are merely fabricated to lure the worker off total temporary disability status. These latter jobs are often summarily closed, and the workers are

moved insidiously and inexorably toward the original job, whether
they are ready or not. The physician must be very suspicious of
such arrangements.[23]

According to Dobyns, "it is always a necessary part of the physi-
cian-manager's task to protect the patient from exploitation," especially upon return from treatment. The physician should make
clear that the return to work "is considered a 'work trial' period
and will be discontinued swiftly if health problems develop or if the
agreed-on conditions are changed without concurrence."[24]

Other occupational physicians have affirmed the concept that
the physician's first responsibility is to the worker-patient. "The
physician," according to I. R. Tabershaw, "is the agent of the profession and of his art no matter who pays him."[25] Not only does the
physician owe a certain level of care, he must also communicate
with his patient to seek information, to reassure the patient, and to
arrive at a mutually agreeable plan of treatment.

The concept that the patient should have some input into his
own treatment has evolved rather slowly as the level of patient
education has developed. Medical ethics questions evolve from the
interaction of the medical and legal professions as well as consumer groups. The medical profession watches and adopts the rationale of court decisions, while the legal profession examines the
ethical code of the medical profession seeking opportunities to protect their clients' interests.

Medical negligence (malpractice) cases historically revolved
around what the norm of care was in the area of treatment, or
what a person could expect of an average physician in his or her
locality. The evolving issue in most jurisdictions is now what the
"reasonable person" expects in medical care, the relationship is
seen as one of a partnership achieving together the appropriate
treatment of a single individual.

Shortly after the turn of the century, courts began applying
the standard of consent. For example, if a surgeon operated on the
wrong limb he was liable for assault and battery as the patient
had given assent to the opposite limb. Negligence suits developed
throughout the first half of the century, generally on the basis that
the standard of care was inferior compared to the standard of the
community. That concept has been called the "professional rule."
Some jurisdictions have imposed a different test, called the "patient rule," which holds that prior to giving assent to a procedure,
a patient must have been given sufficient information to be able to

make a rational decision. Most jurisdictions now embrace the concept of informed consent, or the "patient rule." In Iowa the new standard was upheld by the state Supreme Court in *Pauscher v. Iowa Methodist Medical Center.*

The court had previously endorsed the "professional rule," but in the *Pauscher* ruling, the court recognized "the inherently paternalistic and authoritarian nature of the professional rule of disclosure," and that "an expanding number of jurisdictions have rejected it for a judicially fashioned standard." It continued:

> The decision to consent to a particular medical procedure is not a medical decision. Instead, it ordinarily is a personal and often difficult decision to be made by the patient with the physician's advice and consultation. In order to make his or her informed decision, the patient has the right to expect the information reasonably necessary to that process will be made available by the physician.[26]

Medical ethicists are in general agreement with this concept, and recommend their colleagues confer with patients in developing treatment plans.[27] In general, the *Pauscher* decision and medical ethicists discuss informed consent as an issue arising prior to a given surgical or diagnostic procedure. If, however, such a procedure eventually becomes necessary due to a decision made early in the treatment process, it follows that informed consent would be appropriate earlier in treatment, at the time a choice was viable, rather than when surgery was unavoidable.

VII. Strategy Development

Federal law mandates the employer provide a workplace free of recognized hazards that are likely to cause death or serious injury to its employees.[28] Clearly some employers do not comply with the Act. The problem then becomes how the worker and his union can encourage, persuade, or otherwise force the employer to accept this responsibility. Various options exist and should be explored. These options could be used individually or in concert as part of a multifaceted approach.

This section is designed to be used as a guideline rather than a blueprint. Ideas, options, and suggestions are available to be integrated, where practical, with the local union's own tactics and methods to develop a comprehensive program.

Employers have millions of dollars at stake in workers' compensation costs, engineering changes, and lost productivity. They cannot be expected to fold easily or quickly. This approach may seem overly complicated but it should be thought of as a step-by-step way to reach long-term goals. As grievance processes, which include arbitration, bring long delays, it is doubtful that a fully implemented program can reach complete effectiveness in under two years.

Underlying the recommendations made here are two basic goals. First, to provide the union with several choices to meet developing circumstances, as well as an opportunity for complete victory even though one or more approaches may fail. Second, to make the employer aware that the union's position is firm and unwavering, and that, at some time, they will have to address it seriously. Undergirding the union's position is the increasing awareness of the problem by the public, the medical profession and perhaps, most important, the federal government, especially OSHA. Documentation is also vital to each part of this series. The same documents will focus the attention of an arbitrator, an OSHA inspector, and the physician. Just as important, it will prevent the employer from evading his responsibility with vague defenses.

In concert with more traditional tactics, a physician-oriented approach should be designed so that worker-patients can be removed from injury-producing jobs until their symptoms have subsided. If successful, this approach will provide significant incentives to the employer to modify those unsafe jobs, and thereby eradicate the prime cause of RTDs.

1. Those involved must gather enough information to determine the scope of the problem, through OSHA 200 logs, and interviews with stewards, safety committee members, affected employees, and other appropriate parties. Interviews with management and safety personnel can give additional insight into their view of the problem.

2. Determine which techniques are most appropriate for the current circumstances.

3. Identify problem areas or jobs, selected by incidence rates, availability of medical records, or other methods.

4. Gather whatever information is available regarding the key jobs. It is important to obtain time studies, medical records of affected operators, and interviews with operators, whether affected or not. Any recent job load increase or production problem should

be noted. Other information that will help the case would be all medical records of affected persons, safety committee minutes, meeting notes of union-management discussions of the problem, and accident reports. It is also important to record environmental factors, such as temperature, sound levels, working heights, and any other conditions which adversely affect worker safety.

There are several advantages to targeting specific areas, rather than raising wide-ranging goals. The approach leaves the union with a back-up position: if unsuccessful in one group of jobs, success may come later with a different group. Compiling and handling information will be easier, and the parties involved will be better able to understand a fixed set of issues and facts.

Available strategic options include grievance procedures, OSHA complaints, informal discussions with the employer, safety committee actions, and education-legal campaigns.

1. Grievance Procedures

Most contracts allow grievances under either safety language or working conditions. Careful consideration should be given to the particular language and all options should be evaluated, as separate grievances may be possible under various contract provisions, or for each individual or job. Various combinations may be tried at different times to determine the most effective approach.

Whatever the provisions of the contract, a grievance should be filed regardless of the possible outcome. Grievances provide an opportunity for discussion of the issue and a chance to inform management of the union position on high incidence rates of RTDs. One of the most persuasive reasons for filing a grievance is the opportunity to obtain information from the employer that may be otherwise unavailable. Even confidential medical records may sometimes be obtained through the procedure. If the procedure ends in arbitration at least one expert witness will be necessary.

2. OSHA Complaints

Another likely approach is an OSHA complaint. Employers usually resent "outsiders" being brought in, which of course can upset the relationship between the parties. It should probably be reserved for a later time, when progress has been stymied. The OSHA complaint does have the advantage of communicating the union's commitment to safer working conditions for its members, particularly when other, less disruptive methods have failed to bring satisfactory results. As in the case of the grievance process, careful analysis should be given to the breadth of the complaint. The threat of a union complaint is always present, but a plant-wide complaint, if unsuccessful, removes the threat, leaving the union with one less alternative.

Court decisions, medical opinions, ergonomic factors, and administrative procedures will all play a part in the preparation process. OSHA and state-administered occupational safety programs have extremely limited resources. Inspectors are not always completely versed in each discipline they have to deal with, so any guidance the union can provide will enhance the chances for a satisfactory outcome.

It should be made clear in the original complaint that job loads and chain speeds are excessive so that in any settlement discussions the union can press for immediate relief from those conditions. The alternative could be an ergonomic study that would provide relief over months or years, if at all.[29]

Recent developments indicate that OSHA complaints may be more effective now than in the past. Huge proposed fines were recently levied against IBP, and against John Morrell Co. for underreporting injuries, and for RTD incidence rates. Both Houses of Congress have held hearings on safety in meatpacking, and OSHA is placing special emphasis on meatpacking inspections. Future complaints may thus prove to be even more effective.

3. Education-Legal Campaigns

A. PHYSICIAN RELATIONS-EDUCATION

Developing a rapport with the treating physician can help make the physician a real partner in the effort to provide safer workplaces. Most physicians have a real interest in preventing injuries, but have little knowledge of the problems unions face in representing their members. The physician would probably welcome an invitation by the local union to visit the plant and observe the targeted jobs. If not, it would provide documentation that the doctor had a cavalier approach to his patients, evidence which could prove useful if litigation ensues. Similarly, if the employer refused permission for such a visit it would indicate this uncooperative attitude to an arbitrator or an OSHA inspector.

A plant tour could also be an opportunity to discuss the union's concerns about its members, the workplace, and the difficulty it has in solving these problems. Depending on local circumstances, it would probably be wise to request the employer to participate. If the facility has a "light-duty" program that the employer is abusing, a tour would be an excellent opportunity to demonstrate the difficulty of modifying jobs or performing "one-handed" jobs.

Once a dialogue has been established with the physician, the union will be in a much better position to discuss particular patients and appropriate treatment, particularly for those workers from the targeted jobs. As the relationship develops, further opportunities may present themselves to open communications.

B. WORKER-PATIENT EDUCATION

Whether on targeted jobs or not, all members being treated by the physician should be contacted. Those unhappy with their treatment may be advised about other treatments, as well as their rights to such options. The information could be provided through handouts from safety committee members or stewards, or through mailings to affected members. The document could include a description of RTDs and CTS, and an outline of patient rights. It would be more effective to train a union representative who would be available to inform worker-patients and to accompany them on medical appointments.

If the worker opts to be relieved of the injury-producing job, and no light-duty program is available, the worker should inform the physician. If he resists, then a request should be made to see another physician, preferably a specialist. One option for workers in Iowa is the Center for Occupational Medicine at the University of Iowa which accepts patients without physician referrals; a worker-patient who is unsuccessful with the company doctor may go directly to the university.[30] Other states may have similar programs.

The worker's medical records should contain these requests, as well as other information such as reported symptoms. It is important to keep the records current, so that the worker or a representative can write follow-up letters reiterating the requests. Such communications serve a two-fold purpose: the first, to set the record straight and make sure the request is in the files, and the second, to inform the physician that the worker-patient is unhappy with the treatment and intends to follow through. These documents can also be an important factor in any proceedings, including OSHA, workers' compensation, or civil litigation.

c. Member Education

Some type of continuing education program should be instituted, whether by newsletter, meetings, or seminars. The education should emphasize early identification of symptoms, treatment options, the present quality of health care, the injury rate at the plant, and recommended procedures to follow if affected. The local union may also wish to include the official union position on these matters, as well as the steps being taken to eliminate them. Frequent progress reports will help strengthen membership resolve.

d. Legal Options

Under Iowa's Workers' Compensation Law, workers may change physicians, but most attorneys report that it takes up to a year to accomplish. By that time, however, it is usually too late to provide much help to the patients. It should be noted that union representatives cannot practice before the Industrial Commission in Iowa. Complaints can be filed with the Iowa Department of Medical Examiners for unethical conduct by physicians, though it is unclear whether failure to provide informed consent is unethical. Some disciplinary action would probably be taken if it could be shown that the physician repeatedly falsified medical records.

Civil litigation may be possible in cases where a physician did not provide informed consent. Since the *Pauscher* decision is rather recent, case law in this area is undeveloped in Iowa. The decision would seem to provide at least some hope to the injured worker.[31] Finally, a class action suit might be sustainable in some cases where several members were damaged in a similar manner by the same individual. Attorneys do not agree in this area, but court rulings should be monitored for further developments.[32]

VIII. Conclusion

CTS has an insidious onset. In the absence of an early detection program, coupled with appropriate treatment, the afflicted worker faces a very unpleasant future. Workers on high force, highly repetitive jobs are likely to be unable to continue any stressful activity of the hands or arms into their middle or later years. Taking into account the potential for unsuccessful treatment, whether conservative, surgical, or both, and the possibility of complications or recurrence, the long-term outlook is discouraging. Extending such minimal chances over a person's entire work life indicates an infinitesimal possibility that the afflicted worker will ever enjoy a normal retirement.

The lessons from sports medicine provide a promising but reasonable approach which may offer many guidelines for those concerned with occupational health. The program centers on the patients' subjective complaint of pain, and the judicious matching of treatment to the level of injury. A methodical, patient approach, coupled with modified activity and exercise, is most effective in treating RTDs. This program will result in quicker recovery, fewer recurrences, and a significant reduction in suffering, which would seem to be in everyone's best interest.

The program outlined above has been put to use by the meat-cutters in the Iowa industry. Though it uses traditional union approaches to the problem, such as contract language and grievance procedures, it also incorporates strategies from outside the workplace, including relief from OSHA, state occupational safety administrations, the courts, and education campaigns. These integrated approaches reflect the fact that the program was developed in conditions where workers and their unions face extremely hostile employers in an industry where more and more workers fall outside of union contracts.

The number of workers losing their jobs due to RTDs may run into the thousands in Iowa alone. While employers' costs are closely monitored, no one knows the cumulative financial burden placed on workers by these injuries and treatment methods. The impact on physical, mental, and family health is huge, both individually and collectively. To treat these injuries as many employers do now is immoral by any definition. Any effort short of humane treatment of victims and eliminating the cause of RTDs is *The Jungle* revisited.

Notes

1. S. Tanaka, P. Seligman, W. Halperin, M. Thun, C. L. Timbrook, and J. J. Wasil, "Use of Workers Compensation Claims Data for Surveillance of Cumulative Trauma Disorders," *Journal of Occupational Medicine*, 30 (1988): 488–492.

2. V. R. Masear, J. M. Hayes, and A. G. Hyde, "An Industrial Cause of Carpal Tunnel Syndrome," *Journal of Hand Surgery*, 11A (March 1986): 222–7.

3. The category includes bursitis, synovitis, tenosynovitis, and other conditions affecting joints, tendons, or muscles, but does not include sprains, strains, dislocation of muscles or tendons, or their aftereffects.

4. Still, these figures must be read with some skepticism. The Cherokee figures may be misleading, if not legally under-reported, as workers are often diagnosed in a given year, and undergo surgery in a subsequent year. Mike Wilbur, President of UFCW Local 179, representing the Cherokee/Wilson workers, reports that at least nine workers in the pace-boning operation were off work in 1988, some for several months. Yet, even though the absences were work-related, the lost time did not show up on the 1988 OSHA 200 logs. The employer's explanation to Wilbur was that since the injury occurred in an earlier year, that year's logs would be updated. While presumably legal, those figures would mislead anyone examining the current year's figures, or those of earlier years, if they were not in possession of an updated copy. Estimates are that had those nine workers' injuries been reported during the current year (1988), the number of lost days in pace-boning would have increased by between 300 to 500 days.

5. D. S. Louis, "Cumulative Trauma Disorders," *Journal of Hand Surgery,* vol. 12A, pt. 2 (Sept. 1987): 823–5.

6. Dr. Rowe effectively describes the effects of overuse on the tendon and sheaths: "With overuse . . . the lubrication system may fail to meet the demand, either by inability to secrete enough lubricant or by the production of a fluid with poor lubricating qualities. This allows friction to occur between the tendon and its sheath. Such friction initially stimulates increased secretion of the lubricant by the existing cells within the sheath. If this is insufficient to meet the demand, the secreting cells multiply and this causes the sheath to become thicker." The thickening and swelling of the tendon sheaths in the carpal tunnel can create high pressure within the rigid tunnel. M. L. Rowe, "The Diagnosis of Tendon and Tendon Sheath Injuries," *Seminars in Occupational Medicine,* vol. 2, no. 1 (March 1987).

7. The large muscle at the base of the hand that affects and controls the operation of the thumb.

8. George S. Phelan, "The Carpal Tunnel Syndrome," *Clinical Orthopaedics and Related Research,* 82 (March–April 1972).

9. G. B. Pfeffer, R. H. Gelberman, J. H. Boyes, and B. Rydevik, "The History of Carpal Tunnel Syndrome," *Journal of Hand Surgery,* 13b (Feb. 1988): 28–36.

10. J. J. Putnam, "A Series of Cases of Paraesthesia, Mainly of the Hand, of Periodical Recurrence, and Possibly of Vaso-Motor Origin," *Archives of Medicine* 4 (1880): 147–162, quoted in Pfeffer, et al.

11. J. R. Hunt, "Occupation Neuritis of the Thenar Branch of the Median Nerve, A Well Defined Type of Atrophy of the Hand," *Transactions of the American Neurological Association*, 35 (1909): 184; J. R. Hunt, "The Thenar and Hypothenar Types of Neural Atrophy of the Hand," *American Journal of Medical Sciences*, vol. 141, no. 2 (1911)2: 224; J. R. Hunt, "The Neural Atrophy of Muscles of the Hand, Without Sensory Disturbances," *Review of Neurology and Psychiatry*, 12 (1914): 137; and J. R. Hunt, "Thenar and Hypothenar Types of Neural Atrophy of the Hand," *British Medical Journal*, (1950): 642, quoted in Pfeffer, et al.

12. M. W. Woltman, "Neuritis Associated with Acromegaly," *Archives of Neurology and Psychiatry*, (1941): 680–682 quoted in Pfeffer, et al.

13. B. W. Cannon and J. G. Love, "Tardy Median Palsy, Median Neuritis, Median Thenar Neuritis Amenable to Surgery," *Surgery*, 20 (1946): 210–216, quoted in Pfeffer et al.

14. G. S. Phelan, W. J. Gardner, and A. A. La Londe, "Neuropathy of the Median Nerve due to Compression Beneath the Transverse Carpal Ligament," *The Journal of Bone and Joint Surgery*, vol. 32A, no. 1, (1950): 109–112, quoted in Pfeffer, et al.

15. Gout myxedema, amyloidosis, multiple myeloma, and other diseases unfamiliar to the layman are also noted in medical journals as predisposing conditions. Other factors include wrist fractures, oral contraceptives, menopause, pregnancy, and hysterectomies. L. J. Cannon, E. J. Bernacki, and S. D. Walter, "Personal and Occupational Factors Associated with Carpal Tunnel Syndrome," *Journal of Occupational Medicine*, (23 April 1981): 255–8.

16. V. R. Masear, J. M. Hayes, and A. G. Hyde, "An Industrial Cause of Carpal Tunnel Syndrome," *Journal of Hand Surgery*, 11A (March 1986): 222–7; and R. M. Szabo and M. D. Gelberman, "The Patho-Physiology of Nerve Entrapment Syndromes," *Journal of Hand Surgery*, 12A (Sept. 1987): 880–4.

17. Armstrong uses devices to scientifically measure force, repetitiveness and position. Electromyography is used to measure muscle activity, which has a direct relationship to the amount of force necessary to perform certain jobs. Video cameras are also utilized so that posture and repetitiveness can be studied; cameras are placed in such a way that EMG readings will be displayed on the screen during playback. The tapes can then be studied frame by frame to examine each movement. These methods provide valuable data to evaluate a given job. Over a period of time, when high incidence jobs have been identified and data gathered, the information can be used to evaluate current jobs and proposed changes for prevention purposes. T. J. Armstrong, D. B. Chaffin, and J. A. Foulke, "A Methodology for Documenting Hand Positions and Forces During Manual Work," *Journal of Biomechanics*, vol. 12, no. 2 (1979): 131–3. Armstrong

has also developed a force-repetitiveness test to evaluate jobs for the determination of likelihood of RTDs. A job is likely to be at risk if both the force and repetitiveness is high. T. J. Armstrong, L. J. Fine, S. A. Goldstein, Y. R. Lifshitz, and B. A. Silverstein, "Ergonomic Considerations in Hand and Wrist Tendinitis," *Journal of Hand Surgery*, 12A (Sept. 1987): 830–7. These methods and others are proven predictors of incidence rates.

18. R. Arndt, "Work Pace, Stress, and Cumulative Trauma Disorders," *Journal of Hand Surgery*, 12A (Sept. 1987).

19. J. Erdreich, "VWFS Threatens Your Most Valuable Tools: Employee Hands," *Occupational Health and Safety*, (June 1989): 26–7. VWFS causes periodic spasms which often follow exposure to the cold. When these occur, parts of the fingers turn white and the hand may have a bluish appearance. Attacks usually last from 15 minutes to an hour. After the attack, hands usually become flushed as the circulation returns. VWFS can result in gangrene and, ultimately, amputation of one or more fingers. Vibration may increase the risk of chronic tendon and nerve disorders by increasing the force necessary to grasp the tool. T. J. Armstrong, L. J. Fine, R. G. Radwin, and B. S. Silverstein, "Ergonomics and the Effects of Vibration in Hand-intensive Work," *Scandinavian Journal of Work and Environmental Health*, vol. 13, no. 4 (August 1987): 286–9. By reducing the feeling, and stimulating the muscles to contract, the grip force automatically increases. The amount of force to perform the required work may increase the risk. Other studies have associated vibration with CTS. Cannon et al. 1981; G. Wieslander, D. Norback, C. J. Gothe, and L. Juhlin, "Carpal Tunnel Syndrome (CTS) and Exposure to Vibration, Repetitive Wrist Movements, and Heavy Manual Work: A Case Referent Study," *British Journal of Industrial Medicine*, vol. 46, no. 1 (Jan. 1989): 43–7.

20. Since surgeons consider themselves successful if a procedure merely relieves rather than eliminates symptoms, a success rate of 87–90% may not seem so miraculous to a patient with continuing, though improved symptoms. S. J. Blair and J. Bear-Lehman, "Editorial Comment: Prevention of Upper Extremity Occupational Disorders," *Journal of Hand Surgery*, 12A, vol. 5, no. 2 (Sept. 1987): 821–2.

21. D. S. Louis, "Cumulative Trauma Disorders," *Journal of Hand Surgery*, 12A, vol. 5, no. 2 (Sept. 1987): 823–5.

22. J. C. Puffer and M. S. Zachazewski, "Management of Overuse Injuries," *Practical Therapeutics*, vol. 38, no. 3 (Sept. 1988): 225–32.

23. J. H. Dobyns, "Role of the Physician in Workers' Compensation Injuries," *Journal of Hand Surgery*, 12A (Sept. 1987): 826–9.

24. Dobyns severely criticizes the "fabricated job," the famous "one-handed" jobs that are often requested by physicians and honored by the company. Dobyns viewed a videotape from a turkey-processing company interested in displaying the great variety of one-handed jobs they could

provide. The effort backfired, as "the videotape dramatically displayed how impossible it is to convert bi-manual jobs to one-hand tasks without overburdening the working limb, abusing the rest of the body, adding ridiculous levels of inefficiency, or increasing the safety hazards." Dobyns was "sufficiently disturbed by watching this unknowing travesty that I will never order a "one-handed" job again."

25. I. R. Tabershaw, "Whose 'Agent' is the Occupational Physician?" *Archives of Environmental Health*, 30 (August 1975): 412–16. See also M. Bundy, "How do We Assure that the Workers' Health is the Occupational Physicians' Primary Concern?" *Journal of Occupational Health*, vol. 18, no. 19 (1976): 671–6.

26. *Pauscher v. Iowa Methodist Medical Center*, 408 N.W. 2d 355 (Iowa 1987).

27. C. A. Haney and A. C. Colson, "Ethical Responsibility in Physician-Patient Communication," *Ethics Science Medicine*, 7 (1980): 27–36; and D. J. Mazur, "What Should Patients be Told Prior to a Medical Procedure?" *American Journal of Medicine*, 81 (1988): 1051–4.

28. *Occupational Safety and Health Act of 1970*, 29 USC § 654.

29. Time studies are theoretically able to determine the amount of work an average person is capable of performing in a given period of time, but mountains of documents have been produced to discredit that theory. It is arguable that unless time studies acknowledge the amount of force necessary then accurate assessment cannot be obtained. It seems obvious that probable injury to the individual must be included in any equation measuring a worker's capacity to perform.

30. The Center for Occupational Medicine, University Hospitals and Clinics, University of Iowa, Iowa City, Iowa 52241.

31. Attorneys generally refuse medical negligence (malpractice) suits unless damages exceed $100,000 by a considerable degree. One of the reasons given is the expense of a medical expert witness, though it is debatable whether experts are necessary in informed consent cases.

32. One indication that the Iowa courts are becoming more sympathetic to the plight of injured workers is the recent case, *Springer v. Weeks and Leo Co.*, 429 N.W. 2d 558 (Iowa 1988). The court held that even though Iowa still held to the "employment at will" principle, an employer who files a workers' compensation cannot be legally fired.

Editors' Suggested Readings

Berman, Daniel M. *Death on the Job: Occupational Health and Safety Struggles in the United States*. New York: Monthly Review Press, 1978.

Cherniak, Martin. *The Hawks Nest Incident: America's Worst Industrial Disaster*. New Haven: Yale University Press, 1986.

Davis, Mike. *Prisoners of the American Dream*. London: Verso, 1986.

Derickson, Alan. *Workers' Health, Workers' Democracy: The Western Miners' Struggle, 1891–1925*. Ithaca: Cornell University Press, 1988.

Green, Hardy. *On Strike at Hormel: the Struggle for a Democratic Labor Movement*. Philadelphia: Temple University Press, 1990.

Noble, Charles. *Liberalism at Work: The Rise and Fall of OSHA*. Philadelphia: Temple University Press, 1986.

Rosner, David and Gerald Markowitz, eds. *Dying for Work: Workers' Safety and Health in Twentieth Century America*. Bloomington, IN: Indiana University Press, 1987.

Sinclair, Upton. *The Jungle*. Urbana: University of Illinois Press, 1988.

Smith, Barbara Ellen. *Digging Their Own Graves: Coal Miners and the Struggle over Black Lung Disease*. Philadelphia: Temple University Press, 1987.

Starr, Paul. *The Social Transformation of American Medicine*. New York: Basic Books, 1982.

Stevens, Rosemary. *American Medicine and the Public Interest*. New Haven: Yale University Press, 1971.

Smith Steel Workers and A. O. Smith: New Directions in Safety and Health

*Jonathan D. Rosen**

I. Introduction

This is a story about a local union in Milwaukee,[1] Wisconsin, and a conservative employer, A. O. Smith Automotive Products Company. It is about new approaches that are being implemented to improve the safety and health of the workforce through joint labor-management activities. Eleven joint safety committees were formed in the late 1980s throughout the Milwaukee works. Some of their activities include conducting safety inspections, monthly departmental safety meetings, ergonomic projects, and "hazard communication" training. Although dramatic reductions in injury statistics and workers' compensation costs have not yet been realized, the development of organization and resources to meet these goals is a major step toward their attainment.

The first part of this report will review the history of the employer and the union and their safety and health activities. The single most important event in the history of dealing with workers' physical well-being in this country was the passage of the Occupational Safety and Health Act in 1970 and the formation of the OSHA Administration. Union involvement in safety and health increased by leaps and bounds on the heels of the birth of OSHA. The persistent and dedicated work of the union safety committee over the past 15 years laid the foundation for the advances that are now

I would like to thank all the people at A. O. Smith from the company and the Union who took time out of their busy schedules to be interviewed. I would like to thank my wife, Annie, who spent hours typing the transcripts and proofreading the manuscript.

taking place. For the most part, these workers volunteered their own time, and with sparse resources and little recognition, brought much needed attention to the issue of safety and health of the workforce. However, their effectiveness was limited due to management opposition and scant resources.

The second section of this chapter will relate how the restructuring of A. O. Smith in the 1980s, based on a joint labor-management philosophy, created a great opportunity for the union to improve safety and health. In response to Japanese companies gaining 30% of the domestic auto and truck market, both American auto companies and labor are attempting joint efforts to secure market share and jobs through joint management efforts, team concepts, and quality circles.

A. O. Smith began converting from a management-driven system of shopfloor organization to one of team production. The underlying philosophy was that the people closest to the work can do the best job of managing their affairs and improving the quality of the processes and products for which they are responsible. The new emphasis on human resources has created an environment where union demands for training, empowerment, and a voice in decisionmaking were being recognized. It was in this atmosphere that the pioneering joint safety committees at A. O. Smith were formed.

Our experience has shown safety to be a subject of common ground with the company. The union wanted to end the disabling injuries and illnesses that the membership experienced, and improve working conditions. Some managers shared these goals, but an even greater motivation on management's side appears to have been its desire to improve productivity, quality, and reduce the millions of dollars of annual workers' compensation costs.

The final section will focus on the new safety and health activities. Numerous new methods are being attempted to resolve problems such as patterns of strain and sprain injuries, hot and cold environments, poor air quality, noise, and to conduct safety training and education. These efforts have brought some results, but the entire health and safety program has been put at risk by management's larger investment strategy, aimed at downsizing the Milwaukee works and shifting production to non-union satellite plants. The union's success in joint decisionmaking on health and safety issues has not led to similar cooperation on major decisions which directly affect the future of the Milwaukee plant itself.

II. Historical Background

1. The Company

A. O. Smith Automotive Products Company, Milwaukee's second largest employer, can trace its origins to 1874, when C. J. Smith established his Carriage Works and Machine Shop. In the nineteenth century the company's main product lines were baby carriage parts, and by 1899 it was recognized as the largest producer of frames for bicycles in the world.[2] In 1903 the company made its start in the automobile industry by producing 200 sets of tubular frames, axles, and other parts for Studebaker Electric.

With the death of A. O. in 1913, his son L. R. took over the company. Always a pioneer in technology and engineering, the firm developed the world's first fully automated assembly line and put it into operation in 1921. The line, which produced more than 10,000 frames a day, was in use until 1958.

A. O. Smith has produced more than 100 million auto frames, 40 million truck frames and 65 million control arm sets for customers such as General Motors, Ford, and Chrysler. Over the years the company has diversified, and now has plants worldwide. Total corporate sales in 1988 were over $1 billion, while sales for the Milwaukee plant alone amounted to more than $400 million, or 39% of the total.

Due to the shift to unibody construction in the auto industry, away from full perimeter frames, the Milwaukee plant has been converting to production of truck frames and side rails since 1979. A. O. Smith had made 100% of Cadillac's frames since 1902, but the last car frame production was phased out entirely in the summer of 1990.

Total employment at the Milwaukee plant dropped from a peak of 7,800 in November 1973 to 3,500 in November 1989 due to lost business, automation, austerity measures, and shifting of work to new plants. In 1973, A. O. Smith was hiring more than 200 workers a month and paying $5 an hour, among the top wages for blue collar work in the nation at the time. Back then, good paying factory jobs were so plentiful that many a new hire would quit after just a couple of hours of sweating it out in the infamous press department 1732. Less than 10 years later, however, 15,000 unemployed workers waited in sub-zero weather at Wisconsin State Fair

Park for up to 24 hours to apply for 300 jobs that opened up at the plant in February 1983.

These jobs lasted four years, and came to a halt on December 4, 1987 in the most dramatic restructuring event in recent company history. The day, known as "Black Friday," was the first and most brutal cutback ushering in a period of continuous reorganization. On that day some 850 workers were laid off, along with 65 foremen, as the "G" (mid-sized automobile) frame production was discontinued. "Black Friday" represented the end of an era, as the "G" frame had been the company's main product line for over 20 years. The workforce has never recovered; in late 1989, there were 1,094 people on layoff.

About half the trucks in North America contain Smith components, making the company the largest producer of truck frames in the world. The sprawling facility stretches over eight city blocks. In 1989, the company was ranked number 322 in the Fortune 500.

2. The Union

Smith Steel Workers Federated Local DALU No. 19806 was organized by the American Federation of Labor in 1934 amid the rising tide of industrial unionism, and the local's first contract was ratified December 6 that year. In 1935 the membership reached 700, and later that year the union won double-time for Sundays and holidays, advance notice of layoffs and a minimum shift of five hours in case of a major breakdown.

The years after the war until the late 1970s were marked by continued gains. But in my first year at A. O. Smith (1973), President Nixon's Cost of Living Council held increases to 5.5%. Most workers haven't experienced a comparable raise in the last 10 years. In 1974 the union went out on strike for the first and only time in its history. There was a wave of strikes throughout the country, and although ours lasted only three weeks, it achieved significant gains: a fully paid dental plan, a 30-years-and-out pension plan, return of the cost of living allowance (COLA), and an agreement that the union president would be made a full-time position to be paid by the company. Gains in the 1977 negotiations included an escalator clause for the pension plan, elimination of deductibles for dental coverage, and the formation of the joint safety committee.

1980 marked the last of the "easy" negotiations. It was also the first time that the union demanded a full-time union safety representative. The recession of 1980 caused large layoffs at the plant, bringing employment down to 2,800 from over 5,200 just a few years earlier; but by early 1981 most people had been called back. Ronald Reagan had just been elected to his first term of office, and throughout the country concessionary bargaining became the name of the game. A. O. Smith demanded a concession in the COLA payments, claiming that its bid for the General Motors "G" Frame could not be secured without it, and in June 1981, a temporary concession was granted for a one-year period. A total of 65 cents an hour was conceded over four quarters. However, this was soft compared to the demands the company made in the 1983 bargaining talks. It wanted a freeze on wages, a one-year freeze on COLA, elimination of personal days (five paid days off), reduction in vacation time, and elimination of the vacation and Christmas bonus payments.

While none of these items were approved, the tenor of negotiations had changed from making new advances, to defending what had been achieved in the past. A significant provision in the 1983 negotiations was a letter of understanding on improving Milwaukee works quality, productivity, and competitiveness. This committed the union and management to a joint study effort directed towards identifying and resolving problems inhibiting competitiveness in the Milwaukee works. This led to the labor management participation Program (BEST—Bringing Employee Skills Together) that has changed the way A. O. Smith runs its business.

3. Safety and Health History

In the old days when the city bus used to pull up to the factory gate, the driver would call out "butcher shop" or "slaughter house." Before World War I through the mid-1960s, presses were operated with foot pedals and the workforce suffered the consequences: amputation of fingers and arms. Union president Paul Blackman[3] recalls the following:

> When I first got hired back in 1959 I came in as a driver and one of my first jobs was to service a 3,000-ton press. I can remember sitting around the lunch table with the people from that press and everybody at that table, there must have been seven or eight people, had a finger or something missing. Believe it or not, people felt that it was kind of like a badge of honor that they had a finger missing and that would be a topic of conversation. They would discuss how much they got compensated which I thought

was really tragic and kind of nerve-racking. Right after that I decided that I didn't want to wind up on the press and they needed welders so I signed up and that's where I spent the majority of my working period.

James Pinion[4] reminisced:

When I first got hired in 1951, out in the streets you could tell the person who worked at Smith. He or she had one finger missing, or two. That's the truth, you could absolutely tell. If you saw someone with their hand on the table with a finger missing you'd say, "You work at Smith, don't you?" That was attacked about three years after I was hired when they started putting on guards. I was working on a press in D–1132 and they had a sling guard that would knock your hand out of the way when the press came down. From the time I got hired the safety program has come a long way. I can remember when every week someone was missing fingers, missing hands, until they started doing those things. A lot of that came from the ideas of the people working on the presses.

Yet, Earnest Spivey, administrator of safety and security for the company,[5] had this to say about the history of safety at the plant:

The Smith family was concerned about people and we had a really bad history of hurting people. It wasn't unique to A. O. Smith, in our industry it was a common thing that people lost hands, fingers, and arms. But the Smith family had a concern about that and instituted a safety program, a safety policy, and hired a full-time safety person to administer the safety programs.

The first organized safety activity began on February 1, 1913 with the establishment of the Welfare Department, primarily a hospital or first-aid room. A monthly publication, *Shop Safety Bulletin*, was published from April 1915 until 1918. The safety activities were co-ordinated by a central committee appointed by the general superintendent. Serving on this committee were foremen, engineers and the superintendent of welfare. In a column called "Jots on Safety," the *Bulletin* of October 1917 cautioned: "The Crane men should not be in too great a hurry pulling up loads in order to keep from pulling off the thumbs and fingers of the hookers."

In another article from the August 1915 edition of the *Bulletin* the author writes:

Some men are naturally safety men and others must be taught. Joe Wood has always taken care of himself as can easily be seen by the picture. Joe does not always hold his hands this way but we had him do so this time to prove to you that a man can run punch presses for twenty years and not lose fingers or hands.

Pinion talked about conditions in the 1950s:

I didn't hear much of the union doing anything about safety at that time. We had one safety person that I knew of, he was management. If you had a safety problem, by the time he would get there you may not have an arm, because it would take two or three weeks for him to get there because of the area he had to cover. Roger Rahn replaced him. When Roger came in you could see a difference. He went to work in saving fingers.

When I asked Isiah Lee[6] about the company's safety department in the early days, he said: "There was no such thing. If there was we never knew it." Describing safety at this time, Lee related:

I started to work for A. O. Smith on July 24, 1950 and I stayed with the company for 31 years. Throughout that time I saw so many accidents that could have been avoided if somebody had thought and taken a little time to work safely. They were looking at the dollar more than the man who was working. When I first started here I had to take the job that no one else wanted. If a job was dangerous, that's the job we got cause we were so few. If a press repeated and the white man didn't want to operate that press he'd leave it and they'd put you on it.

In the mid-1960s, Smith engineers developed a "two-hand trip" system for operating power presses. This prevents the press from tripping unless the operator has both hands on the buttons (located away from the pinch point of the dies in a power press), greatly improving safety. This system was largely adopted throughout the industry, and subsequently made a part of OSHA's standards. This was five years before the formation of OSHA and 10 years before the adoption of major power press standards. However, the loss of fingers and hands continued due to presses repeating and faulty brakes.

When a proposed OSHA standard for "hands out of dies" was being debated in 1974, A. O. Smith lobbied to extend compliance over a 10-year period. The company spent $350,000 developing special shuttle feeders, transfer systems, Unimate robots, universal feeders, and other devices.[7] The OSHA standard was never enacted, partly due to the company's success in development of an effective "brake monitoring device" which was made a part of the power press standard 29 CFR 1910.217. Over 100 groups of presses were equipped with brake monitors at a cost of over $2 million. This has virtually put an end to presses repeating, and the gruesome injuries caused therein.

4. The Union Safety Committee

There was virtually no organized union safety activity before 1974 when a standing safety and health committee was formed. According to Paul Blackman:

> In 1972 there was a low priority in terms of safety. In fact I think there's a rap that the lowest priority in a union portfolio is community services. I would venture to say that safety was probably below community services in terms of any real activity going on or promoted by the union.

Enactment of OSHA caused a flurry of safety and health activity in the plant. A "hearing conservation" program was implemented to control noise levels, the "hands out of die" issue was raging, and various other measures were induced by the newly adopted standards. Jim Poulter[8] organized the first union safety committee and initiated efforts to establish it as a standing organization.

> I thought there was a lot of safety hazards here at A. O. Smith that weren't being looked at. I thought that by getting a degree in safety I could help the worker. I wanted an independent safety committee that wasn't involved with the company, but after I got involved with it I realized it would work better as a joint venture. The company didn't oppose it to begin with, but they wanted it to be a joint committee. I ran into problems when we wanted to be out there by ourselves. When we decided we would work jointly then things started turning around. The company didn't want us out there, running around the plant doing this and that, going here and there, and raising hell. I lost my chairmanship due to being laid off. I was really zealous before I got laid off. I think I cited the company for 43 violations of OSHA standards. I'd give them a period of time to correct the violations and threaten to bring OSHA in.

In 1975 the company first recognized the union safety committee. The issue of controlling and limiting its involvement was as much a concern as recognition of this newly formed force for improving safety in the plant. The company formally acknowledged the union safety committee. However, it clearly denied safety observers and safety committee members the right to time off the job to investigate safety complaints, health hazards, or accidents. This was strictly the province of management. Employee input was discouraged and safety was considered strictly a management function.

5. The Joint Union-Management Safety Committee: Powerlessness and Hostile Relations

Only two years later the company agreed to form a joint union-management safety committee. Monthly meetings of this committee were limited by the labor relations of that period. For the most part, union representatives would point out problems, and it would be entirely up to management to resolve them. If the safety administrator felt that the issues were legitimate, he would assume an apologetic demeanor, amid guarantees of quick abatement. On the other hand, if he felt the union reps were nit-picking, he would scold them.

The strength of these sessions was that they provided the union president and safety committee with a forum for discussing and resolving safety and health problems. The weaknesses in the committee were inherent in the fact that this was a small group which met infrequently and had limited resources. According to Isiah Lee: "My really honest opinion about that group is nothing. And when I say nothing that means nothing . . . we'd have meetings, but the meetings weren't about people. We talked about safety but it wasn't suppose to get back into the shop what was said in the meeting."

In the 1983 negotiations the company and the union agreed to increase the joint safety committee meetings to twice a month to strengthen the group's activities. I was brought into the committee by chairman Lee in 1979 to invigorate the group. We began a campaign to recruit safety observers to get broader rank-and-file involvement. Posting for volunteers exhorted the workers to participate.

The campaign was on and over 100 safety observers signed up. Green union safety buttons were a visible sign of the rank-and-file movement. Because the observers were restricted from investigating complaints and taking strong action, they were provided with a union safety complaint form for documenting problems. We presented these to management for action.

Some safety problems were acted on through the safety observer network, the use of the union safety complaint form and the committee meetings, despite the fact that we had to "fight" the company. For example, the asbestos paper used in the paint shops was finally eliminated. Another major concern, hazards in the glass coating department, was corrected when this operation shut down in late 1979. Yet, the company continued to resist union involvement in the safety program. This led to a sense of powerlessness and frustration and the union leadership was blamed for the refusal of the company to allow greater involvement of the safety committee.

The end result of these activities was to make the issue of safety and health a greater priority for the union's membership and leadership. Since 1980 the bargaining committee has been trying to negotiate for a full-time union safety representative, walk-around rights, and greater involvement in the safety program. Despite the hostile labor relations of this period, the union safety committee and management safety personnel displayed an ability to work together to accomplish solutions. These developments helped to raise the importance of worker safety and health at A. O. Smith. The current joint activities are based on this foundation.

III. Developing a Joint Labor-Management Organization

1. *Economic Changes and Industry Restructuring*

The dramatic changes in the auto industry during the 1980s also affected its suppliers, redefining labor-management relations and the very face of the workplace. Theories of joint management and worker participation were employed in an attempt to catch up to the Japanese whose competitive advantage was well understood. Their success in carving a 30% share in the U.S. auto market was due to delivering better quality products at a lower cost. The American market for automobiles is the largest in the world, and consumers have grown tired of shoddy products at ever increasing prices.

One of the key features of the Japanese strategy was a new system of workplace organization, pioneered by Edward Demming after World War I. Central to the concept is the elimination of needless layers of management, and empowerment of the workforce to take charge of its operations. Giving workers ownership of their jobs presumably will create the motivation and dedication necessary to improve performance in safety, quality, and productivity. Training, shopfloor teams, participative management, and pushing responsibility downward are key elements of this emphasis on human resources.

Corporations are motivated by a desire to return to profitability and maintain market share, while unions desire job security and workplace democracy. The days of checking your brain at the factory gate have become unacceptable from both sides of the table. Unions have long denounced mismanagement, poor product quality, and the refusal of companies to listen to front-line employees. The joint program is seen as a way of overcoming this dilemma and securing employment at a time when jobs in the industry are diminishing at a dizzy speed.

A. O. Smith's management style was typical of the conservative American corporation. For decades, excellent profits had been rendered by emphasizing volume at the expense of quality. Large amounts of product were made incorrectly: holes off location on the frames, parts not fitting, cracked steel, and shoddy welds. Millions of dollars a year were spent on scrap and repairs. The maniacal pace this encouraged led to repetitive motion injuries on an epidemic scale.

When workers complained, they were often ignored or insulted by a management that placed a higher value on control above all else. The role of the worker was to do the job and "keep his mouth shut." Labor relations were appalling. Over a thousand grievances a year were filed concerning job assignments, pay disputes, harassment, discrimination, and discipline. (Discipline was imposed primarily due to a chronic absentee problem. On average, more than 10% of the labor force was absent from work.)

In a union study conducted on the company's safety performance for 1985, it was estimated that on any given day 103 workers were off on workers' compensation due to job-related injuries. Statistically, A. O. Smith has experienced high accident and incidence rates. In 1987 there were 14,291 lost workdays due to occupational injury and illness. There were 224 reported cases of disorders associated with repeated trauma, including Carpal Tunnel Syndrome and hearing loss. There were 1,858 days of restricted work activity.

Total workers' compensation cost in 1986 (including roll-over from 1985) was more than $3.7 million. According to Michael Baggot, for every actual dollar spent on workers' compensation, there are two dollars in hidden costs. On this basis one can estimate real and hidden costs for 1986 at more than $11 million. Overall, safety and health problems have a demoralizing affect on the workforce which tends to hurt productivity and quality.[9]

Chronic morale problems emerge when workers have no voice in their jobs, are continuously blamed for the problems of the company, and yet, are powerless to do anything about them. The goal of team concept and "operator control" is to unleash the many talents and skills of the workers to yield exciting results. The experience at the Milwaukee works is that such change is not easily accomplished. A total change in the culture and traditions in an established institution of this size requires a revolution from top to bottom.

2. Participation Programs

The company first began the process of worker involvement in January 1982 when quality circles were established. The formal name of the program was the Quality Participation Program (QPP). It was launched unilaterally without the involvement of union leadership. The company erected trailers throughout the acreage for use as meeting rooms and invested heavily in assigning management personnel to coordinate this program. However, by 1985 the program was dead in its tracks.

At its peak there were over 350 groups on paper. Some improvements were made, but there were many difficulties with this approach. The exclusion of top union leadership in the administration of the program created distrust and resentment. Problem-solving was not integrated into the day-to-day running of the factory and little could be accomplished in a weekly, one-hour meeting. Training was reserved for management leaders, not group members. Probably the biggest drawback with QPP was that the old attitudes that quality, productivity, and safety are the domain of management, created a roadblock to new ideas.

The real accomplishment of QPP was to alert the workforce to the need to work jointly to overcome the plant's problems. The company's effort to improve quality did not rest on QPP alone. In August 1982, a full-time staff was assigned to implement Statistical Process Control (SPC) methods in the Milwaukee works. Training for management and hourly workers was conducted in a five-day general SPC class, and a three-day advanced SPC class. Over 900 employees took advantage of this training.

In 1985 the company and its seven unions launched a joint employee participation program. This was an outcome of the Smith Steelworker's 1983 negotiations in which a letter of understanding on improving quality, productivity, and competitiveness was agreed upon. Participative Systems Inc. (PSI), an established consulting firm in the area of labor-management participation, from Princeton, New Jersey, was hired to establish a meaningful joint program. A contest for a name and slogan for the new program attracted over 120 entries. BEST was selected, and the slogan was "Securing Tomorrow . . . Today."

The organizational structure of the program featured the top leaders of the unions and company officers on the policy committee. At the plant level, below the policy committee, were advisory committees composed of plant managers and their staff members, a few supervisors, union stewards from the plant, and the full-time union grievance committee representative of that area. Under the advisory committees are the BEST teams, composed of a mixture of labor and management personnel from a given area. Five full-time coordinator-trainers were appointed, two from management and three from labor. They received two weeks of training from PSI in New Jersey. All employees were given 40 hours of problem-solving training, conducted on site by PSI and the coordinator-trainers.

Many of the same problems that plagued QPP also afflicted the BEST program. One-hour-a-week meetings did not permit rapid development and resolution of concerns. All too often meetings would be canceled due to production requirements. Where time and resources were sufficient, there were still old attitudes to overcome and a management organization that was dominated by red tape and buckpassing. Often, teams did not have the training in project management to do the research, cost analysis, and other work required to see a proposal through to its conclusion; thus frustrating the program, and frequently turning initiative to demoralization. Yet, many improvements were made in quality, productivity, and safety.

It was during this period that the first plant level joint safety committee was initiated. A joint Building 70 safety committee was formed in the fall of 1986, even before the BEST program had come to Building 70. This very active body was composed of representatives from management and labor, and served as a pilot for the launching of joint plant safety committees through the BEST organization in November 1987. The strength of this pilot safety committee was communicating with the area management about safety and health concerns.

3. 1987 Negotiations

The August 1987 contract agreement was marked by several important changes. The piecework incentive system was terminated and replaced by hourly compensation to improve quality by ending a method of pay that rewarded workers and supervisors for producing large quantities of scrap and parts in need of repair. Job classifications were reduced to permit more job flexibility. While there were no outright concessions in wages and benefits, the contract set the scene for developing the "lean and mean" joint management process. The company opened its books and explained the legitimacy of its competitive pressures. The union hired University of Wisconsin professors to do an independent study of the company and industry trends. It validated its claims.

Restructuring of the auto industry involves longer-term contracts with a smaller select group of suppliers. The companies that are surviving this shake-out have had to make major unit price reductions, improve product quality, and provide just-in-time delivery. In agreeing to the contractual changes, the union showed it understood these realities. Joint efforts and cooperation were viewed as the way to help A. O. Smith become one of this select group of survivors.

The union had high hopes right after the negotiations concluded. Union involvement in all facets of the business was promised. However, the organization for this to take place did not exist, and problems of poor quality, productivity, and safety continued to affect the operation. Union powerlessness exacerbated morale problems. The implementation of the controversial changes was dizzying. In a few short months the pay system was totally changed, classifications redefined, and finally the entire plant restructured.

4. Black Friday and the First Restructuring

December 4, 1987 soon became known as "Black Friday" among workers on the shopfloor: the day massive layoffs took place as "G" frame production came to an end.

Before this the company decentralized its operations, dividing the Milwaukee works into six plants. Each plant is run by a plant manager and his staff and many central functions were placed into the new plant organizations. These included labor relations, now referred to as human resources, engineering, purchasing, and maintenance, to name a few. The BEST organization was adjusted to mirror the restructuring. At offsite meetings the advisory committees discussed the design of the new streamlined organization.

The new organization is designed to provide for direct two-way communication. The union was told that only two levels of management would remain: the plant manager and the line foreman. The goal was to push authority down to the lowest levels and, in so doing, make people more responsible. By eliminating needless layers of management, the organization laid the groundwork for improving its accessibility and effectiveness.

Concerning the reorganization of the safety department, Human Resources vice-president Randy White[10] observed:

> The restructuring decentralized the central safety function. At the same time decentralization was going on, two things were happening. We were rearranging what various management people did, plus we were rearranging what any management person did versus what production workers did, stewards did, and union representatives did, and persons on special assignment did, so we really were re-deploying work across all sorts of different functions. Decentralization caused us to look at who could do work most effectively, most efficiently, on a broader basis without being constrained. Secondly, at the same time we were moving rapidly towards more consultation between labor and management, supervisor and employee, things like that, and more use of committees, task forces, and that sort of thing. It was natural for safety to emerge as one of the things that made sense to be done on a labor-management basis, that was one of the earliest breakthroughs, and then we brought it into our BEST labor-management structure.

Since then over 40% of management and 30% of hourly workers have been eliminated. A second restructuring occurred in 1988 that eliminated one of the six plants altogether and organized the others around product lines as follows: GM Products, Ford Products, Chrysler Products, Small Parts, and the heavy truck division. The heavy truck division, unlike the rest, was established as a self-contained operating unit that reports directly to the Milwaukee Automotive chairman.

5. Empowerment, Training, and Shopfloor Teams

BEST was an advance over QPP, because the program included union co-administration, full-time union and management coordinator-trainers, and 40 hours of problem-solving training for all participants. However, like its predecessor QPP, BEST did not integrate the day-to-day decisionmaking processes of the factory into its employee involvement organization. The BEST advisory committees came closest to accomplishing this in their weekly meetings, many of which featured direct communication between plant managers, staff members, grievance committee members, and area union representatives. However, most decisions and projects could not wait for a weekly forum, and remained the province of management. In many cases subcommittees were formed to solve this problem, but the fundamental obstacle of having no day-to-day mechanism to embody the union members' input continued. All too often this resulted in poor group dynamics on joint committees. Finger pointing and accusations from both sides blocked progress.

In a pilot area in 1986 a team was established to develop an "operator control" training program and manual. The goal of this effort was to develop standard documented work procedures, and to train the operators in all facets of their jobs. The team, consisting of two inspectors, a tool and die maker, and a supervisor, spent six months putting together the manual and training program. The skills taught included set-up, trouble shooting, inspection, writing of maintenance workorders, taking care of production counts and paperwork, and contacting of appropriate resources when required. This pilot project was highly successful, and the rest of the plants began assigning teams to develop "operator control" training programs.

Under this program, workers were told that if they detected a quality problem they could shut down the line. Yet, all too often the ideas taught in the classroom did not find their way back to the shopfloor. For the most part, the first line foremen were left out of the process and had received no comprehensive training. Combined with the organizational deficiencies of BEST, this led to frustration. The lack of training and participation in management decisions was reaching a boiling point as reflected in quotes from this union flier:

> We have asked the company to enforce the agreement that we obtained in the last negotiations: That training and empower-

ment be given to the workers on the shopfloor. The BEST advisory committees in all six plants and central have been assigned the task of developing plans for accomplishing this goal. They have been met with resistance and indifference from some plant managers, middle managers, and first line supervisors. . . . The managers' idea of shopfloor empowerment is for all of the managers to meet separately, decide on an issue, then call the stewards and other workers in and tell them what is going to be done. If there is any opposition from the stewards and workers, the managers say try it anyway.

The demand for shopfloor teams came from the union leadership. The logic of this initiative was that the only way for the worker to gain control over the shopfloor, and therefore his destiny, was with a team system of production. Despite the joint program, contractual changes, and elimination of large numbers of foremen, traditional roles had not been transformed. Foremen, especially in the large production departments, still held a tight reign of control, and most workers continued to call on the boss to act on problems whether it was a quality issue, a safety item, or maintenance.

One of the main obstacles came from foremen and middle managers who felt threatened by the new approaches. Some just did not want to share power with union members. Others became negative and bitter after seeing management jobs eliminated or management functions carried out by union members. In reaction to these problems, in early 1989, comprehensive training was offered to the foremen, including in-house training by managers, use of participative systems, and seminars from area management training institutes.

6. Summary

It was in this environment that the proposal to form joint plant safety committees was adopted. The new approaches conform to the program of empowerment and team work that the top leadership from management and labor were implementing. This, combined with the foundation of concern over safety that was built over the years, created the opportunity.

The transition, over eight years, to a system of joint management was critical to building a consensus on new approaches to safety and health. The old attitude, that safety is strictly a management function, was an obstacle to effective problem-solving.

Only with proper resources (time, training, and personnel) can the goals of reduced injuries and lowered workers' compensation costs be achieved. Conversely, union members require training to be effective in their new role as co-managers of safety. It is one thing to point the finger at a problem, and quite another to research and implement a solution. The effect of this endeavor has been to raise the priority of safety and eliminate some of the resistance to making specific safety reforms.

IV. New Directions in Safety and Health

1. Leadership Support and Safety Education

In 1986 I was reappointed chairman of the union safety committee by the executive board. Since then the union leadership has encouraged safety activities in a number of ways. It recommended sending members of the safety committee to safety education programs, approved purchasing safety and health publications for a union safety and health library, and established a $2,000 budget for the first ever safety observers training program. Subjects covered were OSHA standards and procedures, ergonomics, the union's internal safety and health procedures, and a workshop on hazard communication.

The tactic of holding the regular monthly union safety committee meetings at the end of the Saturday union meeting increased attendance. Our strategy was to build the union safety program by involving as many people as we possibly could in the committee's pursuits. We held open meetings that were frequented by a dedicated core of activists. Anywhere from six to 20 people participated in these planning sessions in which ideas for many of the programs that are now in place were germinated.

A policy of nonsectarianism has made the safety committee a model for involving a broad spectrum of unionists. Young, old, black, white, progressive, and conservative—all share the goal of advancing worker safety and health. There has been none of the factionalism or infighting that often plagues union efforts. Organizationally we have used a variety of logistics, including monthly meeting announcements sent to the homes of safety observers, preparation of an agenda, and maintaining minutes of meetings.

Extensive safety and health training, conducted at the University of Wisconsin's School for Workers' Extension Program, has been very beneficial. Safety committee members have attended three-day or one-week programs on ergonomics, OSHA rights and responsibilities, industrial hygiene, and workers' compensation. Hands-on experience with noise monitoring devices, air sampling equipment, and participation in actual plant inspections have been invaluable in dealing effectively with these concerns in the plant. The staff of the school is made up of a core of experts who are dedicated to worker education with a union perspective.

The union finances program fees and lost wages. This investment has been paid back in the successes of the safety program. In the past, only the full-time officers were given the opportunity to attend these sessions, but with their other duties and responsibilities, they were often unable to use the knowledge obtained in any concerted efforts. Our experience has shown that the union's safety effort is greatly strengthened by training our shopfloor representatives.

In addition, the Wisconsin Committee on Occupational Safety and Health (WISCOSH) has been an important source of information, assistance and training. Our union is a member of this coalition of unions, professionals, and safety activists. Safety education has helped to put us on an equal footing with the safety professionals that we work with at the plant by providing a common language and understanding of the standards and procedures. The organization of the union safety committee has given us a mechanism for putting this knowledge to use.

2. Carpal Tunnel Project

In May 1986, union president Blackman encouraged the committee to investigate the problem of repetitive motion injuries and CTS at the plant; the union's main representative for workers' compensation cases had made him acutely aware of these problems. Many workers were having surgery and some were becoming permanently disabled and unemployed. Indeed, several members at that initial meeting showed their scars from carpal tunnel surgery. The committee began an aggressive investigation.

We invited Denise Tyson, the safety committee chair from Industrial Workers of North America (AIW) Local 232 at Briggs and Stratton Corporation, to our next meeting. She shared information with us about the disease, surveys that her union had taken of the workforce, her local's request for a health evaluation survey by the

National Institute on Occupational Safety and Health, and highlights of their work with the company.

Concurrently, we sent three members to the School for Workers'
three-day class on ergonomics and learned of our right to request
information, specifically the OSHA 200 log of injuries and illnesses. A written request for this information was submitted to the
company. The union analyzed the data. A spreadsheet of all cases
that involved lower arm injuries and that appeared to be related to
repetitive motion was drawn up. Lost workdays, restricted workdays, departments, and job classifications were evaluated as well.

We decided to present the analysis to the joint central safety
committee. It showed that many repetitive motion injuries were
being classified incorrectly on the log and the company acted
quickly to rectify this situation. The company representatives were
very impressed with the union analysis and agreed to work jointly
on a project to reduce these injuries. The joint committee agreed
that we should focus on the four departments identified as causing
50% of the injuries. This was an effective strategy in working with
management representatives because it eased their apprehensions
of an uncontrolled broad campaign. Earnest Spivey brought to the
joint committee the names, dates, and fixture numbers of the injured workers from two of the departments. This information came
from the OSHA 101 log that is not accessible to unions under the
law.

We narrowed our focus further when it was decided to place on
hold development of ergonomic analyses for press department 1732.
Because people constantly move from one machine to another in
this department, it makes it difficult to determine which jobs cause
the problems. In contrast, the other two departments were assembly lines where people had permanent assignments, and definite
patterns of lower arm repetitive motion injuries were associated
with specific fixtures.

Union vice president Jerold Heidtke and I put together a survey and interviewed the injured workers.[11] The company arranged
for us to be released from our regular jobs on the line for this purpose. Because fellow union members were conducting the survey,
interviews were relaxed and frank. The survey helped to verify the
problems with the fixtures and to get input from the injured workers
on how to solve them.

Another important step taken by the joint committee was the
making of a videotape of the jobs involved. We met with the
welders before we started taping to explain the purpose of the proj-

ect. Over the din of the power units, I asked this group of men in coveralls how many of them had experienced wrist problems. All but one raised their hands. I then asked how many had surgery, and three of them responded affirmatively.

To garner the forces needed to implement ergonomic improvements we put together an ad hoc committee from the welding department composed of the plant manager, his assistant, a plant engineer, the steward of the area, and representatives from the joint safety committee. We shared the analysis, the videotape, and the results of the survey with the ad hoc group. Brainstorming from the videotape resulted in three ideas for solutions. They all involved simple modifications that would relieve wrist strain.

There was a serious concern on the part of management that implementation of the recommendations would cause a loss in production. The industrial engineer on the committee was assigned to study this. Meanwhile, a reduction in the car frame business resulted in major changes taking place on these assembly lines. Instead of 750 frames a day, they were redesigned to produce 450 a day. Other modifications and a redistribution of this work resulted in putting the project on hold. The other factor involved in the recommendations not being implemented was that at this time the joint safety committee had a minimal amount of influence on the plant's leadership.

The experience gained in this project, however, helped identify the need for localized plant safety committees. Although the project was never completed in the way intended, it marked the beginning of a new era for the joint safety efforts. It was the first meaningful cooperative activity undertaken and marked a departure from the finger pointing and "bitch" sessions of old. It lent credibility to the joint safety committee in that we identified and attempted to solve a problem of importance, magnitude, and real mutual concern.

3. Formation of Joint Plant Safety Committees

In November 1987, the joint safety committee submitted a proposal to the BEST policy members to form safety committees throughout the six plants. I personally visited each of the advisory committees to explain the proposed purpose and composition of these committees.

As mentioned earlier the real forerunner of these joint safety committees began years earlier in Building 70. This committee

kept a weekly list of projects, most of which were fix-it things: exposed electrical wires were covered, fans were repaired, and the
like. However, several problems frustrated the committee. The
maintenance work was slow in being accomplished; and even more
significant was the fact that the company was not set up for joint
management, and so the actual work of the committee fell to supervisors.

The experience of this group had demonstrated the potential of
localized joint safety committees. The Carpal Tunnel Project identified the need to have plant-based teams for successful completion
of such undertakings. This approach was unanimously endorsed by
the BEST policy committee in November 1987. The formation of
the committees had given each plant their own group that is dedicated to improving safety and health in "their" departments. The
sheer numbers involved-92 people-provide greater resources for
success in this work.

4. Negotiations and Safety

In the 1987 negotiations, the union safety committee successfully promoted the development of a union safety observer's
manual that was presented at a three-day stewards' training program, and monthly monitoring of the progress of the newly formed
joint plant safety committees. Lastly, we campaigned for a full-
time union safety representative.

For 15 years the union's safety personnel had been trying to
achieve walk-around rights, a voice in safety decisionmaking, and
resources for raising awareness and safety training. They were
convinced that for real progress to be made the union must have a
full-time safety representative. The negotiating committee approved the proposal, and a major attempt was put into developing a
document backing up the demand. An analysis of the company's
injuries and illnesses in relation to national averages showed the
depth of A. O. Smith's safety and health problems. Workers' compensation costs were in the millions of dollars, and the demand for
a full-time representative was put in the context of solving these
problems. Union president Blackman gave his perspective on these
events:

> I have to give credit to the tenacity of a lot of people who were
> really interested in safety. I think the thing that really turned
> things around and took the safety movement out of the adver-
> sarial position was when we showed the company that we were

not just after dumping on them, but rather we wanted to join them to try and resolve the safety problems. We weren't concerned about the notoriety. We just wanted to create a safe place for people to work.

The company put the establishment of a full-time union safety representative on the table, but the catch was that the union would have to take back some 33 supervisors who, under the current language, had no rights to return to the bargaining unit. This created a stalemate, and, given the complexity of these negotiations, the item was not resolved. It was agreed, however, that the union would develop a proposal after the talks concluded for improved handling of safety and workers' compensation problems. This eventually led to the creation of the new full-time position of union safety coordinator, to which I was assigned.

5. Survey and Analysis of Committees

I suggested that we put together a survey to assess the plant safety committees. It had been a year since they were formed, and this appraisal gave us information concerning who was on them, how often, when, and where they met, and what their strengths and weaknesses were. Gathering these facts was critical to devising a plan for fully involving the safety teams in the rejuvenation of the hazard communication program.

The survey revealed that there were nine plant safety committees in existence as of November 1988. A total of 63 employees participated on the teams. But two committees had folded due to layoffs and reorganization and a number of the plants were not doing safety inspections (while those which did function tended to deal with short-term items). Only a few buildings were doing safety sampling inspections, and departmental safety meetings in some plants had been disrupted by the latest reorganization. The program also suffered from lack of training, the failure to establish priorities, and differing amounts of representation and participation by maintenance and management. The committees' strengths have been their enthusiasm, initiative, and willingness to assume responsibility.

6. Hazard Communication Training Update

While the evaluation of the plant safety committees was taking place, much of my time was spent developing the plans for the

Hazard Communication Update. I gathered publications from unions, the School for Workers, OSHA, A. O. Smith's previously prepared documents, and WISCOSH, and selected the best of the materials to be used in training. I met with Ernie Spivey daily to discuss the plans. Based on our suspicion that many of the people who had been trained did not know what was required under the standard, we decided to retrain the entire workforce. The first step was to put together a training manual to educate the plant safety committees in a comprehensive four-hour session.

Plant 1 was selected as the pilot area to introduce the program. The safety committee audited the materials in each department by doing "walk-around" inspections, comparing the old list of hazardous chemicals with what was actually on the shopfloor. Forms were developed to simplify and standardize the reporting of additions and deletions to the departmental chemical list.

The training sessions held for people in the plant featured a brief presentation by coworkers in plain language. In preparation the safety committee had several dry runs, printed handouts, and presented an agenda. Notices addressed to the supervisor, team leader, and steward were sent out from the safety committee announcing the time, date, and place of the hazard communication training sessions. The training agenda included a review of the chemical families used in the plant, explanations of procedures for reporting suspected health problems, and demonstrations of the proper protective gear to be used and of the safety and health emergency equipment. An emphasis was put on the spirit of the law so that people would understand the importance of this program.

Don Little[12] relates the effect that the training had on him:

> When I first started I thought keeping your hands, fingers and all your limbs was very important, but I wasn't aware of the hazards of the chemicals out there until we got involved with hazard communications. I can 'off' myself by messing around with the wrong chemicals, putting my hands where they shouldn't be. You could get hurt out there by not being aware that all these dangerous things are out there. What I found out is that everything is safe, but if handled wrong you can get in trouble.

These efforts raised the workers' awareness of the hazards in the workplace, educated them on what to do if they suspected a problem, and put the plant in compliance with this standard. Both plant and union leadership have praised the safety committee for independently managing this project to a successful conclusion. Participation in organizing and conducting this program raised the self-esteem of the safety committee members involved.

Concerns about specific health hazards arose as an outcome of this program. Complaints about welding fumes, paints, solvents, and diesel exhaust were investigated. Most of these exposures are not beyond OSHA's permissible exposure limits (PEL), and in the past this was the company's main determinant on whether to take corrective action. However, because health afflictions such as headaches, nausea, and stomach pain precipitate workers' complaints, we tried to look beyond whether the exposure was within OSHA standards. A quality product cannot be made productively if people are experiencing gross discomfort.

Walter Fanning[13] addressed the Building 70 safety committee's involvement in these matters.

> Just because a thing hasn't been analyzed or researched doesn't mean it isn't hazardous. We're trying to be innovative as a committee, and when people complain, we are saying let's test it, let's find out. With these diesel fumes the jury is still out. We recognize we have a problem now. The trucking department at A. O. Smith recognizes that they have a problem. We've been trying to do something with the trucks. They are trying to idle them down when they come into the building. We still have our winter to go through and when the building is closed, that's when we're going to take the tests. We have to save our own health.

Several factors made this a difficult issue: verification that a problem exists, cost-benefit justification in a time of scarce dollars, and a lack of understanding of the potential benefits in improved quality and productivity which could result from solving these questions. Moving forward on these issues was one of the critical challenges to the program.

7. Plant 2 Ergonomics Project

The shopfloor team from the 55013 and 55014 presses raised concerns over the many injuries that were generated from the unloading operation on these large blanking and drawing presses. These included CTS, shoulder and elbow strains, knee problems and back injuries. In response, the union leadership and plant management formed an ad hoc joint committee to work on the resolution of these problems. The group began meeting every other week in April 1989 to develop long-term and immediate solutions. Larry Donahue,[14] a worker on these presses for half of his 20 years at Smith, discussed the start of the project:

> There were people getting hurt out there, going on sick leaves, and having surgeries. One of the employees was off again having surgery and at that point we decided something had to be done. People just weren't holding up. It is interesting that a lot of the people who are in the department right now are not affected by carpal tunnel, even though the method that they are using to run the job is the same. It seems that the people who are affected are people who have been in there for a number of years.

Using the skills learned at the School for Workers, I put together an analysis of the injuries which revealed direct workers' compensation costs over 3.3 years of $117,000. Combined with the hidden costs of replacing people, paperwork, and training, the real costs are at least twice as high. The analysis was crucial in convincing the committee of the value of moving forward on this project.

Engineering was working with the ad hoc committee to evaluate the use of an automatic unload system or robotics for the presses. They also were considering employing an outside ergonomic consultant to suggest temporary solutions while the engineering project proceeded. However Donahue expressed some concerns about the proposed solution.

> Whenever you're talking about making an engineering change because of injuries, what you're going to get is new technology. The way society and industry is geared, state of the art means fewer people. That's one thing that I'm against. I understand and I realize that these things happen as you move on with technology. But I don't want to say, 'yeah just get rid of everybody, and just put robots in there and then nobody will get hurt,' because that's not the answer. Robots and computers are only as smart as the people who program them. I'm concerned that the new technology for the 013 and 014 presses is going to cause a manpower reduction. We as union employees, and our union leaders, have to take a hard look at what the company wants to do.

I am hopeful that the success of this project will help prove the value of redesigning the equipment that is causing strains and sprains for the membership. The new organization of safety must move in this direction to gain the anticipated results in injury reductions and cost savings. Future success in eliminating injuries from poor ergonomic design of equipment demands broad training of safety professionals, engineers, safety committee members, and orientation of the workforce at large.

8. Job Security Connection

What is the future of the joint safety efforts? What is the direction of the joint labor-management program at A. O. Smith? The issue of job security has always been a primary motivation for union involvement in QPP, BEST and shopfloor teams. Other factors such as better job interest, more of a voice in work decisions, and improvement of the quality of worklife are also important aspects of the appeal of the new workplace organization. However, maintaining one of the best paychecks for blue collar work in the country is the number one concern. Further discussion of the economic changes in the industry and how they affect A. O. Smith can clarify the connection of the job security issue to the success of labor-management cooperation.

Throughout the last eight years both management and union leaders at A. O. Smith have effectively pointed to the competitive pressures in the auto and supplier industries to convince the workforce to adopt the revolutionary changes taking place. The threat of job loss has been reinforced in the greater Milwaukee area by plant closings at businesses that once employed thousands, such as Allis Chalmers and American Motors. Undoubtedly, the radical changes would not have been embraced in a relatively short period of time if the threatened job loss was not made abundantly clear. Although this is a somewhat negative motivation, it has provided a real incentive for change.

Despite the turnabout in quality, productivity, and safety the Milwaukee plant continues to downsize, and repeated attempts by the union to negotiate job security measures have failed. A major aspect of the Japanese system is to provide employment guarantees. The theory is that in so doing you can build dedication in the workforce and stabilize manpower, and utilize excess manpower for training or continuous improvement efforts. Blackman placed this issue on the table in October 1988 at the same time that he proposed the start of the team concept and increased training efforts. In this regard, Donahue offers a rank-and-file perspective:

> The bottom line for each plant seems to be to reduce manpower. They feel that reducing manpower is the only way to improve

profits and I don't agree with that. What they have to do is re-
think their work habits and attitudes . . . which will increase
profits and production. All we can do is express our opinion, but
as far as job security, and guaranteed employment and the future
of A. O. Smith is concerned, we don't know where it's going.
Maybe corporate knows what they expect five years from now.
Whatever that is, if that means loss of employment they owe it to
us to share their plans. If they do, the people whom it will affect
could do something about making changes in their lives now.
Let's face it, if it's A. O. Smith's projection to be functioning here
with a thousand fewer people five years from now you'd like to do
whatever you can to ensure more business so that doesn't happen;
but if that is going to happen let us know so that people can get
some schooling or training and continue with their life. This is a
traumatized thing in their lives.

Two obstacles account for the company's refusal to deal with
the job security issue. First, there continues to be a focus on the
quarterly report which results in short-term planning. Plant managers who do not meet the plan have to face the music at monthly
and quarterly review meetings. Such pressure has led to strategies
of severe cutbacks to meet short-term budget priorities, cutting
into the muscle as well as the fat of the operations. Training and
other investments in human resources generally do not show a
quick payback. Thus, there is a reluctance to "waste" the hundreds
of thousands of dollars that these programs cost.

The other obstacle is the investment strategy of the corporation which to a large degree has been dictated by the restructuring
of the auto industry. Ford, General Motors, and Chrysler are all
demanding their suppliers set up shop for new product lines within
100 miles of their assembly plants. They are demanding large unit
price cuts and other concessions, such as suppliers providing their
own tooling. In return for this they are offering longer-term contracts to fewer manufacturers. The winner takes all.

To maintain its market share and establish a position for
growth, A. O. Smith corporation has been building satellite plants
in places like Corydon, Indiana, and BelKamp, Maryland. These
plants are small and easier to manage. Of at least equal importance to the company is that they are non-union, and provide much
lower pay rates and benefits. Training is conducted up front for
workers who have been selectively hired. Team concept and flexible workrules are established before the first frame comes off the
line.

These moves have been complemented by a gradual downsizing of the Milwaukee plant despite its posting a modest profit in 1988, when a several million-dollar loss was predicted. The corporation has made it clear that the satellite plants are A. O. Smith's wave of the future.

These trends have not sat well with the rank-and-file of both management and labor. In the spring of 1989 concurrent announcements of work that was being phased out, and new work that was not coming in solidified the job security dilemma. Without hope for a future, many in the workforce became demoralized. Chronic morale problems perpetuated the inefficiencies, quality problems, and incidents of injuries. Instead of concentrating on producing a quality product, minds drifted toward thoughts of life after A. O. Smith. Among many, a bitterness began to set in.

The effect that these events will have on the joint safety effort is unclear at this time. Undoubtedly, management and union leadership share a common goal of reducing injuries and workers' compensation costs. The new safety organization at A. O. Smith is establishing a program that can deliver dramatic improvements. However, without a commitment from management to bring new work into the Milwaukee plant, the union's role in the joint management process is on shaky ground. There are a number of factors which will determine the future of this effort: the ability to sustain the safety committees through a period of layoffs, bumping, and transferring; the stability of labor-management cooperation during a period of downsizing; and the continued allocation of time and resources.

Notes

1. Smith Steelworkers Directly Affiliated Local Union 19806 is the largest of the unions and it represents the production workers, secretarial staff, and plant guards. The local is not affiliated with an international union and is served directly by the national AFL-CIO. There are two International Association of Machinist Locals; Lodge 78 represents the tool and die makers and Lodge 1668 the machine repairmen and lubemen. Steamfitters Local 601 represents the fitters, the Carpenters District Council for Southeast Wisconsin has a nine-member unit, the International Brotherhood of Electrical Workers Local 663 represents 70 electricians, the Firemen and Boilermakers are represented, and lastly the Technical Engineers Association has a bargaining unit.

2. John P. Kelley, "Early Shop History," *Shop Safety Bulletin* (August 1915).

3. Paul Blackman, President of Smith Steelworker's Union Local 19806, hired in 1959, personal interview, Milwaukee, WI, May 1989.

4. James Pinion, Plant 1 Safety Committee member, union steward, Union Executive Board, hired in 1952, personal interview, Milwaukee, WI, May 1989.

5. Earnest Spivey, Administrator of Safety and Security for A. O. Smith, first hired in 1964, personal interview, Milwaukee, WI, June 1989.

6. Isiah Lee, the second union safety committee chairman, former steward, hired in 1950, retired, personal interview, Milwaukee, WI, June 1989.

7. *A. O. Smith and OSHA—A. O. Smith's Position Comment, The Automotive Division Safety at A. O. Smith Technical Problems Press Compliance Summary* (1975), a publication outlining the company's efforts and views on "Hands Out of Dies," presented to Congress.

8. James Poulter, the first Union Safety Committee Chairman, union steward, former grievance committeeman, hired in 1965, personal interview, Milwaukee, WI, May 1989.

9. Jonathan Rosen and Ernest Spivey, *Joint Labor/Management Safety Committee Proposal for Improved Handling of Safety and Health and Workers' Compensation Problems* (1987). Also compare A. O. Smith's *Accident Experience at a Glance* for 1987 to the industry averages as reported by the Bureau of Labor Statistics (BLS) for 1984. BLS total cases for *Motor Vehicle Parts and Accessories* (SIC code 3174), was 11.1. A. O. Smith's recordable injury incident rate was 21.4. BLS lost workday case rate was 4.9. A. O. Smith's lost workday case rate was 8.3.

10. Randy White, vice-president of Human Resources, hired in 1963, personal interview, Milwaukee, WI, June 1989.

11. A total of 21 employees were interviewed. Of these, 18 identified their injuries were caused by repetitive motion. The OSHA-200 reports had listed these employees as having missed a total of 469 days, while the employees reported missing a total of over 668 days. Similarly, the OSHA 200 log reports had listed these employees as having a total of 85 days of limited duty, while the employees reported in excess of 400 days total. Obviously, these injuries are even more severe and costlier than we first estimated. All 18 employees reported some period of limited duty. Ten of them reported having missed work due to their injury, in periods ranging from 15 to 126 days. Seven of the employees reported having had surgery, and 15 reported some type of drug therapy, often cortisone shots. Thirteen employees reported receiving whirlpool treatments or other hydro-therapy. All but one had to use some kind of wrist brace, splint, or other support following their injury.

12. Don Little, Plant 4 Safety Committee Chairman, union steward, hired in 1964, personal interview, Milwaukee, WI, May 1989.

13. Walter Fanning, Building 70 Safety Committee member, union steward, hired in 1965, personal interview, Milwaukee, WI, June 1989.

14. Larry Donahue, Plant 2 Trainer, union steward, hired in 1969, personal interview, Milwaukee, WI, May 1989.

Editors' Suggested Readings

Berman, Daniel. *Death on the Job: Occupational Health and Safety Struggles in the United States* New York: Monthly Review Press, 1978.

"Carpal Tunnel Syndrome," *Occupational Hazards*, February 1987.

Feldman, Richard and Michael Betzold, eds. *End of the Line: Autoworkers and the American Dream.* New York: Weidenfeld & Nicolson, 1988.

Halberstam, David. *The Reckoning.* New York: Avon Books, 1986.

Humphrey, John. *Capitalist Control and Workers' Struggle in the Brazilian Auto Industry.* New Jersey: Princeton University Press, 1982.

Jaffe, Dennis, Cynthia Scott, and Esther Orioli. *Stress Management in the Workplace.* Washington, D.C.: U.S. Public Health Service, 1986.

Kinney, Joseph. *Faces: The Toll of Workplace Deaths on American Families.* Chicago: National Safe Workplace Institute Press, 1989.

Mancuso, Thomas. *Help for the Working Wounded.* Washington, D.C.: Machinists Union, 1976.

Tolliday, Steven and Jonathan Zeitlin, eds. *The Automobile Industry and Its Workers: Between Fordism and Flexibility.* New York: St. Martin's Press, 1987.

Viscusi, W. Kip. "Market Incentives for Safety," *Harvard Business Review* (July/August 1985): 133–138.

Adversary Participation in the Brave New Workplace: Technological Change and the Bakery, Confectionery, and Tobacco Workers' Union

Raymond F. Scannell

I. Introduction

In the following pages the mandate, research, findings, and conclusions of the Bakery, Confectionery, and Tobacco Workers' (BC&T) technology task force will be discussed. It is the story of one union's effort to understand the transformation of the workplace now under way in North America and to learn from its own experiences and those of other unions in order to forge a strategy for the future.

The union's study is placed in the context of the debate which began in the last decade over how unions should respond to the reorganization of production in U.S. manufacturing. However, this is not intended as an extended review and/or critique of the experiences and writings of others on the topics of technological change, new forms of work organization and union renewal. This paper instead focuses on how the task force, through its field work, readings and discussions, gained insights into the issues raised in that debate and ultimately sought to address them.

It has done so through a technology policy and program which advocates participation by workers and their union in what has traditionally been viewed as managerial decisionmaking processes through collective bargaining, an approach referred to here as "adversary participation."

The production of knowledge is a collective enterprise. The work described here, and in many cases the very words used, are part of the continuing project involving the members of the technology task force and others in the BC&T. While the author accepts full responsibility for the form this paper has taken, credit for much of the content belongs to the committee as a whole.[1]

II. The Debate

The 1980s were tough on organized labor in the U.S. Unions were faced with difficulties, and the labor movement's ability to meet those challenges was questioned and strategies debated. In manufacturing, the most fundamental of these challenges were, and continue to be, the reorganization of the production process[2] and the institutional decline of unions.

While the introduction of new technology and the reorganization of work have often been discussed as if they were two distinct phenomena, in fact, they are part of a common process. The institutional decline of unions likewise has often been addressed in isolation. But, as others have perceived, the issues are linked.[3] The collapse of traditional manufacturing has spurred the crisis in traditional unionism, yet, within American labor's response to the reorganization of production is a key to arresting, and perhaps reversing, its institutional decline.

1. "No Way" vs. "Okay"

If one were forced to rely on the public media for a discussion of labor's response to the reorganization of the workplace, one could be excused for believing that the strategic choices available amounted to "no way" vs. "okay."

New "cooperative" or "participatory" systems of work and governance which brought the promise of enhanced productivity and competitiveness in world markets[4] were the focus of increasing media attention throughout the 1980s. The argument within labor over these new systems of work and workplace governance appeared to drive participants into two warring camps: hard-line opposition to any change in the status quo against acceptance and/or defense of any and all changes.

Similarly, the question of new technology and labor's response often seemed to be posed as a choice between all out resistance (decried as "Luddism") or the supine acceptance of progress.[5]

While the public coverage of these questions was shallow at best, the controversy over the stance of unions toward changing technology and the reorganization of the work process has gone to the heart of the historical ambivalence within American unionism; the opposing approaches of corporatism (job, industry, or craft consciousness) vs. class consciousness.

Viewed through this lens, on one side are the advocates of cooperation. While some in this camp are clearly motivated by a progressive belief in the capacity of workers to manage themselves and the industrial enterprises,[6] others have been motivated by a more straightforward "corporatist" interest in securing the survival of a particular plant, firm, industry, or specific set of jobs during a prolonged period of industrial decline and intensifying competition. Their concern for the viability of the corporate whole seems founded in light of the dizzying rate of collapse of North American manufacturing.

Some academic observers have welcomed what they perceive as a decline of "adversarialism" in the U.S., making possible a new system of industrial relations more suited to survival in the new global economy. These writings and the vigorous endorsements of the U.S. Department of Labor and various other federal and state agencies have legitimated the stance of union advocates of cooperation.[7]

Arrayed against "cooperationism" have been those who are motivated by a vision of class solidarity and struggle as the basis for unionism. This vision has led to a critique of cooperation and participation which emphasizes the real and perceived dangers to the unity of workers in a shop or an industry in abandoning adversarialism and engaging in what they claim amounts to class collaboration.[8]

Others, less ideological, have also been driven by an equally strong commitment to an "us vs. them" relationship between workers and managers.[9] They view adversarialism as the traditional bedrock upon which unions as institutions stand and have rejected any involvement in the affairs of the firm other than bargaining over traditionally defined terms and conditions of employment.

Where have these divergent paths led unions? To neutral observers in the labor movement each argument has some merit. But each is limited in its ability to address the challenges facing organized labor.

"Jointness" or cooperation in the auto industry, telecommunications, and elsewhere has seemed unable to stem the loss of manufacturing jobs and the shrinkage of the unions in those sectors, or to win greater job security for many workers.

Quality of worklife and similar programs have, in fact, been sometimes used to extend managerial control, divide workers, speed up work and bust the union.[10] The real goal of managers has often been to replace visible, bureaucratic, authoritarian control with a more intimate authoritarianism[11] that is harder to resist.

Yet, at the level of the local union or on the shopfloor, with the club of the "competitive environment" and a shutdown hanging overhead, the alternatives to cooperation and acceptance of the reorganization of work have appeared less clear. At times it has seemed that the opponents of cooperation and participation were making a principled defense of Taylorism and expecting a revolution or some other sweeping change in the political and economic balance of power to resolve all problems.

Few unions can wait for such "salvation" even if they desire it. And, because in many ways new work practices have improved the lives of workers, unions completely ignore or reject them at their own risk.

In crucial ways, critiques like those of Parker and Slaughter have left trade unionists at loose ends, searching for solutions. For example, in their response to Banks and Metzgar, Parker and Slaughter call for more pattern bargaining and the establishment of national and international standards.[12] These are goals worthy of support, and the BC&T and other unions continue to work toward them. But what is to be done in the meantime, in the face of a determined employer offensive,[13] since generations may pass before those goals are achieved?

If an employer fails to meet the pattern, Parker and Slaughter believe that the employer "should be allowed to fail," and "other ways found to save the workers' jobs." What other ways? And in those parts of the country where the competition for union companies is virulently anti-union, or where employers can readily shift production to non-union shops (or move abroad) what is a union supposed to do?

Of course the difficult solution is to organize, both in the U.S. and internationally. But, in the meantime, is the pattern to be pursued at all costs and the unionized employer allowed to fail, leaving the market to an even stronger non-union (or foreign) competitor?

Parker and Slaughter also argue that unions should "take our livelihoods out of the competition game" (true enough), "and force companies to compete in other areas [such as] customer need, technology," etc. Yet within these areas are precisely the forces transforming the way work is done in BCT industries and subjecting workers' livelihoods to the competition game. We are ultimately left where we began, searching for a response to the changes under way.

2. A Third Way

The debate embodied, for example, in the division within the UAW between the Administration Caucus and New Directions, has not only eluded resolution, but threatened to tear some unions apart. However, in practice, across the continent and abroad, union officers and activists over the last decade have been trying to create their own pragmatic yet principled resolution of the two positions.

Several unions[14] have sought a third, alternative path providing workers with a voice in the introduction of new technology and work systems without subordinating labor's agenda, and allowing a degree of influence over innovation. Much attention has also been focused on buffering the impact on workers and their unions through a variety of measures such as retraining and early retirement.

Labor has also been fortunate to have available the work of academics sympathetic to the labor movement who have argued for an assertive approach to changing technology that seeks to shape the new machines, software and applications and secure for shop-floor workers a degree of control over the computerized work process.[15]

In Canada, Scandinavia, and the European Community, unions have struggled with the same issues, leading to several innovative approaches intended to give labor significant control over new technology. In Western Europe, for example, a new conception of the union's role is emerging. In several countries (including Sweden and Germany), the unions are retaining their traditional, "adversarial" position in defense of the members and the working class, but demanding the opportunity to participate in the decision-making process governing the design, use, and installation of new technology and other non-traditional areas. As a consequence, skill-enhancing, worker-centered technologies are being actively pursued.

Rather than being subordinated "partners" cooperating in the ratification of management decisions, the unions approach the decision process as a new arena in which to struggle for worker rights and an alternative vision of the workplace and production process. The efforts of the Italian Metal Workers are especially noteworthy since they operate in a labor relations climate traditionally as "adversarial" as any in the industrial world.[16]

David Jacobs, drawing on the experience of French workers with workplace councils, named this approach "adversary participation." French unions maintained a traditional adversarial posture and independence from management while they participated in the arenas created by the legally mandated "cooperative" works councils, and through them sought to extend worker and union control further on the shopfloor and within the firm itself.[17]

Banks and Metzgar have further elaborated on how a union can, through participation, extend the workers' reach and power into crucial and strategic areas of corporate decisionmaking without abandoning the independence of the union as an institution, or the class interests of its members.

They outline a union-empowering strategy of worker participation which could achieve both the economic goals of increased efficiency, productivity, and competitiveness while expanding worker power and the role of the union. They also advocate a shift from the service orientation developed by unions during the era of the social contract to an organizing model which would build union power and arrest decline.

Drawing explicitly on the American tradition of collective bargaining, they distinguish between participation and an ideology of "cooperationism" which denies or ignores the clash of interests between the managed and their managers to the disadvantage of workers and unions. In contrast, through a bargaining approach, unions have participated in making decisions over certain issues and extended a cooperative hand to management in return for real, concrete gains for workers. Unions need not jettison this approach, they argue. Instead unions should expand the workers' agenda to include issues like the design and deployment of new technology and work systems and extend the process into new managerial decision arenas where critical choices are made.

Such innovative action and thought has remained, until recently, relatively invisible, overshadowed in the public eye by the cantankerous debate within the labor movement. Perhaps as a consequence, even such a veteran observer of industrial relations and unions as the Dean of Cornell University's Industrial and Labor Relations School could, in a 1989 round-up of major forces at work to change labor relations in the next decade, only cite credit cards, group travel plans, and anti-raiding procedures as innovations within organized labor.

The restructuring of the economy, forced by globalization, heightened competition, and greed, and the consequential restructuring of the workplace through the introduction of new technologies and work practices have permanently altered the environment within which unions operate. The balance of power achieved in the fifties and sixties between labor and capital has been destabilized. Caught with structures and strategies developed in and for a different time, unions have found it difficult to respond and adapt and have gone into absolute decline. The historic task of unions, now, is to change as work and the working classes change. They must become more creative to be able to continue as the collective tool of working people in the struggle to win justice and dignity on the job, and to elevate the material conditions and quality of life of the vast majority.

The struggle to respond to new technology and work practices, and resolve the debate over "jointness" provides an opportunity to forge a new unionism. The third path continues that tradition of strategic and tactical "cooperation" with employers on defined terms for specific periods (which is collective bargaining) while retaining the independence of the union and its critical "adversarial" distance from the employer. It promises real "partnerships" between labor and management based on equality and offers a union strategy for empowerment rather than capitulation or blind rejection.

The third way is built on a proactive approach to the changes taking place in the workplace, and has as its primary goal organizing workers to keep them and their unions at the center of the brave new workplace.

III. The Technology Task Force and Its Study

1. Looking Back . . . and Forward

In the summer of 1987, John DeConcini, International president of the BC&T, and the other International executive officers, initiated a comprehensive review of the union's experience over the decade since the merger of the Bakery and Confectionery Workers and the Tobacco Workers in 1978, and of future prospects.

While the review was to be conducted by International staff, the leadership chose outside consultants to guide a study of the union's current and future situation. Such a strategic review and planning process was uncommon but not unprecedented within the labor movement, although such efforts had received scant attention from the general press. Many had been inspired by the effort of the AFL-CIO's committee on the future in the first half of the decade. Strategic planning on the scale to be undertaken was, however, new to the BC&T.

In explaining his initiative, DeConcini pointed to fundamental internal and external changes which were creating new challenges for the union. During the 1980s the ownership structure of virtually all the major companies with contracts with the BC&T had changed, sometimes more than once. The number of companies in the core industries had declined, as had the number of manufacturing plants. Most companies had either become subsidiaries of larger conglomerates or been taken over in highly leveraged transactions.

In virtually all cases, the new owners brought higher expectations of cash flow and profitability to industries which had long been considered mature and, with the exception of tobacco, relatively low margin businesses. In most cases, new owners meant new faces across the bargaining table. Relationships which had taken years to build threatened to evaporate. Internally, after a long period of stability at the local level, an apparent, dramatic rise in turnover rates among local officers indicated possible problems. Further, throughout the union, the most stalwart leaders were aging. Many were clearly nearing the ends of their careers and there seemed to be a dearth of well-prepared successors.

On the whole, however, the union was strong. It had succeeded in repelling most of the demands for concessions which had bedeviled other organizations during the previous decade. Its finances were sound and the rate of membership decline was slowing. The union's basic strength made a study of potential problems and solutions easier.

Klein and Company of Cambridge, Massachusetts, were hired as the consultants to guide the study. In the fall and winter of 1987–88 they conducted in-depth interviews with BC&T vice-presidents and staff, general executive board members and other key leaders. At the same time, they did an initial study of the major BCT industries. They also engaged Peter Hart to conduct a poll of members' opinions of the union and to identify pressing issues in the eyes of the membership.

The first results of that study were presented to the leadership of the organization in the spring of 1988. A report was also presented to delegates at the national education conference that summer.

Based on the report, a number of recommendations were presented to the International officers. Among them was the suggestion that three task forces be set up to study further the most salient issues identified in the interviews and polls. These task forces were structured to represent the key leadership groups within the International union, and they were formally charged with analyzing the issues and recommending a future course of action.

One of the three was the task force on new technology. In their initial study, Klein and Company had identified a rising tide of capital expenditures in BCT industries. At about the time the study was being conducted, Nabisco Biscuits, the union's largest employer, announced a major new investment program in state-of-the-art production technology. The announcement promised to trigger a round of rising investments in the biscuit industry.

The public reports of Nabisco's plans indicated the baker's parent, RJR Nabisco, planned to use cash from its tobacco subsidiary to accomplish a technological leap forward. A new, "high-tech" bakery was to be built in Raleigh, North Carolina, which would have led, it was later revealed, to the closing of several unionized facilities and the loss of thousands of jobs. The new bakery and equipment installed at remaining older facilities promised to lower dramatically the costs of production of the U.S.' leading biscuit maker. This, in turn, would have put enormous pressure on Nabisco's competitors.

The concentration of ownership in the hands of corporate parents willing and able to make relatively long-term investments to achieve lowered production costs, and a cursory review by Klein of the production technology being introduced and planned, suggested that a major upheaval in the workplace loomed. New investment promised to make the 1990s decisive in reshaping the way goods are produced in BCT industries. The union's experience with new technology in the early and mid-eighties showed that traditional workplace organization and collective bargaining structures and processes would be challenged by this change.

The other key insight gained in the initial study was the recognition, through the poll results, that the majority of BC&T members and officers did not perceive technological change as an issue of importance to them or their union. Fifty-four percent of those polled in 1988 believed that future automation would have only minor affects on their lives at work.

This low level of concern about the potential impact of new technology seemed to be, in part, a consequence of the relatively small and incremental steps by which new equipment and work practices had been introduced in BCT workplaces during the 1980s.

What disruption there was tended to be comparatively isolated to the specific department or plant where a machine or new line had been installed. Job losses were often externalized, occurring in another plant where investment did not occur.

The specifics of contracts had not generally been altered by the introduction of new technology. The focus by the International and the bargaining groups it led on wages and benefits, and the relative separation of bargaining over these issues from language and "noneconomic" issues meant that the experiences of different shops or locals were not widely known or understood.

A third factor contributing to the lack of recognition of technological change as an issue was the relative autonomy of the tobacco sector of the union. While the tobacco workers had long grappled with the issue of technological change and had confronted it repeatedly during the eighties, there were no forums through which their experience and awareness could be broadly disseminated within the BC&T.

In short, the freight train was coming but the whistle wasn't recognized by most of the workers astride the tracks.

Despite the general lack of awareness, some people heard the whistle loud and clear. The announcement of Nabisco's plans in 1987 was just one example which signaled that the process of modernizing and reorganizing production was already well under way. Other warnings that the pace of change was quickening had also been sounded. Union staff who had attended the 1985 International Baking Industry Exposition in Las Vegas, or were increasingly encountering new machines, or hearing rumors of planned investments, raised questions.

In headquarters, staff tracking the industry press kept a file of trade articles which both described the coming brave new world of computerized baking and reported the start-up and performance of newly computerized plants and lines. The adaptation of the microprocessor to the hot and dusty environment of the bakery and other advances in production and distribution technology had, in fact, unleashed a continuing stream of innovation.

2. The Tobacco Workers' Experience

As the task force was taking shape, the experience of the tobacco workers in the 1960s was on people's minds.[18] Having been exposed through their international contacts to the experience of European tobacco workers with the introduction of high speed, automated cigarette-making and packaging machinery, and faced with the introduction of the same machines into the U.S. and Canadian industry, the Tobacco Workers International Union (TWIU) had convened a committee to sort out the union's response.

That committee had realized that the introduction of new equipment by North American companies was unavoidable. If the union resisted, industry would simply go forward with new, greenfield factories in different sections of the south and staff them with new, non-union workers who would be difficult to organize in the face of vigorous company opposition.

Rather than court certain extinction, the TWIU accepted the new machines[19] and pursued a three-fold strategy of negotiating some degree of control over the new equipment (e.g., speeds); a share for current workers in the increased productivity and profits derived from the use of the new machines (higher wages, shorter workweeks); and severance provisions in contracts and plant-closing agreements which used some of the wealth created to buffer the impact on the displaced. As one tobacco worker leader explained it, the union became very adept at negotiating "funeral arrangements."

While this approach led to the acceptance of absolute, large-scale employment losses in the industry over the long run, it also assured the survival of a unionized workforce whose members became among the best paid industrial workers in North America. Further, the union succeeded in establishing the introduction of new technology as a bargaining issue, assuring the union an arena to continue to influence the change process.

At no point did the Tobacco Workers abandon the structure of collective bargaining and formal "adversarialism." Their leadership extended an open hand to the companies in the industry and sought to improve relations. At the same time, they continued their efforts to build greater unity and strength within their organization to confront what they knew to be multinational giants interested ultimately only in the most profitable course, whether that be cooperation or industrial conflict. As technology in the industry evolved the union's approach also changed, but the tobacco workers remained committed to accepting technological change, bargaining over its introduction and impact, and sharing in the profits it created.

Part of the legacy of that approach has been the continued ab-

sence of "quality circles" and similar structures of formal "cooperationism" in tobacco plants despite overwhelming support among tobacco members for labor-management cooperation. This does not
mean that the structure of work has remained unchanged. At the
same time, through collective bargaining at the larger cigarette
manufacturers, giant steps have been taken toward reducing the
number of job classifications and (with extensive, jointly super-
vised training programs) achieving greater flexibility in workforce
utilization.

Another aspect of the legacy is the contemporary BC&T. Their
study and understanding of what the future held moved the Tobacco Workers to explore merger options while still an attractive
merger partner and eventually to join with the bakery and confectionery workers. The TWIU's experience in studying and addressing technological change was considered a success by BC&T leaders,
to be learned from if not exactly replicated.

With this history in mind, the BC&T task force on new technology was explicitly set up to serve as "a forum for members of
the tobacco sector to share their considerable experience on technology" with the rest of the union. The industry vice-president for
the tobacco sector was appointed its chair.

3. The Technology Committee's Mandate

In the fall of 1988, the technology task force (or committee, I
shall use the terms interchangeably) was appointed by president
DeConcini and set about its work.

Klein and Company, in consultation with the International
president, officers and headquarters staff, prepared the mandate
for the technology committee. The two-page document identified
preparation for the introduction of new technology as "perhaps the
most important medium- to long-term task for the BCTWIU."

The hope expressed in the mandate was that "the wide ranging introduction of new technology in large companies like RJR/
Nabisco [is] far enough in the future to allow adequate preparation
by the union" so it could (somewhat paradoxically but hopefully)
"take the initiative in responding to the introduction of new technology in all sectors."

The "long-term objective" for the committee was to "fashion
effective policies for the BCTWIU to participate in the develop-

ment, introduction and operation of new technology as well as dealing with the impact." Both consultants and staff hoped that technological change would not be a *fait accompli*, with the union's marginalization and decline inescapable.

The mandate also recognized that the reorganization of production was not likely to be a finite process with a clear beginning and an end. From the initial study of BCT industries, the consultants and headquarters came to understand that there would be an extended time line for change and the union's response would also be, by necessity, continuous.

The committee was instructed to build "a comprehensive understanding of the current and forecasted technologies to be introduced in the major industrial sectors represented by the union, understand the impact of those technologies on the production process; how changes in the production process will affect BCTWIU's members; and existing responses to those impacts."

Technology's impact was to be considered in relation to existing contract language, the history of the union, the experience of other unions and possible new approaches. There was a clear invitation to study experiments in new forms of work organization and, from the outset, the committee's work was understood to include a study not only of equipment, but of the entire "brave new workplace" of the future.

Finally, the committee was explicitly asked to "explore alternative methods of approaching the issue of technology such as joint labor-management efforts or involvement in the design and/or introduction of new technology." While an exploration of new forms of work organization and labor relations was to be undertaken, the committee was cautioned not to abandon familiar trade union forms. "The task force should consider participation through traditional collective bargaining settings as well as in non-traditional settings such as labor-management joint efforts."

By definition then, the committee found itself considering the central controversies of contemporary labor over the role of unions and the future of the labor movement.

The members of the committee charged with this task included a local union officer of a mid-Atlantic bakery local, a local officer and general executive board member from a southern biscuit and bread local, an international representative from Quebec, and the author. A consultant from Klein and Company, a former welder and student of technological change at MIT, advised the group.

4. The Committee's Research

In November 1988 the committee embarked on what was to become a three-phase study of our subject. In the first phase, the focus was on gathering plant-level information. The emphasis was to find out what was really happening on the shopfloor. Members of the committee went in person to visit BC&T-represented production facilities in every sector in the U.S. and Canada. They interviewed rank-and-file members about how they did their work, learned the skills to do their jobs, and how they were assigned to them.

Using secondary sources and trade literature, the committee members further analyzed existing conditions in BCT industries. This helped orient committee members[20] and determine the extent of technological innovation and specific types of equipment and forms of work organization in use.

In the second phase, information was gathered through interviews and analyzing union contracts on the union's formal and informal responses to technological change, the role the union had assumed in different cases, the contract language adopted and its enforcement. Committee members interviewed vice-presidents, International staff and principal local officers about how they negotiated contracts, and stewards and staff about how they were enforced. We visited various training programs and plants with new forms of work organization.

The committee's involvement with every level of the union formed the basis for the eventual recommendations made in the final phase of the study. A draft technology policy and an initial course of action for the union were developed and brought to the executive officers, International president and local leadership for feedback.

After incorporating the comments of the top officers, and with their support, the committee's recommendations went to the general executive board, which approved them. The committee's report was then presented to the 1990 convention for adoption. It was accepted unanimously.

5. Research Phase One: What's Happening? Site Selection

Anecdotal evidence, a review of industry trade journals and the literature on technology introduction, along with Klein and Company's research and competitive analysis of the bread, cake, and biscuit industries all confirmed that significant changes in the production process were indeed under way or on the horizon in the U.S. and Canada. Further, the pace of change seemed likely to accelerate.

Even those firms whose capital expenditures were constrained by debt incurred in leveraged buyouts and/or by rising corporate hurdle rates were likely to look, as soon as feasible, to "rationalize" production and boost productivity by altering the way work was done. Those that lagged risked being left completely behind in the race for "low-cost producer" status which had begun in the late 1980s.

What remained unclear was what was actually happening in the plants. Unlike steel, auto and other heavy industries, very little had been written in the academic or commercial press about the food industry, with the exception of meatpacking. What was available in the trade press was, while enlightening, generally laudatory. Seldom was the role of the union or the stance taken by workers in reaction to the new technology discussed. Problems, the nuts and bolts of the decisionmaking process, and the impact on the union and the workforce[21] were generally not reported.

At the very beginning, the committee chair had decided that on-site visits and discussions with members and local leaders would give committee members an understanding of the dynamic situation in BC&T industries that no survey could provide. Committee members agreed. Few locals would have responded to surveys anyway, even if the committee knew precisely what to ask.

The then-current state of the production process and work organization in two of the union's core industries, wholesale bread and cake[22] and biscuits,[23] were to be investigated by studying sample bakeries. Sites were identified and selected for visits which were expected to represent "old," "advanced state-of-the-art," or "mainstream" technology plants. The age of a physical plant was generally assumed to be an indicator of the state of the technology inside, an assumption that proved, to our surprise, to be wrong in several cases.

Because technological change and consolidation had long been under way in cigarette manufacturing (the heart of the tobacco industry), there were few plants left in the industry. Most of the major plants had equipment less than a decade old. Therefore, the cigarette plants selected represented the mainstream and the newest of facilities. They promised to offer insights not only into the future of tobacco but other sectors as well. In the candy and confectionery sector a facility was chosen that offered under one roof the gamut of candy-making technologies from hand preparation to computer-controlled processes.

In all, some 15 plants and training centers were visited between the spring of 1988 and the fall of 1989. Task force members were instructed to note "what is in place now" and asked to produce, where possible, detailed maps of plants, noting the location of various types of equipment, the number and skills of workers staffing them and the nature of the jobs being done (actual manual labor, monitoring and adjustment of machine controls, etc.).[24]

Special attention was given in the list of questions to the production machinery and process, the types of machine controls, and their locations. The span of control of the device, and the job classification and role of the human operators or monitors were noted whenever possible.

Committee members asked about product lines, their markets, how production was scheduled, how often products run on specific lines were changed and how long changeovers took. The flexibility of workers and equipment was noted. We also asked about plans for purchasing new equipment or reorganizing work.

The committee was particularly interested in learning about existing contracts, their various provisions, and the impact change was having or would have on them. Specifically, job classifications, as defined contractually and in practice, job assignment procedures, the actual tasks done, and the required skill levels of those performing those tasks were studied.

As the committee began its work, we assumed (or "hypothesized") that BC&T contracts, like those of most unions, contained extensive job control and job security language. We expected long lists of specific and narrow job classifications that limited the work one did, as well as seniority, job bidding and bumping language which controlled who could do what work and limited management's ability to move workers from job-to-job, even temporarily. We were generally right, on paper.

Other job control and security provisions typical in BC&T contracts guaranteed a minimum number of hours paid in a day if called in at a shift's start, an eight-hour guarantee if one was sent home after a specified period worked in a day, and a workweek guarantee and other measures limiting the use of part-timers and assuring that full-time workers would receive a minimum level of pay regardless of hours worked.

While these kinds of provisions regulate the intensity and duration of work and preserve work and jobs for union members, in fact, they generally represent the structure of work and the codification of work categories defined by previous managements and technologies following Taylorist principles.[25]

They were developed in an era of relatively stable markets, limited product variety and constant technology. The union, using its right to bargain over terms and conditions of employment, had incorporated them as part of a framework of protections for workers to guarantee some minimum level of equity and income and also to minimize the physical exploitation to which bakery workers were subjected.

From the early 1980s, these types of provisions had been attacked by management demanding flexibility. While the attacks initially simply aimed at lowering labor costs and raising margins, changing markets created increasing pressure for eliminating traditional job structures. Programmable automation made this more possible.

The union's experience with firms like Nabisco had suggested that new forms like quality of worklife programs and quality circles did not necessarily require new technology as a reason for their introduction. But we expected that the arrival of new machinery would, in fact, be seized on by management as an opportunity to reorganize the way work was to be done, and be freed from the job control and security provisions of the contract. We also expected that, the stronger the contractual job control and security language, the greater the incentive for management to innovate.

Because we assumed the existence of traditional job structures and enforcement of job control and security provisions, committee members asked little, initially, about job control language. Instead the focus was on training and advancement patterns to determine whether existing contracts and practices provided for the training and retraining which our initial review of the literature indicated would be necessary when computer-controlled equipment was introduced.

Much to the committee's surprise, one of the first, and most stunning of our findings (which I will return to later) was the divergence between the contractual and actual job structure in plants. Job control provisions, while as extensive in writing as we had expected, were not always enforced. They did not always reflect the reality of the way work was organized and done, except when labor and management were in conflict. The change process had already begun to challenge traditional ways of structuring and controlling the workplace.

6. Phase Two: The Union's Response, Tiered Interviews

Informed by the findings in phase one, phase two of the study focused on studying the union's responses to the changes under way, the role it had assumed, and formal and informal relationships with managers at different levels of the firm. During this phase, interviews were conducted with union representatives involved in bargaining and administering the same or similar contracts, and in some cases with the members who worked under those agreements.[26]

Questionnaires tailored for each level of the union guided the interviews. Several identical questions were asked of vice-presidents, local union leaders, shop-level leaders and members.[27] As mentioned, during the first phase of our investigation the committee had found reasons to doubt its assumptions about contract language. By asking the same questions of people at each level of the union we sought to learn how accurate a reflection of the existing work organization the contract was, and how the union's goals and policies (as embodied in contract language) were in fact carried out, or differed from level to level.

IV. Findings

1. Changing Environment, Changing Workplaces

The first two phases of the committee's work revealed that BCT industries have entered a period of technological transition and innovation which will profoundly affect our members and our union. In all sectors of the union (bread, cake, candy, snacks, pasta, and tobacco) the committee found production processes being altered, and job and skill requirements changing. In facilities large and small the brave new workplace of the future is being created everyday. While some plants, companies, and industries are more technically advanced than others, there is no industry where technological innovation is not occurring.

These changes are part of the response of corporate leaders to profound changes during the 1980s in major BCT industries which set in motion new competitive pressures on corporate and plant management. Market shifts and segmentation (brought on in part by changing demographics, and in part "self-inflicted" by the drive to increase sales) have encouraged the proliferation of new brands. Greater product variety and demands for quality require greater flexibility and precision in industries which were built on mass production of limited product lines. The high proportion of production costs which ingredients represent also has provided an incentive to reduce waste and improve product quality.

During the decade, companies had, in fact, increasingly responded to these conditions with changes in the production process. Many had introduced new machinery accompanied by new work practices. But as expected, our research also found that new machinery and work organization are not always linked.

In some cases new work practices and forms have been introduced without major hardware changes, as in quality and productivity programs. In other instances, broadened job classifications or other arrangements meet demands for flexibility without major changes in the production equipment used.

We found that companies in core BCT industries can alter both machinery and work practices in small, incremental shifts, or major, across-the-board changes. Most commonly, new equipment is introduced piecemeal with what appears, at least initially, to be minimal alteration to the way work is organized. For example, plants that were visited because they were examples of "older" facilities had, in fact, new computer-controlled equipment or lines which were gradually transforming the production process in those facilities.

We found that changes which often seemed minor to the union when they were made, in reality wrought profound changes without the union knowing or understanding their implications. Job and skill requirements are being changed, new jobs created, and others eliminated. New work practices have been introduced which allow workers to cross train and move from job to job as production requires, work in autonomous teams, or participate in quality circles. These innovations challenge the traditional structure and distribution of power within BC&T workplaces.

While incremental change seemed more common than the wholesale introduction of new equipment and construction of new plants, it seemed likely that this would change. As the experience of Nabisco instructed, greenfield construction and great technological leaps forward can run headlong into the constraints on capital spending that leveraged buyouts and other financial maneuvers have imposed. But if those constraints are lifted, there could be a proliferation of greenfield plants and the rapid transformation of the industries. By the end of the millennium, the workplaces of bakery, confectionery and tobacco workers may be very different places than those of today.

2. Multiple Strategies

Other strategies have been pursued in BCT industries in response to the changing environment. Companies with limited marketing areas have devoted plants to the production of a few product lines to achieve economies of scale, then "cross-ship" products to plants and depots to permit distribution of a full range of products. Other responses to lower employment costs have included two-tier wage demands, deunionization (by running away from union shops) and contracting-out production (usually to non-union plants). But as the example of non-union Pepperidge Farm (which opened a state-of-the-art bakery during the committee's study period) indicates, employee-bashing alone is, at best, a temporary step. Labor costs represent a relatively small percentage of total operating costs, and gutting the union does nothing for a company's ability to produce several different products where once it turned out only white bread.

While new production and work processes had generally been pursued in union shops as an alternative to the above,[28] the technology task force was aware that the two approaches to cost reduction, technological innovation, and union-busting, are not incompatible. In at least one example, a company chose to escape rather than deal with the union and existing workforce by opening a high-tech facility with a new, non-union workforce. This illustrates how a company willing to spend money on a greenfield approach could shed the union,[29] making it clear that unyielding opposition to new processes could likely hasten deunionization.

Nonetheless, while labor cost savings and control appeared to be important factors in technological innovation (and a central consideration in the type of innovation chosen by management), they were far from the only factors. Technological change is not something simply being done to workers. The drive for increased flexibility in production is part of an ongoing process driven by capitalist competition as much as by class conflict. These pressures may wax and wane in BCT industries, but they will continue. Simply opposing change will not stop it. The transformation of the workplace can be resisted but it cannot be halted. Since innovation involves choices, during this "moment of transition we have a unique opportunity to influence what the workplaces of the future will be like."[30]

3. Types of Change

Technological change has had negative and positive effects on BCT workers. The impact has depended on a number of factors, including the design and implementation of the innovations in production and work organization; the training, if any, offered to workers; and the awareness, ability, and strength of the union.

The committee found that the central changes under way involve two processes which are not new. First, incremental changes in machine design and layout are achieving increased production speed and volume of output. Thus, although high-speed bakeries may now turn out 150 loaves per minute, the near-term goal of machine and process designers is the 400 loaf per minute baking line. Secondly, new machines are being designed to extend automation into areas like packaging that have remained relatively labor-intensive. As the cost of labor rises and the cost of microprocessors, robots, and sensors falls, capital continues to be substituted for labor. The machinery may be new, but the process is not.

It is the third and fourth aspects of the current wave of technological change in BCT industries that make it revolutionary, and distinguish it from historic processes. Technologies which were introduced in machine tool, aerospace, auto, and other heavy industries in the late 1970s and early 1980s evolved and migrated in the second half of the decade to food processing. The development and introduction of programmable, computer-controlled, "smart" machines which "infomate"[31] as well as automate have given management the ability to gather and centralize information and operational control of equipment. This provides, in theory, the opportunity to eliminate people from the shopfloor altogether and secure greater control over all aspects of production.

Smart machines make possible the advent of computer-integrated manufacturing (CIM) and flexible manufacturing systems in baking, candy-making, and other food and tobacco industries. Programmable automation makes possible continuous-flow production[32] characteristic of, for example, the chemical industry,[33] and "continuous batch" production. These represent new levels in "automatic" production, especially in food.

Through CIM, continuous-flow production lines, dedicated to a single high volume product and maximizing economies of scale while minimizing downtime and labor inputs, are achievable. In an even greater leap, programmable automation promises the continuous production of smaller batches. Using smart machines, production specifications can be rapidly reset from a central point, minimizing the changeover and downtime. These changes virtually allow product after product to flow down the line one after another, maximizing the use of capital and labor.

Thus, smart machines mean not only that Nabisco can run endlessly Ritz crackers on a line with minimal human intervention, but that Pepperidge Farm can produce profitably dozens of different breads with a limited number of production lines in a single facility serving Florida and the southeast.

4. The Heart of the Smart Machine

At the heart of the smart machine is the computer and the software which controls it. The computer is known as a programmed logic controller, PLC. (It is also known as a "programmable controller" or "process controller.") A PLC can run a single machine or set of machines. Electromechanical switches (characteristic of earlier automation) are replaced in the smart machine with electronic switches, which, combined with sensors and connected to the PLC, provide a steady stream of digital information about the production process to the PLC. The PLC, in turn, uses the information to correct and maintain the process. Because they are, in theory, self-regulating, they reduce or eliminate the need for humans to operate or adjust them.

PLCs, other computers and electronic devices can themselves be controlled by larger computers in a hierarchy of command to monitor ever larger segments of production and collect and process information. A hierarchy of control is central to CIM. Local machines are linked to more powerful computers which control and monitor the process from ingredients handling to packaging, shipping, order forecasting, and production scheduling. CIM and flexible manufacturing systems are advertised by equipment manufacturers as the basis of the "workerless factory."

Computer hierarchies make possible the "Taylorist" dream of real remote control. Depending on the costly investment in sensors and other sophisticated devices, the software running the machines, and the degree of access to information and "override" capabilities allowed, workers on the shopfloor can control the machines and the production process locally or managers can control it from a remote location. Knowledge and control can be separated from workers and placed in the hands of managers. Many plants we saw placed controls in a room in the plant, off the shopfloor.[34] Equipment vendors even talk, theoretically, of the ability to locate controls in another city.

The workerless factory would not, in fact, be totally workerless. But, as envisioned by the vendors, the remaining jobs might be limited to a handful of highly skilled maintenance workers, and a hybrid "fixer" (as exists in the tobacco industry) who monitors production and performs minor repairs on the shopfloor. The work of skilled or "semi-skilled" production workers (mixers, machine operators) would be eliminated or done by supervisors or non-union "technicians." Engineers, software programmers, and managers decide whether smart machines enhance skills or deskill workers in the design and procurement decision process. The actual choices made seem limited by the degree of success designers and programmers have in accounting for the variability inherent in food processing, and the amount of money companies are willing to risk on ever more complex and sophisticated software and equipment.

Given the cost and practical limitations on optimizing a totally automatic, workerless approach to production, the committee decided that the union should be able to exert some influence over technology and other workplace changes by gaining information and access to the decisionmaking process. The opportunity exists, through training and cross-training workers and giving them access to machine controls on the shopfloor, to reintegrate application and knowledge. Jobs would be preserved and new kinds of work created for unionized workers. We also realized that, although most of our members can learn to do the jobs of the future, productivity gains make some displacement inevitable. Thus, necessary steps must be taken to buffer the impact of lost jobs.

5. New Forms of Work Organization

In the course of its study, the committee also encountered a variety of new forms of work organization and governance. To an extent we had not anticipated, we found traditional structures of work changing. While a majority of plants may retain old structures and processes, increased flexibility, cross-training and "teams" are becoming a reality. In many shops, BC&T members were able to move from job to job as production required, sometimes contractually, sometimes informally.

An example of how competitive pressure created innovative work processes despite a traditional, formal work structure was found at a northern U.S. bakery. It had been chosen as an example of an old plant, and in fact its equipment was archaic. The union contract reflected the minute division of labor, range of classifications and job control provisions one might expect of a relatively labor-intensive, 1950s facility. What we found, however, differed radically from the structure contained in the contract.

Because plant supervision had generally risen from the ranks and employees had many years of seniority, many of the workers were familiar with a wide range of jobs within the facility. Managers, workers, and the local union had agreed informally to allow workers to move around the shop as needed to fill vacancies. Thus, if a mixer was idle because a roll line was down, and the bread line was short a machine operator, the mixer might be asked to fill in on the bread line rather than be sent home. Or a worker might be asked to help clean the facility even though sanitor was not in the worker's job description. Because of this flexibility, the company was able to keep staffing levels and labor costs down. In turn, layoffs and shortened workdays were kept to a minimum, the plant remained open, and a high degree of job security existed.

One could search in vain through the contract for language authorizing this arrangement. But, because of the longevity of the workforce, the familiarity of senior workers and supervisors, and the good relations between the company and the local union, this informal arrangement was allowed by local officials. The union simply refrained from grieving as long as the informal agreement was adhered to and beneficial for the workforce.

This arrangement was built not only on good personal relations between the local and the company, but also on a straightforward recognition of mutual interests. The common assumption of advocates that cooperation in and of itself invariably and automatically yields "win-win" solutions is rightly criticized as ignoring the very real and recurring conflicts of interest that inevitably arise between workers, owners, and managers. We found that even in the most civilized of labor-management relationships, conflict, and the need for "adversarial" resolution processes (like bargaining and grievance and arbitration procedures) remain indispensable as a means for reconciling differing interests.

Our own experience in the late 1970s with a union-initiated quality of life program at a major biscuit bakery had shown that the failure of management to acknowledge the legitimacy of conflicting interests led inevitably to the subordination of workers' needs and concerns to those of the company, and consequently the withdrawal of the union from the program. When the workers in a single plant, company, or industry subordinate their agenda and adopt management's in pursuit of security they also become vulnerable to whipsawing.

The dangers of whipsawing and other tactics which pit worker against worker hit home. During the period of the committee's study the long established process of pattern bargaining in bread and cake broke down in two regions because of agreements to "save" plants, which were reached without the International's knowledge. The nature of bargaining in major BCT industries virtually assures that measures agreed to by the union which might provide one producer with a significant competitive advantage over another will lead to demands for similar steps at other companies. In such circumstances, the International union must be concerned about avoiding the initiation of a downward spiral leading to the degradation of conditions for all workers.

It was apparently to avoid just such a spiral that the locals (such as in the example above) kept arrangements to achieve flexibility informal. It was also clear that such an informal agreement could, if it "got out," undermine standards and practices throughout a company or region. Thus, even as we saw that BCT workplaces could become more flexibly structured, we could see the danger in that process occurring haphazardly without a guiding policy.

Because they represent a snapshot of the production system at the time of negotiation, traditional contracts have proven less than adequate as a vehicle for addressing and influencing workplace changes. Few BC&T agreements have technological change clauses, and those that do generally fail to recognize the impact that changes will have on other parts of the collective agreement and the work process. Although many contracts have strong job control and security provisions, these generally leave the union reacting to changes already initiated by management. The contracts lack a framework for ongoing involvement in decisions governing change.

6. Opportunities

New forms of work organization offer opportunities, as well as dangers. In our study, we were struck by the enthusiasm expressed for work teams by union members in some of the locations visited. Younger members in particular, expressed appreciation for the opportunities offered by cross-training within a team.

Contrary to the accepted wisdom in some sections of the labor movement that production jobs in factories have been and will forever be boring and monotonous, and workers are resigned to or actually prefer the limited responsibility, thought, and/or physical labor they require, we found that many of our members were positive about the variety and responsibility cross-training and work teams offered.

We saw that all age groups were capable of working under the new regimens, yet it was generally younger, less senior members who wanted jobs that were more varied and who appreciated the challenge involved in mastering the different tasks. There also appeared to be a shrewd calculation at work in the minds of some workers. The more jobs one learned, the more skilled and valuable one would be in the job market of the future. They were therefore more willing to embrace new technology and to volunteer for any and all training opportunities. In more than one shop these attitudes among younger workers tended to divide dangerously them from older workers. However, a union ignores or rejects such sentiments among the young at its peril, especially if, like the BC&T, it has identified involvement of younger workers as one of its paramount concerns.

The efforts of management to protect workers who have received training on computerized equipment from traditional bumping and bidding by seniority tends to confirm the perceptions of those workers that "high-tech" jobs are more secure.[35] Perversely, by defending traditional seniority, the union may become ensnared in a dilemma. Since unions are supposed to be a mechanism for promoting job security, the failure of the union to adapt to opportunities presented by new technology and workforms raises questions of credibility in the eyes of younger union supporters, and seems to confirm the perception that unions are "old fashioned and out of touch."

Of course, the question of opportunity can cut both ways, as in the case of the baking company which opened a high-tech, non-union facility near its existing plant. The company claimed that it had to have a new workforce because the workers at the older plant would be unable to adapt to the new work process. The issue the union stressed among the members in the old plant (many of whom were young) was that they could learn the jobs of the new plant, but were being denied opportunities and long-term security by the company's effort to go non-union. While we were frustrated by the obtuseness of the NLRB, the issue helped to rally our members at the plant.

Other positive factors which members in some teams appreciated were the relative freedom from direct supervision, and increased autonomy and responsibility for product quality and for the smooth operation of their lines. This pride in "craft" hearkened back to the earliest days of the bakers union which was founded by skilled journeymen who promoted unionism by showcasing the ability of union workers and the quality of their products.

It was also true that many of those who were eager to embrace new opportunities and more interesting and challenging jobs were solid union activists. They saw no contradiction between wanting to be on the cutting edge, do a good and interesting job, learn new skills and be a union stalwart.

Despite the pitfalls,[36] the technology committee concluded that new work practices like teams could be positive or negative for workers and unions, depending on how they are designed and implemented. Even as they threaten to extend management's control over the workforce, speedup production, and pit workers against one another, new work practices also have the potential for reintegrating a work process which management, following Taylor and his successors, has disintegrated. More interesting jobs, the development of career paths, reinvention of a craft for union members and real autonomy and increased influence over their lives at work are possible results.

The fundamental question is not the rearrangement of jobs and tasks, per se, but the agenda pursued in the reorganization process and the locus of real control over the worker and group. Has management abandoned the central insight and goal of Taylor, the separation of knowledge and control over the process of production from the work itself? To the extent that new forms of work "empower" workers only to reveal their secrets about efficient methods, and to "Taylorize" themselves through "peer pressure" in competitions to be ever more productive, the answer is no. Taylor's original goal, to reduce worker control over production, is achieved.

In contrast to this intimate authoritarianism is the legacy of the craft worker:[37] multiskilled, flexible and capable of outproducing those less skilled when properly equipped and compensated. The craft worker controlled the production process. Whether new work forms and "reintegration" reflect neo-Taylorist goals or a more humane alternative is the result of conscious choices over control. Only through union participation in making those choices is there hope.

7. Union Structure

The technology task force also found that the union's structure limits its ability to respond to workplace changes. There was significant variation between levels of the union in the interpretation and application of contract language, and inadequate communications within and between regions and sectors regarding workplace change.

This lack of a common approach regarding workplace change was a result of the low degree of union awareness of technological change, and also because of the structure of bargaining and servicing within the union. In general, leaders had not received enough guidance from the International.

In such an environment of uncertainty, bargaining does go on, often informally and sometimes without the knowledge of others, even within the same local union. The outcomes of these informal negotiations are almost totally dependent on the good will, principles, and smarts of the bargainers. Sometimes they will do the right thing. Other times, operating with limited information and understanding of the issues, they will agree to things which might undermine standards and patterns.

The experience of tobacco and biscuits, the sectors which have had the greatest success in confronting technological and work organization change are instructive. Company-wide and national bargaining, led by the vice-presidents, characterize those sectors. Servicing is also more centralized under International leadership. Consequently, while some informal bargaining has gone on, the International has generally been able to provide leadership, and have greater influence over workplace change in those sectors.

8. Conclusions

The reorganization of the workplace is not to be stopped; its direction must be shaped and controlled. The union must be a conscious and effective participant in making the choices shaping the brave new workplace. This requires awareness and understanding to understand fully the options available, the choices being made, and their ramifications. A program of education and "conscious-ness raising" is required to prepare the union to play a decisive role in determining the future. The change process must be brought above ground, formalized, and placed in the context of a union-wide policy which lays out the fundamental principles and aims of the union.

Union structures must be adapted to make this happen and provide the International with a more active leadership, coordination, and oversight role. The task force concluded that the International must develop a union-wide policy to guide the leadership at every level and the membership. These measures would be part of a program to empower the union to participate in the decisions shaping the brave new workplace.

As the new technology task force turned to transforming these insights into policy and program recommendations, we faced several questions. On what basis should the union seek to participate in managerial decisionmaking? What should the vehicles of participation be? What are the fundamental principles upon which the union's program would rest?

V. Adversary Participation: Extending Collective Bargaining

The traditional approach to technological change has been to bargain over the impact after the equipment has been delivered and installed. Unions have often assumed a passive (even if hostile) posture regarding changes in work organization. To have real influence, the union must gain access to corporate decision arenas and participate in the decisionmaking process. In many plants, the BC&T has the ability to mount an all-out campaign of resistance to new equipment and new forms of work organization. Marshalling that capacity to keep in reserve has to be part of any strategy, for where reason and negotiation fail there must be a means to compel. But to what end should that power be employed?

Considering the history of various experiments, the best alternative is not participation through some structure of formal "cooperationism" which supersedes or subsumes the contract. Rather than being passive partners in a process essentially controlled by management, the task force felt that our goal should be to pursue a framework in which the union can be an active player meeting management as equals to influence the decision process. In doing so, the union would remain first and foremost the advocate of the workers' interests.[38]

We looked to the experience of our biscuit and tobacco sectors. Technology and workplace reorganization had been addressed in the major companies in those industries through company-wide collective bargaining, as part of negotiations for national agree- ments, or within the context of contractual mechanisms for dis- cussing issues during the course of the agreement. This framework had proven advantageous for labor and management. The biscuit and tobacco sectors of the BC&T had achieved many of their goals regarding technological change. At the same time, the companies had been able to pursue modernization. Real partnerships and co- operation have been possible.

The technology task force proposed seeking, where possible, a role much earlier in the managerial decision process than the union had heretofore pursued. Such participation should remain within the context of "the collective bargaining process and the contract." Maintaining traditional bargaining forms and relation- ships makes sense.

> Collective bargaining is a process *through which adversaries coop-*
> *erate* . . . a negotiating process between adversaries with conflict-
> ing interests. As an adversarial process, each side is expected to
> pursue its own interests, and the common interest will be arrived
> at through the give and take of negotiations. . . . Though adver-
> sarial, collective bargaining does not exclude cooperation with
> management. In fact a labor contract sets the terms and condi-
> tions upon which labor and management agree to cooperate for a
> designated period of time. But . . . [it] is not some touchy-feely
> encounter group with labor and management representatives in-
> terspersed in a circle. Labor is on one side of the table and man-
> agement, on the other. Both management and labor realize that
> the terms of cooperation they negotiate will be determined by the
> relative strength (and bargaining skill) of each party. If the union
> is weak and members are not united, the terms of the contract
> will favor management. If the workers are united . . . the new
> contract will favor the union.[39]

The traditional bargaining model has been criticized because, while remaining on familiar ground regarding its relationship with management and the membership, the union generally abdi- cates any role in decision processes during the course of the con- tract. This need not be so. Bargaining need not occur after change has taken place, nor for that matter be confined to the end of the contract cycle. Workplace reorganization is continuous; high capital costs generally make incremental change preferable to massive new greenfield investments. With adaptations, collective bargaining can be ongoing too.

The major adaptation is to modify a model which is traditionally time-bound (contract expiration dates) to a process that is continuous by creating a framework within the contract for ongoing negotiations. The collective bargaining process, then, should serve as the key forum for participation, and be used to define other vehicles for ongoing union and member participation in workplace decisionmaking and work practices during the life of the contract. Experiments and new arrangements should remain within the guidelines of the contract and under the traditional oversight of union officers and the grievance procedure.

Bargaining has gone on in the BC&T during the term of the contract despite the collective agreement, but the approach of the union representatives conducting these informal negotiations was ill defined. We proposed that the process be formalized and subject to the oversight of local and International officers and the membership. To achieve these ends, the committee concluded and recommended that technology and workplace change also become part of the union's broader bargaining agenda. Ideally, the union could secure the right to early notice of proposed changes and to information. Because no single technology clause in a contract can be comprehensive enough to cover all situations, language would focus on the right to participate and bargain on an ongoing basis over the choices to be made.

In the best of circumstances we envisioned a bargaining process that would have two phases. In the first phase, the union would win enabling language giving it the right to be notified and informed of management plans. The union would also have the right to bargain over and offer alternative plans, and there would be a mechanism to resolve impasses should the union and management fail to reach an agreement over the proposed workplace changes. In the second phase, the union would "administer" the contract, invoking the enabling language to initiate bargaining when it became aware or was notified of changes being considered. Bargaining would cover all aspects (including design) and implications of the proposed change.

Since few changes happen without adverse impacts, the union could negotiate ways to buffer and help members who are negatively affected. Traditional and innovative proposals could all be considered within the bargaining context. Management's rationale for change is subject to challenge through the independent bargaining mechanism, and the union can get the best agreement and bring it to the membership. Union leaders can be held accountable for the agreements they make. Management is forced by the bargaining process, contract, vigilant leadership, and militant membership, to resolve its internal struggles before bargaining and is bound, as a whole, by the outcome. Adversary participation keeps the decision process "honest." By remaining in the context of a collective bargaining approach, power (its legitimacy and its exercise) is recognized and a resolution of conflicting interests is pursued. If the union recommends acceptance of an agreement governing change, the change is more likely to be accepted and to proceed smoothly.

Committee members were realistic enough to expect that this "ideal" process would not soon be won, or that it would ever come to pass in some companies. Nonetheless, articulating the model has value as it provides a yardstick against which one can measure the union's progress. Decisionmaking would be transformed and opened up with both parties being equal, in theory. In reality, equality partly depends on the organizing effort undertaken by the union, and the ability of management to walk away from the union and the facility. Depending on the strength of the union, its alternatives will be considered, prying the company open to innovations that may have been suppressed in the internal political arenas of the firm.

These recommendations fulfilled one of our mandates. We had explored the brave new workplace, alternative forms of participation and the experience of our union and others and concluded that the traditional bargaining approach, adapted to the more dynamic process of workplace change, would serve our members better. It was also an approach that was true to our traditions as an organization and would be understood by union leaders, members and, for that matter, our employers. The BC&T had never found traditional union structures and formal adversarialism to be an impediment to civilized cooperation with employers where it was warranted and goodwill and good deeds prevailed.

By maintaining a posture of adversary participation in a collective bargaining framework, we felt the union could avoid the shortcomings of "formal cooperationism" and still achieve the benefits of participation in decisions reshaping the workplace. Finally, to achieve the right to bargain and successfully exercise it, the union must organize in the workplace to empower workers and make them into actors in the process of workplace change, rather than spectators, or victims. Empowerment is at the center of the process of workplace reorganization; not only can the union shape the brave new workplace, but it can also revitalize itself.

VI. Operationalizing Adversary Participation

The program the technology task force proposed involved four key elements: a formal technology policy statement; the appointment and training of regional technology representatives; a bargaining program; and an education program.

1. BC&T Technology Policy Statement

The task force proposed a technology policy statement that outlines our conclusions, and articulates the bedrock principles and standards of the union and lays out its goals. The first section addresses the realities of changing industries. The first section, "Competitive Arena," acknowledges the pressures on employers which are generating demands for flexibility. The union accepts change so "that companies . . . stay competitive." Yet, in a rebuke to the worshipers of the workerless factory, the statement asserts that "the production process is most productive when run by skilled, experienced workers . . . our members."

The second section, "Technology and Work Organization," discusses the task force's conclusions and views on the change process. During a five to ten year period of experimentation, the workplace of the future will take shape and the union has a "unique opportunity to influence" what it will be like. The issue must be addressed immediately, it notes, for once the investments are made, the opportunity is lost.

Technology itself is not always good or bad. Rather, the emphasis is placed on influencing its application to minimize the negative effects. Implicitly cautioning against a "silver bullet" approach and emphasizing the local application of technology, the section concludes by asserting "there can be no single right response. Therefore, while BCTWIU principles can be identified centrally, identifying specific goals to achieve must be done locally."

Those fundamental principles intended to guide the union and establish standards are the subjects of the next two sections. The key role of training is emphasized, including the claim to fair, equitable and guaranteed access to training. Long-term job security is essential, and the task force affirms the desire of members for a "lifelong relationship to their work and their work community" and calls for the development of new "career paths" within BCT industries with the union taking the lead, if necessary. For example, this section refers specifically to the potential, with cross-training and job rotation, for the recreation of a baking craft. However, where the journeyman baker of the early 20th Century knew all the jobs involved in baking a loaf of bread, the craftsperson of the 21st Century will be able to control all the machine processes involved in making that loaf.

In "The Union's Role," the union's principles are expressed: "The union must remain first and foremost the advocate of the workers' interests. As an institution, the union must not be replaced or displaced as the primary agent of the workforce in dealing with the company. . . . [T]he collective bargaining process must remain the key forum." The intent is that both bargaining mechanisms for negotiating over workplace change and new organizational forms remain in the context of a bargaining, i.e., adversarial relationship. Put another way, nothing should be given away without something being returned.

The task force's position on deal-making without the union's knowledge, and other efforts to bypass the union, is staked out when it asserts "new arrangements must remain under the traditional oversight of union officers and the grievance procedure." The establishment and maintenance of standards of fairness, equity and shopfloor justice are affirmed as a continuing top priority for the union, because they "determine the kind of community we will have and the kind of life we will have while at work." Finally, the union's responsibility for pursuing all avenues to buffer the impact on those who are displaced by change is confirmed.

The final section reveals the overall goals the task force recommends. First is to establish, wherever possible, "a clear and guaranteed right for the BCTWIU to influence change in the workplace through contract language asserting the union's right to early notification of company plans, full disclosure of relevant information and the requirement that the company bargain over design as well as impact of these changes." A training program to "develop expertise and understanding of technology and competitive issues" is also advocated, as well as the incorporation of discussions of workplace changes in the union's structure and processes.

2. Technology Representatives

The committee embraced the suggestion of the International union president that a member of the International staff in each of the union's regions be designated as a technology representative. "Tech reps" were envisioned playing a multifaceted role including increasing the International's involvement in addressing workplace change issues, improving coordination and communications between levels, locals, regions, and sectors, and providing leadership.

Representatives will respond to local union requests for assistance, and intervene where workplace changes are being contemplated. They will implement the bargaining program, and lead negotiations and/or other discussions with management. They will also be responsible for monitoring their regions, keeping abreast of the developments in the various sectors and exchanging information with other representatives and the International. Finally, the representatives will organize and lead technology committees in the regional and bargaining conferences of the union to educate local leaders and to promote an exchange of information and their experiences with the new workplace.

The committee also recommended the establishment of technology committees in regional and industry councils (where bargaining coordination occurs). The tech reps and technology committees represent significant adaptations in the union's structure. But they are changes which remain within the basic structures and ideology of traditional "adversarial unionism" and do not compromise the union's ability to remain true to the principles spelled out in the policy statement. In fact, the most significant role of the tech reps is to assure that those bedrock principles remain at the core of local union actions to address workplace change.

3. Bargaining Program

The committee also recommended a bargaining program to secure the union's participation in decisionmaking. Technology language was to be put on the agenda in all future negotiations. As mentioned earlier, in the first phase of the ideal bargaining program the International union would introduce "enabling language" into pattern-setting and national negotiations. In many cases, the union recognized it would be unable to win the right to bargain over workplace changes. In those cases it might accept other forms of participation, including informal consultation and non-binding discussions of both sides' concerns. However, if necessary the union could pursue a program of concerted "non-cooperation" to force discussions.

In support of this aspect of the program, the committee developed "model" contract language. The draft language contained enabling clauses outlining union rights to early notice, information, independent technical advice, and the right to bargain over proposed changes and specific procedures for implementing those rights. For example, one clause calls for the company to meet with the union within two weeks of notice to discuss the need and justification for the proposed change, the evaluation and selection of the appropriate equipment or work practices, and the implementation of change and its effects. The model language also outlines grounds for maintaining the status quo such as failure to follow contractually mandated procedures or to reach agreement with the union.

A suggested impasse resolution mechanism is included based on the language currently contained in some BC&T biscuit sector agreements. Should the union object to a change, it would, first, negotiate at the workplace level, then, barring resolution, top officers of the company and International union would get involved. Failing at that level, mediation followed by arbitration would be invoked. In addition, suggested language concerning bidding rights, job protections, retraining rights, bumping, transfer, maintenance of unit and jurisdiction, shorter working hours, and gains sharing are included. While many of these clauses are based on language familiar to other unions, when combined with the notice, information, bargaining and arbitration provisions, they represent a more comprehensive approach to addressing change than generally found.

The specifics of a strategy for achieving contractual rights regarding workplace change was not addressed by the committee, as it believed that the "how, and how much" questions were better left to the leadership of the union. But the model language was presented early in 1990 to one of the union's bargaining councils. In response to a request, committee staff later prepared a "short form" representing an initial bargaining proposal presented in the latest round of bargaining in that region. Assuming the union has been successful in negotiating for the right to bargain, the second "contract administration" phase of the bargaining program would involve applying those rights.

At each stage in the process, the local would have to work

closely with the International and its tech reps to evaluate the competitive conditions and the company's goals, understand the company's proposals, explore alternatives and their consequences, develop proposals for buffering change, and organize internally in preparation for bargaining.

4. Educational Programs

The final element in the committee's proposal involves an educational effort within the union to bring the technology policy statement, the conclusions of the committee and the union's technology program to local unions. Tech reps will be urged to form technology committees at the regional conference level to meet annually to review changes and share information. And, where locals request, tech reps and International staff will conduct education programs for local officers, stewards, and members. The programs could review the issues surrounding technology, the specific changes under way in their locals, and the bargaining situations they face. A third element of the education effort involves the inclusion of technology training in the existing steward, membership and leadership programs of the International.

The task force's recommendations represent one possible program for operationalizing adversary participation and a bargaining approach to participation in the decisions shaping the workplace of the next decade and century. Many decisions remain regarding the feasibility and implementation of these suggestions, and other alternatives. As it is put into operation, the limits of the recommended program and adaptations made necessary by the realities of the bargaining environment will undoubtedly become clearer.

VII. Conclusion

At the outset of this paper I argued that within the response to the reorganization of the workplace lies the key to arresting the institutional decline of unions. There are several reasons for reaching this conclusion. If production decisions are left completely in the hands of management, with unions restricting their role to bargaining over the impact, then organized labor will become adept at negotiating funeral arrangements. Control over production, even if it is efficient, will be centralized. If no alternatives strive for a humane, yet competitive, mix of humans and machines, then, in the long run, management will have the incentive, and the designers and engineers the time, to get workerless technologies right.

If workerless "high-tech" plants spread through the BCT industries, the union's leverage will decline. Unionized, but less competitive plants, will be whipsawed against computerized facilities. The downward spiral of wages and conditions will be paced not by the speed of the union's retreat, but by the productivity of the high-tech plant and management's willingness to stay the course to break the union. Even if the union remains within the workerless high-tech facilities, representing the handful of "fixers" and sanitors who may remain within its jurisdiction, their total separation from control will make it difficult for union workers to exercise much leverage.

Further, if the union is not involved in the change process or defining where and how power will be exercised within work teams and other new forms, the solutions that are chosen will, more likely than not, orient the worker toward the goals and priorities of the company, and away from the interests they have in common with fellow workers. The history of intimate authoritarianism at firms like Pepperidge Farm, R.J. Reynolds Tobacco, and Procter & Gamble illustrates clearly that management can make unions functionally irrelevant if it is willing voluntarily to curb its tendency toward arbitrariness and injustice, is able to spend money on decent salaries, benefits and a sophisticated human resources staff, and can impose its own apparatus for "taking care" of the needs of the majority of its workers.

The failure to break out of the traditional posture of "wait till it's implemented, then grieve it," will mean, ultimately, an absolute decline in numbers, relegation to the most marginal sectors of industries, diminished income and capacity to provide services, and a radical reduction in union power in the workplace and in industry.

A proactive approach to the issues does more than just avoid the worst scenario. By becoming actors instead of the "acted upon" in the workplace reorganization drama, the union can help shape the human-machine mix and preserve both jobs and opportunities for their members. Such an organization will have more to offer prospective members than the traditional, narrowly defined bread-and-butter benefits of union membership and can better address the concerns of workers for job security and a life of employment more satisfying than simply punching the clock each day.

The essence of the technology committee's proposals is empowerment. Workers and their unions can become more technologically savvy, and become players in the life of the company. An increased appreciation by field staff, local officers, and members of the options and constraints, and processes and plans of the BCT corporations can only help make the union more effective, as long as we remain committed to the interests of the membership and are not drawn by this new understanding into an unquestioning acceptance of corporate imperatives.

Avoiding the latter is one of the advantages of pursuing "adversary participation" in decisionmaking. While such an approach appears to come down on the "us vs. them" side of the debate, it is, in fact, far more flexible. The collective bargaining system is also more flexible.

In these new arenas, discussions can be held without the pressures and constraints of contract deadlines and preparations for conflict that are a requisite of the formal bargaining process. Accommodation of contending interests can exist while the union remains the independent, collective tool of working people.

Adversary participation and a willingness to pursue entry in a range of new areas makes possible a resolution of the debate over the appropriate role of unions in the new workplace. What has sometimes been lost sight of in the heat of the argument are the goals and principles that specific structures and relationships are meant to secure. Thus, the artificial, numbing division of labor fathered by Taylor ends up being defended by unionists when there might be more humane and potent methods of achieving the same ends.[40] We must not be trapped defending the structures of the workplace which were established in the forties, fifties, and sixties simply because they were the best we could do then. Yet, we must remain critical and involved in reshaping the workplace to assure that the same fundamental goals and principles secured in the old structures are defended and furthered tomorrow.

The work of the BC&T technology committee continues. Implementing the BC&T's program will be an ongoing and evolving process shaped by practice and the realities of the workplace and organizational life. Where we will be in another year may be a very different place than where we are today. But we will remain engaged in the pursuit of a resolution of the question of the proper role of unions in non-traditional realms of American industrial relations, and of building a stronger union for the year 2000 and beyond.

Notes

1. Special recognition goes to the late chairman of the committee, Joe Masterson, who was its driving force; to consultant and member Weezy Waldstein with whom the author spent countless hours discussing the issues addressed herein; to David Jacobs who coined the term adversary participation; and International president John DeConcini who had the vision to establish the task force.

2. Specifically, the emergence of "flexible," "cooperative" and "participative" structures of workplace governance, control and work practices (such as teams, quality circles, quality of work life and "joint" labor-management programs, broadened job classifications and job rotation) as substitutes for traditional practices, and direct and/or bureaucratic forms. Richard Edwards, *Contested Terrain: The Transformation of the Workplace in the Twentieth Century* (New York: Basic Books, 1979).

3. Andy Banks and Jack Metzgar, "Participating in Management: Union Organizing on a New Terrain," *Labor Research Review* vol. 14 (Fall 1989): 1–55.

4. A now fading but related topic of media interest was the democratization of work and the end of alienation promised by these systems, concerns long since eclipsed by the emphasis on productivity and efficiency.

5. In reality, with the club of "international competition" or a plant shutdown looming, outright resistance was seldom a real option open to local union officers and shopfloor activists.

6. These "left cooperationists," best exemplified by the UAW's great social unionist Irving Bluestone and academics like Cornell's Jaroslav Vanek, saw in cooperative programs an opportunity to expand workplace democracy into arenas once the exclusive domain of capital and as a means to win new social benefits and dramatically improve working conditions. They were often inspired by experiments in worker self-management abroad and could be seen as the continuation of the syndicalist tradition which saw in unions the seed of the new social order that would arise from the ashes of the old. While eclipsed by more pragmatic, corporatist and managerialist approaches to cooperation, the insights of the "left cooperationists" can remain valuable to those forging a bargaining approach to participation.

7. Thomas A. Kochan, Harry C. Katz and Robert B. McKersie, *The Transformation of American Industrial Relations* (New York: Basic Books, 1986).

8. See, for example, B. Reisman and L. Compa, "The Case for Adversarial Unions," *Harvard Business Review*, vol. 65 (1985): 22–36.

9. It is one of the interesting features of this debate that "left rejectionists" have often found themselves on the same side as "bread-and-butter" unionists in spurning cooperative programs. This confusion and the presence of the "left cooperationist" current earlier in the debate has made the use of terms like left and right to define the sides meaningless.

10. See Mike Parker, *Inside the Circle: A Union Guide to QWL* (Detroit: Labor Notes Books, 1985); and Mike Parker and Jane Slaughter, *Choosing Sides: Unions and the Team Concept* (Detroit: Labor Notes Books, 1988).

11. Thanks to Dave Jacobs for this descriptive term.

12. Mike Parker and Jane Slaughter, "Dealing with Good Management," *Labor Research Review*, vol. 14 (Fall 1989): 77.

13. Employers, in many industries, are bent on rolling back existing pattern bargaining, among other objectives.

14. Notable examples include the International Association of Machinists (IAM) and Communications Workers of America (CWA).

15. For example, Shoshana Zuboff, *In the Age of the Smart Machine* (New York: Basic Books, 1988).

16. See Euro Institute, *Technology and Collective Bargaining* (Brussels: European Trade Union Institute, 1985); and Francesco Garibaldo, *The Crisis of the "Demanding Model" and the Search for an Alternative in the Experiences of the Metal Workers Union in Emilia-Romagna* (Paper, Bielefeld University, 30 March 1989).

17. David C. Jacobs, "The Concept of Adversary Participation," *Negotiations Journal* (April 1988): 137–142.

18. Stuart B. Kaufman, *Challenge and Change: History of the Tobacco Workers International Union* (Kensington, Maryland: BCT, 1986).

19. Not all local unions followed the International's lead. The local at Brown & Williamson in Louisville, Kentucky, chose to resist the new machines. Brown & Williamson responded by building a greenfield plant in Macon, Georgia, and eventually closed the Louisville facility. While the new facility was organized and many workers transferred from Louisville, the majority found themselves jobless.

20. Because members of the committee had different backgrounds, it was necessary to introduce them to the various industries the union represents and to facilities or equipment with which they were unfamiliar.

21. This impact, however, was hinted at in the discussions of labor savings to be achieved with the new equipment.

22. The single largest bloc of members is employed in the bread and cake industry.

23. While wholesale bread and cake represents the largest of the union's sectors, biscuits (cookies and crackers) is generally viewed as the most advanced in terms of wages, benefits, and contract language.

24. While access to sites was attained relatively easily by cooperating local union officers, managers were sometimes not enthusiastic about union representatives making notes and sketching production lines. In one case in which the author was involved, the visiting delegation was nearly thrown out of a plant, sketchpads in hand. In that instance, all worked out for the best; after swearing not to take further written notes, the committee visitors were guided through the plant by the director of engineering. Although initially suspicious, he eventually provided a far more comprehensive tour than had the personnel director who knew little about the production equipment. As in many other visits, follow-up conversations filled in many of the holes memory left.

25. Harry Braverman, *Labor and Monopoly Capital* (New York: Monthly Review Press, 1974).

26. Interviews were conducted with two or more of these groups at some 20 plants, including several facilities visited during the first round. The interviews were generally conducted in person (and in several cases tape-recorded) or over the phone by committee members. A few interviewees whose schedules precluded personal contact responded in writing.

27. Vice-presidents lead bargaining for virtually all pattern-setting and national economic agreements; local union leaders include business agents who may or may not have come out of the shop they service, but generally participate in bargaining especially over contract language and enforce agreements; and shop-level leaders include stewards who, although they may or may not have participated in bargaining, interpret and enforce the agreement daily through the grievance procedure.

28. This is only a solution for the middle term. The question of how effective these responses will be in the long run if all competitors match one another's efforts remains unclear.

29. The company argued successfully to the regional NLRB that the new processes were fundamentally different from traditional bakery production methods and that existing workers could not be retrained. The case taught us that there was someone who understood the technological change process even less than we did; it was not reassuring that it was the NLRB.

30. Bakery, Confectionery and Tobacco Workers' International Union, *Meeting Tomorrow's Challenges Today: Reports of the Leadership Develop-*

ment, Youth Involvement, and Technology Task Forces (Kensington, Maryland, 1990).

31. These terms are from Zuboff, 1988.

32. For a description of this process see Joan Woodward, *Industrial Organization: Theory and Practice* (London: Oxford University Press, 1965).

33. After all, looked at one way, what is food processing but the combining of agriculturally based chemicals and other additives into a digestible product?

34. Such arrangements are not necessarily efficient. In several cases, because of the absence of and/or unreliability of sensors, management kept workers in the vicinity of the machines. But, even assuming they could detect errors, workers were unable to intervene in the production process to correct them. Instead they had to contact a supervisor, who called the computer room, who had someone confirm the error.

35. See Roy B. Helfgott, *Computerized Manufacturing and Human Resources* (Lexington, Ma: Lexington Books, 1988).

36. See Parker and Slaughter, 1988 and 1989.

37. This is especially true in the baking and confectionery industries where craft workers in retail and catering continue to prove their value and flexibility.

38. As it was explained to the BC&T convention in August 1990, the committee believed that, "where the members' interests coincide with the company's we can and must work together. But where they differ we must continue to be aggressive advocates of what is best for our members . . . The union must continue to set and maintain hard won standards of fairness, equity, and shopfloor justice. Union-set standards determine the kind of community and the kind of life we will have while at work. . . . We want to participate in the decisionmaking process governing technological change as equals, with legitimate interests which need to be fairly addressed. We do not want to repeat the problems with 'jointness' experienced by others. . . . As an institution, the union must not be replaced or displaced as the primary agent of the workforce in dealing with the company. To do so would return us to the time when members had to deal individually with the company and had to fight among themselves." From BC&T, 1990.

39. Banks and Metzgar, 1989, 24.

40. For example, who would defend the narrow classifications and limited opportunities confining a bakery worker if, in return for greater flexibility, the union were able to construct a new craft in which cross-trained workers organized in autonomous work teams (as conceived of by

Banks and Metzgar) controlled the production process, and "management by stress" was prevented by adequate staffing levels, reasonable production quotas and other provisions of a collective agreement?

Editors' Suggested Readings

Alic, John A. "Who Designs Work: Organizing Production in an Age of High Technology." *Technology and Society*, vol. 12, (1990): 301–317.

Bakery, Confectionery and Tobacco Workers' International Union. *Meeting Tomorrow's Challenges Today: Reports of the Leadership Development, Youth Involvement, and Technology Task Forces.* Kensington, Maryland, 1990.

Banks, Andy and Jack Metzgar. "Participating in Management: Unions Organizing on a New Terrain." *Labor Research Review*, vol. 14 (Fall 1989): 1–55.

Braverman, Harry. *Labor and Monopoly Capital: The Degradation of Work in the Twentieth Century.* New York: Monthly Review Press, 1974.

Edwards, Richard. *Contested Terrain: The Transformation of the Workplace in the Twentieth Century.* New York: Basic Books, 1979.

Euro Institute. *Technology and Collective Bargaining.* Brussels: European Trade Union Institute, 1985.

Garibaldo, Francesco. *The Crisis of the "Demanding Model" and the Search for an Alternative in the Experiences of the Metal Workers Union in Emilia-Romagna.* Paper, Bielefeld University, 30 March 1989.

Helfgott, Roy B. *Computerized Manufacturing and Human Resources.* Lexington, Ma.: Lexington Books, 1988.

Jacobs, David C. "The Concept of Adversary Participation." *Negotiation Journal* (April 1988): 137–142.

Kaufman, Stuart B. *Challenge and Change: History of the Tobacco Workers International Union.* Kensington, MD: BCT, 1986.

Kochan, Thomas A., Harry C. Katz, and Robert B. McKersie. *The Transformation of American Industrial Relations.* New York: Basic Books, 1986.

Lazonick, William. *Competitive Advantage on the Shop Floor: Organization and Technology in Capitalist Development.* The Graduate School and University Center of the City University of New York, Center for Labor-Management Policy Studies, Occasional Paper, no. 10 (July 1990).

Parker, Mike. *Inside the Circle: A Union Guide to QWL*. Detroit: Labor Notes Books, 1985.

Parker, Mike and Jane Slaughter. *Choosing Sides: Unions and the Team Concept*. Detroit: Labor Notes Books, 1988.

————. "Dealing with Good Management." *Labor Research Review*, vol. 14 (fall 1989): 73–79.

Reisman, B. and Lance Compa. "The Case for Adversarial Unions," *Harvard Business Review*, vol. 65 (1985): 22–36.

Thomas, Robert J. *Technological Choice: Obstacles and Opportunities for Union-Management Cooperation in New Technology Design*, Cambridge MA: MIT-Sloan School of Management, 1989.

Woodward, Joan. *Industrial Organization: Theory and Practice*. London: Oxford University Press, 1965.

Zuboff, Shoshana. *In the Age of the Smart Machine*. New York: Basic Books, 1988.

Part Two

Rebuilding Labor's Base

The new economic conditions formed by the changing structure of U.S. manufacturing have generated dramatic changes in employment patterns, thrusting new ethnic and gender constituencies into the workforce. Many of these new workers are employed in the largely non-unionized service sector and new industrial sweatshops of the 1980s, while others are trying to get a toehold within more established manufacturing jobs. The authors in Part Two tackle the question of how unions can organize and respond to the needs of women and immigrant groups in the new economy.

May Ying Chen's study of the garment, restaurant, and hospital industries places considerable emphasis on the reconstitution of production and the labor market in New York under the impact of the internationalization of industries once central to the city's economy. In the garment industry, the overseas flight of major, unionized, higher-paying manufacturing concerns during the 1970s and early 1980s led to massive declines in membership in the International Ladies' Garment Workers' Union. The loss of such producers created a lucrative niche for smaller-scale manufacturers serving "the fashion industry's demand for a 'spot market' of last minute orders, unique merchandise, or reorders of staple sportswear items." Asian entrepreneurs were quick to exploit the opening, taking advantage of capital from Hong Kong and South Korea, cheap rents in downtown Manhattan and the outer boroughs, and a new Asian immigrant workforce, growing since 1965 as a result of immigration law reforms. Conditions of workers toiling long hours in the sweatshops of the city's garment industry call to mind pre-20th century workforms. Worksites are located in unventilated, poorly lit, unsafe, and run-down factories, often found in the same buildings and districts of their turn of the century precursors. These immigrant workers do not receive health benefits, job security or even the minimum wage. Indeed, child labor has reemerged as a growing problem in this industry.

These issues are remarkably similar to those which spurred the original growth of the ILGWU 80 years ago, but unions cannot repeat organizing tactics which brought success in the past. Chen

125

argues that organizing among Asian workers poses distinct problems for trade unions, especially as most of the bosses are themselves Asian, and are more closely integrated into the workers' community than is the union. Not only are these workers difficult to organize because of the sweatshop working conditions, but language barriers and cultural traditions require unions to develop more sophisticated organizing strategies beyond bread-and-butter unionism. The ILGWU's educational programs are aimed at making the union relevant to the needs of the workers, who desire literacy and skills training, among other services. In addition, the union needs to increase its visibility in the community. Participation in Chinese committees and social clubs, as well as through sponsorship of choral groups, retiree meetings, immigration services, and political action services, are examples of union responses to the needs of its members which are sensitive to the ethnic traditions of the community. Thus the union increases its prominence as an institution relevant to the lives of Asian workers, and strengthens its position as a force to improve the workers' standard of living.

In developing such strategies, the ILGWU was clearly working to retain its base in a garment industry undergoing massive restructuring, while moving to protect workers from exploitation. Yet these same strategies make sense in other sectors of the economy where the influx of Asian labor has provided a low-wage workforce, including restaurants, hospitals, and hotels. These sectors are difficult to organize under any circumstances and the need to appeal to a new ethnic constituency is a strong challenge to the unions.

Through case studies of the ILGWU, Local 1199, and Hotel Workers, Chen highlights successful efforts and strategies at organizing, yet also explores tensions within these unions that at times suggest they are less than responsive to the circumstances of these workers. Obviously, these community initiatives require extensive commitments of resources, and staff-time, as well as a willingness to risk experimenting with creative strategies and tactics somewhat removed from traditional union concerns. Furthermore, they demand the need for promotion of such members into union leadership positions.

A more thorough commitment on these lines would advance the interests not only of immigrant workers, but of all American workers as well: the elimination of sub-economies and the underclass helps prevent the erosion of living standards of all workers.

Immigrants represent a vital workforce, whose numbers could add weight to unions, while the strategies needed to attract and retain their loyalty suggest paths to democratize and invigorate the labor movement.

If Chen analyzes approaches unions must take to organize new immigrant groups, Susan R. Strauss' focus falls on another group of workers whose particular interests have gone largely unrepresented within traditional union structures: women in skilled manufacturing jobs. Her chapter examines the process and consequences of implementing an affirmative action training program at General Electric's (GE) unionized manufacturing plants around Lynn, Massachusetts. From 1978 to 1984 a strategy negotiated between the government, the union, and the company enabled a little over 100 women to move into skilled, non-traditional jobs.

According to Strauss, women were vastly underrepresented in higher skilled jobs at GE, and had extremely limited access to adequate training programs—the ticket to skilled jobs. Women workers at GE were able to fight gender discrimination in employment and promotion through their access to political resources outside the workplace, namely the Equal Employment Opportunity Commission (EEOC) and the courts, both state institutions with the power to influence corporate policy. In the face of two sex discrimination lawsuits initiated by the union in 1978 and 1982, GE was forced to institute an affirmative action program, although the substance and scope of the program was left largely in the hands of management.

The company and the union, Local 201 of the International Union of Electronic, Electrical, Technical, Salaried and Machine Workers (IUE) designed the program. But, according to Strauss, the company, concerned with its own interests, had an extremely narrow view of what was necessary to advance women into higher grades. Strauss argues that the training programs had built-in structural disincentives, such as low training pay, rigid after-work classroom requirements which cut into family responsibilities, and the possible sacrifice of high paying piecework jobs. These features meant that women inside the plant with seniority and families were unlikely to respond to the new training opportunities. Thus the women trainees were recruited either from outside the plant, or from among recently employed lower-skilled women at GE.

Furthermore, the programs offered "one-type training" for narrowly defined machining operations and were aimed at quickly satisfying GE's expanding labor needs for machining personnel. These

programs could not provide women with the qualifications necessary to gain access to the best skilled jobs. Strauss asserts that the
program design reflected the company's normative goals for a mass
production industry: increased deskilling and restrictive mobility.
Training was not intended to duplicate the experiences men were
exposed to in small machine shops during their apprenticeships.
Rather, the one-type training was limited to providing the minimum knowledge necessary to begin at the lowest skilled rate.
Without well-rounded training, women machine operators were denied job mobility or advancement into the higher ranks, creating
what Strauss describes as skilled female job ghettoes.

These policy choices were determined by company interests in
reducing training costs and maintaining control over wages and
advancement. The power to define arbitrarily skill levels and the
qualifications necessary for advancement, is an important area of
control over the workforce: management can limit worker knowledge, as well as access to higher paid and more secure jobs. But the
union also had a vested interest in maintaining rigid job classifications and skill definitions, motivated by a desire to protect contractual guarantees of internal labor markets and job ladders: the bedrock of job security for members. Women tend to suffer under such
conditions more than men, as they were traditionally excluded
from apprenticeship training in small machine shops, the common
recruitment route for most of the men at GE. And despite the security derived from rigid job classifications, such rules tend to be
conservative fetters on women's development which "restrict the
development of real skill, discourage flexibility, and inhibit incentive."

Even the limited gains of women workers at GE were reversed
by the early- to mid-1980s, when, under the Reagan administration, the federal government abandoned its commitment to affirmative action. Strauss argues that with a declawed EEOC and a less
interventionist judiciary, both the company and officers of Local
201 turned their backs on programs to fight discrimination. The
training programs stopped after 1984 and upgrading of skilled
women was negligible, although skilled men were hired and placed
in high rated jobs. At the same time, GE returned to its previous
pattern of hiring women to unskilled and semiskilled positions.

In 1987 the Lynn factories began massive layoffs due to loss of
defense contracts, transfer of work to other GE plants, and subcontracting. Out of a workforce of 8,300 the layoffs threatened
about 3,000 workers with unemployment. Workers with less than

ten years on-the-job faced possible job changes, shift changes or reduced wages. The economic crunch exposed the problems inherent in GE's recruitment to the affirmative action program. Women lacked seniority, thus they were among the first to go, and the layoffs "threatened to eliminate the vast majority of gains women had made in skilled jobs over the last 10 years." By July 1989, skilled women lost a disproportionate share of jobs in nearly every skilled job category: overall 65% of the skilled women lost their jobs, compared with 42% of the men. Strauss asserts that had the company originally recruited women with longer service at GE, as the union had argued for, they would have been better able to retain their jobs and protect the long-term viability of the affirmative action program.

GE was able to circumvent these programs after Federal government pressure for equal opportunity declined during the Reagan administration, and because from the outset the program was designed to train women in a manner consistent with the company's own production needs, rather than increasing the numbers and security of skilled women. The shortcomings in the plan were identified early by the women themselves, but because of the weak position of the union vis-à-vis the company, the women had to rely on outside agencies for influence. The situation of women workers parallels that described in the previous chapters, where even in the best cases workers were able to influence their company's policies only when management saw opportunities for cost-saving, and, ultimately, such initiatives were limited by management's unilateral control over investment, production, relocation, and employment policy. Thus economic crisis did not in itself undermine programs intended to increase worker rights and promote fairness. Rather, the unequal power between labor and management made it particularly difficult for workers to retain their limited gains once the crisis began. This has been especially true in new areas of negotiations that involve women.

Workers' rights are not always protected successfully by their union. Strauss' paper highlights the limited achievement by her union to institute effective affirmative action programs. More importantly, the union could not convince the company to make women's particular needs integral to the affirmative action drive: it was unsatisfactory to recruit women using techniques which had long been used to recruit young men to skilled positions. In addition, the Women's Caucus within Strauss' IUE local, and the concerns it represents—day care, maternal leave, sexual harassment, and job discrimination—needed to be taken seriously by the union itself.

The problems Strauss identifies are widespread in the labor movement: they are not restricted to unions in traditional industrial or craft sectors, nor to those with a minority female membership. The numbers of working women have grown dramatically as the largely unorganized service economy has expanded, and they represent an extremely important potential base for the labor movement. Women already make up more than one-third of union members, and they are the overwhelming majority of new members. Yet, even where service sector unions have won recognition, women's leadership participation is nowhere near representative of their membership. Susan C. Eaton examines the problem of responding to women's issues as a necessary condition to organizing the growing female workforce in the service sector.

Eaton's paper analyzes current obstacles to promoting women into leadership positions, taking into account cultural, political, economic, and structural conditions which interfere with women's advancement. Eaton argues that unions must tackle the question of why more women don't get into leadership positions, and develop programs to advance women leaders at rank-and-file and top positions. The approach is necessary for practical and principled reasons. Self-interest dictates that unions expand their base, a task better achieved with more women in leadership, but the commitment to women's advancement also fulfills unionism's vision of democracy and equality. The strength of Eaton's paper is that she also proposes a set of realistic strategies to accomplish the goal.

In 1980 Eaton was hired as a staff member in the International offices of the Service Employees' International Union (SEIU) under the union's Research Specialist Training Program. Her experiences and insights inform her criticisms of union efforts, or their lack, to promote women rank-and-file and staff leaders. She identifies five critical stages of leadership development detailing problems and proposing solutions. Although her focus is service sector unions, her analysis applies to blue collar unions, particularly her discussion of the barriers confronting women due to traditional apprenticeship training programs. Echoing Strauss, Eaton points out that discrimination and structural disincentives (low pay, inflexible hours, family responsibilities) within apprenticeship programs work to depress the numbers of women in higher skilled jobs. And, in times of economic instability and contraction, the last hired are the first to go. Picking up where Strauss leaves off, Eaton argues that this situation thwarts women leaders because, in industrial unions, stewards are most often elected from the ranks; thus, "unions have to develop more aggressive affirmative action plans and make revisions to the established career paths."

But even in a union with a stated commitment to affirmative action, women nonetheless face a hard road. When Eaton started in the SEIU she confronted a chauvinistic culture where, for example, new recruits were expected to pass "drinking tests." In addition to sexual harassment and other sexist behavior, her male colleagues let her know that women were not trusted with leadership responsibility, nor were the concerns of women members or staff seen as particularly important. In short, Eaton and other women like her didn't see the union as a place they could call their own.

The problems went beyond culture, however. Eaton found that there were many women stewards, but they balked at moving up, in part due to their own reluctance toward challenging the male hierarchy. While she points out that the lack of confidence is a factor, Eaton stresses that unions can overcome the problem: attention needs to be paid to mentoring, training, and developing appropriate role models so that women see themselves as qualified for leadership positions. Her idea of "guided experience" where on-the-job training is combined with close supervision, networking and feedback is helpful for any new recruit, but is especially useful to help women advance. Union leaders, she suggests, must take a more conscious and pro-active role in encouraging women.

Even where women come forward the demands of the job work against them. Single women might find it possible to be "married to the union," but for those with a partner and/or family responsibilities they actually perform two jobs: at work and at home. Women with such commitments have lower than average union participation, while for men in the same position it's actually higher than average. Unions must recognize the higher price women pay to be leaders and work to alleviate their added burden. Eaton suggests a number of sensible and relatively inexpensive changes: formation of women's departments or inter-departmental groups within unions to advocate their interests; constitutional change mandating affirmative action; closer ties to non-union women's organizations starting with those having an orientation toward women workers such as the Coalition of Labor Union Women and 9 to 5; and finally making union work practices more "women friendly" through provisions for child care at conferences, flexible hours, and conscious attempts to provide a non-sexist work environment.

Reaching for Their Rights:
Asian Workers in New York City

May Ying Chen

I. Introduction

Since 1965, when the restrictive quotas on Asian immigration were lifted, the urban centers of the U.S. have seen a large and visible influx of Asians to American communities, schools and workplaces. A large number of these Asians are first generation immigrants from China, Korea, the Philippines, India, Pakistan, and Southeast Asia. Others are American-born Asians whose parents, grandparents, or even great-grandparents settled in America long ago.

Increasingly, Asian immigrants and Asian American workers are joining America's trade unions. This chapter presents historical and demographic information about Asian workers in New York City, who represent a large, visible, and growing part of the workforce in the garment industry, hotels and restaurants, and city hospitals. Three case studies describe the organization, participation, and services for Asian workers in New York's garment, restaurant, and hospital unions.

Today, a number of New York City's unions are making important efforts to understand and meet the needs of the Asian workers in their ranks. In 1988–89, an Asian Labor Resource Center was founded by Asian labor activists from various unions, and the New York City Central Labor Council initiated an Asian Labor Committee to network with Asian trade unionists around the city. A conference addressing key issues affecting Chinese, Korean, and Filipino workers was held in June 1988. The conference reports and this research reflect the beginnings of a collaboration among Asian American trade unionists to define and tackle the problems of Asian American workers, develop and share programs to meet these needs, and sensitize labor unions to organize and assist Asian workers.

II. Facts and Figures

Data in the 1980 Census showed a population of more than 250,000 Asians in the five boroughs of New York City, with Chinese numbering close to 130,000, Asian Indians at 45,500, and Filipinos and Koreans at about 25,000 each. Federal and city agencies acknowledge a severe undercount in these figures. Nevertheless, these and projected 1990 figures show that New York houses the largest urban population of Asians in the United States. Even though Asians are a greater proportion of the population in a smaller city like San Francisco, the actual number of Asians in New York is greater than in any other city.

Within the tri-state (NY-NJ-CT) area, Asians comprise more than 5% of the population of New York and Queens County, and 2% to 4% of Bergen and Hudson Counties in New Jersey, and Kings (Brooklyn), Richmond (Staten Island), Rockland, and Westchester Counties in New York State. Conservative projections for the 1990 Census (based solely on legal immigration patterns in the 1980s) bring the total number of Asians in New York to more than half a million people. In 1980, 77% of the Asian population was foreign-born, and the proportion of foreign-born Asians continues to increase with continuing immigration.

Twenty three percent of Asians in this region have limited English proficiency, while 7% reported speaking no English at all. The Japanese and Filipino populations have high levels of education, especially Filipino women, but there is also a significant adult population, mainly Chinese and Southeast Asian immigrants, women, and the elderly, who have less than elementary school education. Asian Americans face a sharp disparity between their high educational achievement and their income and employment status. Many highly educated Asian Americans work in small family businesses or in the garment and restaurant industries. Asian immigrant professionals often experience downward mobility upon coming to the U.S.

Labor force participation among Asian Americans is very high especially among Asian women. Chinese, Filipino, and Korean women often assume the dual role of worker and mother. Since the mid-1970s, the rate of Asians becoming American citizens has been very high. Today, half of the tri-state region's Asian American population have acquired U.S. citizenship by birth or by naturalization.

III. Asian Workers and the Labor Movement

As a small minority group composed of many diverse nationalities with distinct languages and cultures, Asian Americans have been neglected and misunderstood in the pages of American history. Though present in America for more than a century, Asian Americans are largely perceived to be foreigners who threaten the American way of life and who hold customs and cultures so exotic as to be inassimilable and "inscrutable" to Americans.

Unfortunately, the pages of American labor history uncover incidents of overt racism and exclusionism towards Asians in America, including massacres of Chinese in the Wild West by the Workingman's Party in the depressions of the 1880s, and strong labor support for the passage of the Chinese Exclusion Act in 1882. Little or nothing appears in American history about the contributions and sacrifices of Chinese railroad workers who built the western end of the transcontinental railroad, or of the wildcat strikes by these same workers. The contributions of Filipino, Japanese, and Chinese workers to organize farmworkers, cannery workers and longshoremen are little known.

Today, a widely accepted stereotype holds Asian Americans up as the "model minority" who have succeeded like no other ethnic or minority group in the U.S. in educational and economic achievement. However, the facts and figures do not entirely support the rosy success stories of a model minority. Discrimination and isolation have placed many Asian Americans in an underclass not unlike the experience of other immigrants and minorities in America. Within this sub-economy, Asian Americans face business and working conditions which tend to replicate conditions in Third World countries. A stereotype of Asians as cheap labor and hard workers reinforces and justifies the second class status of the Asian American worker. There is a need to demystify the Asian American experience and for Asian Americans to break out of the isolation that historical discrimination, neglect and stereotyping have engendered.

Asian American workers have begun to reach for their rights as workers, for the benefits and protection of trade union membership, and for the equality and promise of the American dream. These aspirations are simple and no different from past and pres-

ent generations of other American workers. But the attainment of
these rights and benefits by Asian Americans presents a new challenge and demands the recognition of a special cultural and historical experience.

Increasingly, unions have begun to see Asian American workers join their ranks: immigrant garment workers in Chinatown
and in the New York City fashion district, hotel and restaurant
workers who enjoy the benefits and protection of American union
shops, medical workers in New York City's hospitals and clinics,
schoolteachers, electrical and construction workers, and postal
workers. Some of these Asian American workers have effectively
stepped out of the sub-economy in Asian communities and into
the "American" workplace. But the challenge of organizing in the
sub-economy nags at the organized labor movement; increasing
numbers of non-union garment shops, non-union restaurants, and
non-union construction sites financed and managed by Asian businessmen have appeared in Asian communities. In an interview, a
Chinese immigrant restaurant worker commented, "The Chinese
boss has a 'black heart.' But the American union has given up on
Chinese restaurant workers. We are too small and too much trouble for them."

American labor unions, especially the ILGWU, can play a significant role, as it did for past generations of immigrant Italian,
Jewish, Latino, and other workers, as a protector of a basic standard of living in one of the lowest strata of the workforce, as a
bridge out of the sweatshops, and as a link to American politics
and society. In the Asian underclass, where most employers are
also Asian, the union faces a particular trial of understanding the
culture and community, and reaching out to the Asian worker,
sometimes in a face-off with the Asian boss. The experience of Local 23–25 ILGWU in a 1982 confrontation with 500 Chinese garment contractors who refused to sign the master agreement for the
garment industry demonstrated the massive solidarity of more
than 20,000 Chinese workers for the union. This historic struggle
and the subsequent experiences of Chinese garment workers and
the union are a relevant case study for other unions setting out to
organize Asian workers.

IV. Asians in the Garment Industry

As reflected in the facts and figures above, increased immigration of Asian workers after 1965 and the trend of high labor force

participation of women have brought the newest wave of immigrant labor to the American garment industry. Contracting shops in New York's Chinatown began to join the union on a large scale in the 1960s when the major source of garments had to be obtained from unionized garment manufacturers. Contractors approaching these garment manufacturers and jobbers gladly encouraged their workers to join the union, since this was a precondition for getting the work into their shops.

One Local 23–25 member recalls the following events which brought her into the union. "I joined the union more than 20 years ago. I was working for a brand new shop. When the union came to recruit, the boss thought he would get more work if he unionized. So he urged all the workers to join. As an incentive, he even gave $10 to each worker who joined. So of course we all joined! And we got the union benefits."

Today, the ILGWU is deeply entrenched in the Chinese workforce. Many union staff members and workers interviewed commented that you barely have to ask Chinese garment workers to join the union. They come looking for the union application card as soon as they've worked for a few weeks in a union contracting shop. The health benefits are a major incentive, but many workers interviewed also discussed the importance of job security and protection of workers' rights as reasons for joining the union. Another old-time union member, recently retired, declared: "Years ago when there was no union, there was no job security. The boss could ask you to work until dawn, and if you refused, you were fired!"

By 1982, the structure and economic well-being of the New York garment industry had already experienced tremendous change and upheaval: union manufacturers and jobbers were in decline, going out of business, or shipping production abroad. Chinese contractors who relied on these union companies for work began to feel the pinch, and their formerly cooperative relationship with the union began to turn. Playing on ethnic ties in the 1982 contract negotiations, the Chinese bosses thought they could pull Chinese workers away from the union and refused to sign the union contract. Local 23–25 mobilized the huge Chinese membership in two major community rallies and successfully forced the Chinese bosses to sign the contract.

The 1982 garment contract was an historical turning point for the Chinese members of Local 23–25. Though its full history and the raging debate on its repercussions remains to be written, there is no dispute over the fact that, as one worker put it, the Chinese workers left their mark in the annals of ILGWU history. As a result, many active rank-and-file Chinese members joined the staff, and much greater attention was devoted within Local 23–25 to special programs and services for the Chinese membership and to forging stronger links with the Chinese community.

Today, while the garment industry is still losing major unionized manufacturers and the union is losing thousands of members, the Chinese membership is growing—not only in the New York metropolitan area, but also in Boston and San Francisco where the garment industry's decline has been even more severe than in New York. Presently, there are some 20,000 Chinese members in the New York City locals of the ILGWU, and more than 5,000 Chinese members in other cities. Korean membership numbers in the hundreds. Local 23–25 has seen a net loss of several thousand members since 1982, but has also received a large influx of new immigrant Chinese members, especially in the past two or three years.

Yet, today the New York Chinatown garment industry is situated precariously at the edge of sweatshop labor. In a June 1983 study by a private research firm for the ILGWU, Local 23–25 and the New York Skirt and Sportswear Association, the Chinatown garment industry was applauded as an important factor in preserving New York's historical garment industry. The report stated that this was because it relied on a plentiful supply of workers brought in by the 1965 immigration law, Chinese entrepreneurship, and affordable rents and adequate loft space for manufacturing in Chinatown. Furthermore, the industry was able to respond quickly to the fashion industry's demand for a "spot market" of last-minute orders, unique merchandise, and re-orders of staple sportswear items.

"Sometimes abusive labor practices" were already noted in the June 1983 study, and these conditions have been exacerbated throughout the 1980s by the decline of unionized manufacturers, who introduce large lots of non-union, lower priced work to union shops. (The gentrification of manufacturing loft space in the community has sent commercial rents sky-high, exerting an additional economic pressure on the Chinese contractor and indeed forcing many shops to close or move to cheaper premises in Queens or Brooklyn.) The ILGWU has tolerated the production of "non-union garments" by union members in the contracting shops on the condition that contractors report and pay for union medical and other benefits which were usually provided by the union manufacturer. It is precisely at the point where Chinese contractors must pay out of pocket for union benefits, that the contractor-union relationship chills, and the Chinese employer resorts to many underhanded means of concealment and exploitation for his survival and profits.

In various interviews with garment workers and ILGWU staff, the differences between the Chinese shop/Chinese boss and the American shop/American boss were discussed. Increasingly, Chinese union members are looking for opportunities to move out of Chinatown into shops in the fashion district. Vocational English as a Second Language (ESL) and skills upgrading classes for unemployed garment workers have received strong support and enrollment among Chinese garment workers. The conditions described in interviews with three young Chinese garment workers in American shops like Calvin Klein and Liz Claiborne, plenty of light and air, spotless factories, air conditioning, annual wages of $20,000, a five-day workweek and seven-hour days, sound like paradise compared to the Chinatown factory. American factories also have personnel offices, quality control departments, and rules and structures which conform to the letter of the union contract.

In contrast, the Chinatown shops are much smaller. Several of the interviewees work in shops of 20 to 30 workers and almost all report less than 100 workers in their shops. ILGWU Executive Vice President, Edgar Romney, described the impression of walking into a Chinatown shop, "You look around and cannot necessarily pick out who's the boss because she's often working along with the workers. The office is often somewhere in a corner, sometimes just a desk with a phone, and no secretary, clerical, or accounting facilities. The structure of supervision and management is not formal and obvious. There's a tendency for the media to look at these small factories as sweatshops, especially because the building conditions are so old and run-down."

This is the sub-economy of Chinatown which has "saved" the New York garment industry! Immigrant workers toil in this environment simply because they have little choice, and they expect the union to provide benefits and job protection to save them from total exploitation. Many old-time union members bemoan the terrible decline in their working conditions in Chinatown, "The garments are getting harder and harder. Styles today are very difficult. And the piece-rates do not increase with the difficulty in styles. I'm making less now than I did years ago." In comparing the difference between the Chinese workplace and the American shop, almost every response pointed to "long hours and low pay" in Chinatown. A recently retired member observed, "There's a big differ-

ence between the Chinese and American boss. In Chinatown, the
piece-rates are cheap and workers have to work very long and
hard. The bosses are more exploitative. But the piece-rates they
get from the manufacturers are cheap too. I never worked for an
American boss, but I heard they are more fair." However, workers
in the Chinatown factories also noted the ease of communication,
conveniences, and flexibility of hours in Chinatown.

How should the union draw the line on sweatshop conditions
in the substandard contracting shops in Chinatown? This has been
a constant challenge facing Local 23–25. ILGWU policy-makers
tread a fine line between giving allowances to employers who are
barely surviving and upholding workers' benefits and rights. Obviously, the bottom line for any union serving any population of
workers must be to defend the survival of the worker. The Chinatown garment industry must be no exception. Several union officials point out the tendency of Chinese workers to underutilize the
grievance mechanisms of the union. The different structure and
"rules" of the Chinatown shops suggest that the traditional grievance machinery must be more sensitive and responsive to problems
of blacklisting and other forms of employer harassment that arise
when individual workers file grievances at the union. One member
commented, "For a time I had to keep changing shops because the
bosses didn't like it when I complained to the union. They would
find ways to force me to leave, picking on my work, messing up my
machine, etc." In order to win the trust and cooperation of members in the shops, the union must present a strong and winning
defense for workers' grievances and complaints.

The interviews with union members point out the need for
more consistent elections and training of shop leaders. Many of
these active Chinese members recognized the responsibility of a
shop representative in maintaining decent working conditions and
in monitoring and ensuring the enforcement of basic provisions in
the union contract such as holiday pay and signing up new members. They emphasized the importance of union business agents
visiting the shops more frequently and working together with
members on contract enforcement and union rules. They were committed to upholding decent working conditions in the Chinatown
garment shops and fighting for their rights and benefits.

With few exceptions, the workers interviewed expressed pride
and satisfaction with their work. Their participation in the union
extended far beyond traditional workplace issues. Union staff and
members indicated a very broad role for the union including pro-

viding political, social and recreational opportunities for its Chinese immigrant members. Indeed it has been these programs that draw the largest participation of Chinese members. Medical benefits and the Union's Health Center, ESL classes, trips, the Chinese Choral group, Chinese retiree meetings, immigration services, and political action activities were all mentioned as important union activities which Chinese members support. Susan Cowell, International Vice President of the ILGWU, pointed out the special importance of the union as a social institution for its immigrant members. The participation of Chinese, Latinos and other new immigrant members in the ILGWU's various service and educational programs is quite different from the native English-speaking garment workers in other parts of the U.S. who look mainly to the union to solve workplace problems and do not require language assistance or social services and other support from the union. Additionally, the ILGWU has respected, throughout its history, the importance of ethnic clubs and organizations within the union, from Italian and Yiddish associations to groups like the Chinese and Hispanic Coalition of Labor Union Women (CLUW) Committees in Local 23–25 today. These committees and other clubs (Chinese retirees and Chinese pressers) help build the social support and sense of participation for diverse populations in the union.

Organizing strategies for Asian workers should also include building up the visibility of the union in the community as an organization fighting not only for fairness in the workplace, but also for human rights. A self-described agonizer/organizer, Francisco Chang of the ILGWU's Metro Organizing Department, feels that unions can fight for Korean workers' rights and protect their civil rights in America. Organizing Korean workers in the garment industry must be part of an overall organizing plan which can provide not only union benefits and services to the workers but also some consistency and stability to the shops. This is a very tall order given the general instability of this segment of the garment industry. Out of an estimated 1,400 non-union Korean-owned shops, Chang observed that only 40 are well-established, the others are shaky members of the Asian American sub-economy. Chang also noted that while Korean employers admit that the union is good for the workers, they feel their businesses cannot afford the union. It is important for the union to approach Korean employers and workers carefully. A sharp confrontational approach used by the ILGWU in the past created polarization and very negative feelings by both workers and bosses towards the union. Many Korean garment workers were housewives from middle-class families in Korea, and they did not readily identify with the "working class." The notion of strikes and conflict in the workplace is embarrassing to them.

Since joining the ILGWU staff in 1986, Chang has worked to improve labor education in Korean-American newspapers, has written flyers about the union in Korean, and has kept in touch with the 100 or so Korean members of the ILGWU. Because of the language barrier, these Korean ILGWU members are unable to communicate with the union, and thus are unaware of its many services. However, one service which has attracted Korean members is the ILGWU's English program. Chang is also active in the Korean community in Flushing, Queens, where he meets Korean workers in a different setting, providing community services.

The ILGWU interviews all pointed to the importance of Asian staff members in the union. Most members interviewed recognized the support of the union for affirmative action and its active legislative programs, and expressed the hope that qualified, responsible Asian staff members could be promoted into leadership posts in the ILGWU. Union leaders confirmed the principle of affirmative action in the union, as well as its activism in the legislative arena.

The experiences of the ILGWU in New York with its tremendous concentration of Asian members provides many valuable insights on labor organizing among Asian Americans, especially in the immigrant sector. These include:

1. Because of the depressed economic status of the Asian communities and their workplaces, basic benefits (medical and other) of union membership are highly sought after by Asian workers. Like all immigrant workers before them, Asian workers are anxious to move beyond the substandard conditions of the Asian workplaces and into equal competition and status with other workers. The union must deal affirmatively with contract enforcement, grievance procedures, shop organizing, and leadership training among their Asian members.

2. There is a major language and cultural barrier for unions reaching out to Asian workers. Translation, cultural sensitivity, and the hiring of Asian staff and organizers are critical for success. Asian workers also recognize the language barrier as a major impediment to stepping out of the Asian workplace. Thus, Asian workers welcome the establishment of ESL and other educational programs with bilingual teachers.

3. A labor presence in the Asian community is important to provide basic labor education and to show labor's concern for other community issues affecting Asian workers. Unions must support political action and advocacy for civil and human rights. Labor must take its place within the spectrum of Asian community organizations working for the welfare of the community. Monitoring and utilizing the ethnic press and media are important as well.

4. Many Asian workers in large American workplaces, and indeed in large unions, feel a sense of racial isolation and even discrimination. Asian workers' clubs, social, recreational or political, play an extremely important role in integrating Asian workers into the union.

V. Asians in the Restaurant Industry

While the garment industry has been the major employer for Asian immigrant women workers, restaurants and hotels provide jobs for large numbers of Chinese, Korean, Japanese, Indian and Pakistani men. The restaurant and hotel industry also employs large numbers of Asian women who work as maids and waitresses. Thousands of Asians work in Asian restaurants in New York, and increasingly are seen working in the kitchens and dining rooms of American restaurants and hotels.

Asian restaurants, markets, and other small businesses have been the traditional economic backbone of Asian communities for decades. Today, many Asian businesses have developed far beyond the traditional "Mom and Pop" operation. Most family businesses rarely pass beyond the first generation of immigrants in the family. Although family-owned markets and restaurants still provide a foothold for new immigrants who have accumulated a little capital, these small businesses cannot sustain or attract workers and simply cannot provide a decent living to a second American-born generation of Asians. Today, larger capital brought from Asia has established a multitude of new Asian American businesses. Some new Asian restaurants are branches of restaurants in Asia, part of foreign-owned restaurant chains. Others are the multiple ownings of rich Asian businessmen in the U.S. Asian workers find working in these large restaurants or in American workplaces far more attractive than the old family store. In this new workplace setting, conflicts arise between bosses and workers instead of cousins fighting uncles or grandfathers. Though feudal and family relationships still linger in the Asian workplace, these relations have changed in a direction which ripens conditions for unionization.

Working in an Asian restaurant is a strenuous and labor-intensive occupation. Long hours and a six-day workweek are still the rule, and the pay, when calculated over so many hours, barely meets the minimum wage requirements. There is no health insurance, and no paid holidays or vacation. If a worker is absent he must find his own replacement. He can be fired at any time, for example, if the boss is in a bad mood, or if he wants to give the job to a relative. The Asian worker, striving to make a better life in America, wants job security and benefits, but he also wants dignity and respect.

In 1979–1982, the Hotel Employees & Restaurant Employees (HERE) Union in New York City made an historic breakthrough in responding to Chinese restaurant workers in midtown Manhattan who were demanding unionization. Previous efforts to unionize Chinese restaurants, even in San Francisco, had never concluded in a union contract. At its height, close to a dozen Chinese restaurants (dining room employees only) had joined HERE. Unfortunately, practically none of these remain union shops today due to restaurant closings, anti-union tactics by employers, decertification to a Chinese "independent union," and the union's failure to renew contracts.

Nevertheless, the Asian membership in HERE hotels and restaurants continues to grow. Both Local 6 and Local 100 note the growing presence of Asian workers in the union hotels and restaurants. Local 100 is looking to hire a Chinese-speaking organizer into their staff.

The seven hotel and restaurant workers interviewed for this project expressed strong support for the union. When asked, "Is it good for Asian workers to join a union?" the overwhelming response was positive because of "benefits" and "security." One hotel worker commented, "It's good for any worker to join a union. For Asians in particular and for immigrants, the union is the only way to achieve a standard of living to allow our kids to move ahead." Other responses pointed out that Asians are often a target of workplace discrimination and abuse, and Asian workers need the protection of the union. For these hotel workers, joining the union was "automatic" upon landing the job in a union hotel. Such jobs are prized and often held for a lifetime by Asian workers.

For Asians in the non-union restaurants, especially in Asian restaurants, various obstacles have made unionization difficult. First, it is no understatement to say that Asian restauranteurs are very anti-union. Union benefits and payscales cost more money. But beyond the economics are cultural factors. Randy Wei, former organizer and business representative for Local 100 of HERE, recalled the organizing drive at Hunan Garden, a small restaurant in Chinatown. "The bosses could have paid for union benefits for 10 years with the money they spent on legal fees to fight the union. The main issue wasn't economic, it was the idea of 'face', that the boss is in charge and the boss doesn't want workers telling him how to run his place. The boss felt he would lose face by giving in to the union. He functioned on the old feudal idea, like master and serf." That unionization drive was touched off when a waiter was fired for eating a bowl of hot and sour soup in the kitchen! A union contract was finally signed with Local 100, but over time the original staff of waiters who led the organizing drive were harassed or forced out of work one by one.

An immigrant worker formerly in a unionized Chinese restaurant and now working in a non-union place criticized the union for giving up. The most important attraction of the union was to maintain itself as a "place where the workers can turn to for help." He blamed the union's lack of adequate services and programs for the failure to maintain these Asian shops in the union.

Another obstacle to the unionization of Chinese restaurants was the development of a Chinese independent union (Local 318) which created confusion and divisions among Chinese restaurant workers and their supporters. A Chinese restaurant workers' organization had been created in the Chinese community during the early organizing drives as a community support mechanism for new Chinese union members. The Chinese Staff & Workers' Association (CSWA) was founded for restaurant workers and activists to support and maintain unions in the Chinese restaurants. In the midst of a major labor dispute at the Silver Palace restaurant and its subsequent unionization, different views emerged towards the "established American union" (HERE). The CSWA was split over this issue, with one group leaving to form a Chinese organizing team for Local 6 and the CSWA consolidating its members to reject the AFL-CIO unions in favor of forming Chinese independent unions. Instead of developing an affirmative organizing plan towards the non-union Chinese restaurants, the independent union systematically raided each Local 6 Chinese restaurant at the expiration of union contracts. The independent union played on Chi-

nese workers' dissatisfaction with HERE and on narrow ethnic na-
tionalism. In the end, the entire restaurant unionization effort,
both "independent" and HERE, suffered tremendously in the Asian
restaurants and today is virtually at a standstill.

A hotel worker commented on the situation, "Given the willingness of HERE to accept Asian members, there is no reason to
support the independent union. Asian workers benefit from joining
together with all workers. There's strength in numbers, better benefits, etc. But the union must make and maintain its commitment
to Asian workers. Asians must join the union staff. More education
must be developed for Asian workers and employers about the
union. In this way, the union must create conditions for stronger
participation by the Asian members." The growing Asian membership in HERE could be a valuable resource in promoting and expanding unionization among Asian restaurant and hotel workers.

VI. Asians in the Hospitals

The 1980 Census reported a large proportion of Asians in New
York State working in health services, including 37.4% of Filipino,
26.1% of Asian Indian, and 18.7% of Korean workers. This large
proportion stems from special immigration programs which
brought large numbers of foreign medical professionals to fill staff
shortages in urban hospitals and medical facilities. The majority of
these health-care workers are physicians, nurses, pharmacists, and
clinical lab technologists and technicians with strong educational
backgrounds. Many were doctors and medical professionals in their
native countries. Data compiled in a 1985 article for the *New York
State Journal of Medicine* by Professor Setsuko Matsunaga Nishi of
the City University of New York (CUNY) indicates that sharp in-
equities exist for Asian health professionals in New York. She concludes, "It is possible that many Asian American and other Third
World trained health professionals . . . will constitute a more or
less stable underclass in New York's health-care delivery system."
In a field where Asians have ostensibly achieved success, these
professional employees face discrimination. U.S.-trained health
professionals are favored for promotions, Asians lack training and
advancement opportunities, are tracked into public hospitals and
psychiatric facilities, and are underrepresented in the higher salary brackets.

The findings in Dr. Nishi's study are strongly confirmed by the experiences of Asian workers at a hematology laboratory at New York University-Bellevue Hospital who disputed with management over promotional opportunities. Five Asian workers, including two Chinese and three Filipinos (one is a delegate to Local 1199), were interviewed. They have worked in the same laboratory from four to 15 years, and two of them were medical doctors in the Philippines and China before emigrating to the U.S. They candidly discussed their feelings about the hospital management, especially the insensitivity and discrimination they felt, and their observations about their union, Local 1199. Several of these workers filed a discrimination complaint with the New York City Human Rights Commission charging the NYU-Bellevue management with discrimination in a series of promotional decisions spanning many years.

One lab worker pointed out that more than 80% of the technologists or technicians in the lab were non-white, but for the past 20 years, the chief supervisors have always been Caucasian even though some administrators lacked the educational credentials and experience held by some Asian lab workers. Every worker interviewed felt this injustice very deeply, and some reported hiring attorneys to resolve their specific grievances on the job. A Filipino worker who became a union delegate in the hope of strengthening Asian participation in the union commented, "I feel black people are more organized, and that is why they are stronger. Asians should not remain passive, we must be active. The white boss we have is not qualified and knowledgeable. Most of the promotions are done under the table. In the past, before we complained, the vacancies for supervisor positions were not even posted for us. The union, though they support us, does not want to get involved with this discrimination in promotion."

Other workers expressed disappointment with the union's lack of responsiveness to their plight. Another Filipino worker observed, "Even though an Asian has the proper education, as we have seen happen several times in our hospital, the union was not able to help those people who are supposed to get promoted. White people without the proper credentials were secretly promoted, yet the union wasn't able to correct this problem. The internal organization of 1199 is becoming better under the new leadership. It has been stronger in this contract negotiation. But in terms of grievances, they haven't shown improvements."

Nevertheless, the Asian workers were unanimous in recognizing the need for a union and satisfied with the benefits and job protection provided by the union. "Asian workers must join the union for more security. At the other [non-union] places I worked, there was no security. The boss could decide to pay more to the workers he liked and less to the ones he didn't like. The workers could not complain or fight back."

In 1989, Local 1199 had one active Filipino organizer who was working with Filipino nurses. After the passage of the Employer Sanctions Provision of the Immigration Law in 1986, some New York City hospitals threatened to fire Filipino nurses working in an H–1 non-immigrant status upon the expiration of their work visas. Local 1199 came to the defense of the Filipino nurses, holding meetings and pressuring hospitals and policy-makers to extend the work visas of the Filipino nurses and supporting legislation to legalize their status in the U.S.

In pursuing their discrimination complaint, the NYU-Bellevue workers sought stronger support from Local 1199 to provide information and other assistance for their complaint in the Human Rights Commission, and to follow through on union grievances on promotions and training opportunities. Noting the general problem of Asian hospital professionals positioned in a second class status, the union could collaborate with educational institutions to offer stronger training programs and encourage the formation of Asian worker clubs and other support mechanisms.

VII. Conclusion

New York City's labor unions can play an important role in aiding Asian American workers to break down their isolation and promote their acceptance into the family of American workers. As a conscience, a helping hand, indeed a bridge, a unifier, the labor movement provides the best hope for Asian American workers who are "reaching for their rights." The successful organizing of Asian workers advances the cause of labor as a whole in eliminating the sub-economies and underclass which gnaw at the living standard of all workers. The ILGWU, HERE, Local 1199, and others have begun to address the needs of Asian American workers, and their example and experiences should be studied, copied, improved upon, and deepened.

Asian Americans will remain a growing and important part of the workforce in New York City for generations to come. They need the basic benefits and rights of union membership. Unions must reach out and hire Asian organizers and staff members, provide translations, and develop sensitivity to Asian cultures. The Asian communities in which these workers live are dynamic and growing. Labor unions must be involved with Asian community organizations who can support organizing drives and gain access to ethnic media to promote labor's causes. Political action and advocacy on community issues such as housing, women's rights, and education provide a common ground for labor and community cooperation. Finally, the efforts of Asian workers to build worker associations and labor coalitions such as the Asian Labor Resource Center must be supported and nurtured by labor unions. Through these organizations, outreach efforts and labor education to Asian workers can be strengthened, Asian leadership can be identified and developed, and Asian union members can develop a fuller sense of belonging and participation in the labor movement.

Editors' Suggested Readings

Bailey, Thomas and Marcia Freedman. *Immigrant and Native Born Workers In The Restaurant Industry*. Thesis, Columbia University, July 1981.

The Chinatown Garment Industry Study. New York: Ables, Schwartz, Haekel and Silverblatt, Inc., June 1983.

Chung, Lucie and Edna Bonacich, eds. *Labor Immigration Under Capitalism: Asian Workers in the U.S. Before W.W.II*. California: University of California Press, 1984.

United States Commission on Civil Rights. *The Economic Status Of Americans Of Asian Descent: An Exploratory Investigation*. Washington, D.C.: U.S. Commission on Civil Rights Clearinghouse Publication No. 95, October 1988.

Kinkead, Gwen. "A Reporter at Large (Chinatown-Part I)", *The New Yorker*, 10 June 1991, esp. 71–75.

Kwong, Peter. *Chinatown, N.Y.: Labor and Politics, 1930–1950*. New York: Monthly Review Press, 1979.

New York State Committee on Labor. *New Chapter 764, Laws of 1986, A.3680B/S. 2825B*. Albany: New York State Assembly, 1986.

Outlook: The Growing Asian Presence in the Tri-State Region. New York: Chinese-American Planning Council, United Way of Tri-State and Regional Plan Association, 1989.

Saxton, Alexander. *The Indispensable Enemy: Labor and the Anti-Chinese Movement in California.* Berkeley, Los Angeles: University of California Press, 1971.

Takaki, Ronald T. *Iron Cages: Race and Culture in Nineteenth-Century America.* New York: Alfred A. Knopf, 1979.

U.S. Congress. *Immigration Reform And Control Act Of 1986.* Washington, D.C.: U.S. Government Printing Office, 1986.

Waldinger, Roger. *Through The Eye Of The Needle.* New York: New York University Press, 1986.

Strategy for Failure:
Affirmative Action in a Mass Production Context

*Susan R. Strauss**

I. Introduction

In January 1987, a large unionized multinational corporation, producing aircraft engines, marine turbines, gears, and power generation, announced layoffs affecting one-third of its workforce. The General Electric complex is basically a defense facility with some commercial contracts employing 8,300 people in plants spread over four towns. The layoffs not only threatened about 3,000 workers with unemployment,[1] but created a veritable chain reaction of "bumping," affecting nearly every member of the IUE, Local 201, the main bargaining unit for the complex. All workers with less than 10 years service faced job changes, shift changes, or reduced wages. Most importantly, these layoffs also threatened to eliminate the vast majority of affirmative action gains women had made in skilled jobs over the past decade.

The primary reason for the massive layoffs which began in 1987, was the transfer of work from the Lynn turbine division to Fitchburg, Massachusetts, Schenectady, New York, and Bangor, Maine, and the loss of government contracts in the aircraft division. Work was also lost due to GE's decision to subcontract some manufacturing to smaller companies.

The GE complex north of Boston comprises three plants. They are located in Lynn, Everett, and Medford, and form one bargaining unit which entitles workers to transfer between plants. Two other bargaining units are also part of IUE Local 201. Salaried workers (mostly clerical workers) in these three plants make up

---

*Part of the data for this paper was collected in collaboration with Dr. Ellen I. Rosen.

the second unit. A third bargaining unit is in Wilmington, where aircraft instruments are assembled.

The largest proportion of women employed at GE were concentrated in the Wilmington plant, where they comprise 45% of the workforce, and were employed mostly in unskilled and semiskilled jobs.[2] These women, however, were not included in the study because they had no transfer rights into the Lynn-Everett-Medford complex and, subsequently, were not affected by the displacements in the first bargaining unit.

GE is an ideal place to study the long range consequences of affirmative action programs designed to increase the numbers of women in skilled manufacturing jobs. Most of these programs in the General Electric complex were initiated in the late 1970s, and over a hundred women were placed in nontraditional work before severe industrial contractions led to massive displacements. The experience in Lynn provides the setting for this examination of the flaws in the affirmative action programs, as well as the consequences of displacement for newly recruited women.

The GE complex was the site of nationally known affirmative action training programs which began about seven years before the layoffs. In 1978, as a result of the threat of a sex discrimination suit by the EEOC against General Electric, the corporation signed a consent decree with the federal agency. A major part of the affirmative action agreement was to offer back pay, wage increases, and promotion incentive bonuses to women in both the main complex as well as the Wilmington aircraft instrument plant, and a one-rate upgrade for undervalued jobs. Training programs for women and minorities were also mandated by this settlement.

GE began encouraging women in the main complex employed in unskilled and semiskilled jobs to sign up for its existing three-year apprenticeship course. At the same time, a new, shorter program which took about six months to complete, was developed to address GE's expanding labor needs for machining personnel. This was a one-type training program (MOTP), offered to both men and women, to train them for narrowly defined machining operations. Recruitment for both programs was primarily directed to men and women *who were not currently working in the plant.*

Subsequently, the union, IUE Local 201, challenged the consent decree, arguing that the settlement was inadequate and did not sufficiently address the needs of women in the Wilmington plant. No training programs were even established at this plant at the time of the EEOC settlement. Most importantly for this research, however, the union also challenged the company's policy of recruiting MOTP candidates "from the streets." Low-rated women already working in the aircraft and turbine facilities, as well as women clerical workers, were effectively denied access to skilled jobs; and too, they were not given the financial and structural supports that would make the training programs attractive.

A compromise, now known as the "Krikorian decision," was reached between the union and GE in 1982. By 1983, as a result of both the initial EEOC sex discrimination suit and the Krikorian decision, GE, in cooperation with Local 201, had organized four new training programs in which a significant number of slots were set aside for women. One was a two-year program to train craftspeople (only 10 weeks for ironworkers); another was a five-week program to train welders; the third, an updated version of the MOTP, was to train machinists. Although men were permitted to take these training programs, a substantial number of slots were guaranteed to women. By the end of 1986, just a month before the layoffs were announced, about 100 women had actually been trained and placed in skilled production jobs.

The increase in the number of women who began to work in GE's skilled production jobs enhanced the influence of a pre-existing Women's Committee within Local 201. This committee has continued to be an important advocacy group for women workers within the union, encouraging Local 201 to support day care, parental leave, and policies to deter sexual harassment.

However, the affirmative action training programs did not significantly change the work environment for skilled women. The union and the company believed that allowing women to "gain access" by becoming "qualified" through the training programs was sufficient to provide women with equal opportunity. Yet, pre-existing negotiated rules governing job bidding, advancement, and layoffs remained in place, creating a variety of structural disadvantages for women, particularly when the layoffs began.

II. Methodology

Information for this study was gathered from company-generated data for the Lynn-Everett-Medford locations. This data included information on workers' birthdates, race and nationality, gender, seniority, occupational classification, and changes in job status.

People lose their jobs for a variety of reasons, including illness, pregnancy, accident, retirement, promotion, or personal problems. The company records these "changes of status" using 92 different categories. However, while these categories show whether a lack of work is due to the loss of government contracts or transfer of work from the turbine division, they do *not* indicate if a job is lost due to subcontracting. This may be an attempt to conceal from workers the number of jobs being "farmed out."

Workers are considered skilled by GE if they hold job rates between the categories labeled R18 and R25. The survey included only those workers in the rate range who were directly involved with manufacturing or who were required to have some training or mechanical knowledge to qualify as support personnel. Thus a number of support personnel like tool crib attendants, lab workers, and servicers were excluded. Using these criteria, there were 22 skilled categories where women were found in December 1986, just before the layoffs. (These job categories and rates are described in the Appendix.)

To compare the extent to which men and women were differentially affected by the layoffs, I counted the numbers of male and female workers who were employed in skilled jobs in December 1986 and compared them with the numbers employed in July 1989, after the displacements ended. I calculated the differences between men and women in each job family and for each job rate who had been *involuntarily* displaced between January 1987 and July 1989. I also calculated the numbers of unskilled and semiskilled women employed in 1986, when the layoffs began. A sample of 15 men and 15 women was chosen to participate in in-depth interviews to supplement analysis of the data.

III. Findings

1. Aggregate Data

Research conducted between 1980 and 1986,[3] shows that there has been some progress in increasing the numbers of women in skilled jobs at the GE complex. In 1980, O'Farrell found that women constituted 3% of all skilled workers and 0.3% of the workers at rates R23–25. O'Farrell also found that women hired between 1978 and 1980 were hired four steps lower than men and were disproportionately found in unskilled jobs at rates R14 and below.[4] According to my calculations in December 1986, after six years of affirmative action training designed to give women access to skilled nontraditional jobs, women comprised about 6% of the skilled workers and 1% of the workers at the highest skill levels, rates R23–25.[5] Women had only between three and six years to advance in the skilled rates before the beginning of the layoffs. Even before that, women were restricted by the lack of available jobs at the highest levels, a sign that production was not expanding. Thus, while there appears to have been some progress in placing women in skilled jobs between 1980 and 1986, the state of manufacturing itself largely determined the parameters of women's progress.

2. The Training Programs

As previously mentioned, a total of five training programs was implemented by the company. GE had been running a three-year apprenticeship training program for its highest skilled workers and future managers, primarily men. Only after 1978, when the EEOC consent decree was signed with the company, did GE actively begin to recruit women. Before that time, only five women had participated in the program and, by 1986, these women had been placed on the shopfloor at rates from R22–25.[6] In 1986, women apprentices numbered 27, or 16%, out of a total of 171 trainees.

Despite what seems to be significant progress for women at GE, many of the training programs were seriously flawed. The apprenticeship course required a lengthy commitment, with classes held after regular working hours, in addition to a considerable amount of homework. The first-year participants were required to work at the rate R5, about $5 to $7 an hour. These conditions were most appropriate to someone just out of high school who might be considering a lifelong career at GE. However, a program with this type of structure was not attractive to older women with family responsibilities. Female recruits to non-traditional skilled craft jobs tend to be somewhat older and frequently have children.[7]

The second series of training programs started as a result of the Krikorian decision and provided accessibility to more types of skilled jobs. In response to criticism from Local 201's Women's Committee, the company made an effort to recruit internally and to increase the rate of pay during training. However, data from my interviews with women indicate a number of other problems continued with the programs.

Training wages were increased to a maximum rate of R17 for MOTP participants and a maximum rate of R20 for craft trainees during the second series of programs beginning in 1982. While this new policy was decisively more appealing, it still did not attract the large numbers of women recently hired in unskilled and semiskilled jobs (see Table 1). Between 1950 and 1977, 112 women were employed in these jobs. However, between 1978 and 1980, 210 additional women were hired, increasing the numbers of women in the unskilled and semiskilled workforce by almost 200%. These women were concentrated in semiskilled R14–R17 rates, with many of these jobs paying premium piecework wages.

Some of the semiskilled women were earning piecework wages and were reluctant to leave lucrative positions and take significant cuts in pay during training. For these women, a change could mean losing as much as $100 a week or more in wages. Further-

Table 1
Distribution of Seniority among Non-skilled Women
December 31, 1986

	R18–R19 (support)	R14–R17 (semiskilled)	R8–R12	TOTAL (unskilled)
1986	3	25	25	53
1985	3	47	18	68
1984	2	43	9	54
1983		10	2	12
1982	2	12		14
1981	1	17		18
1980	3	52	9	64
1979	3	62	5	70
1978	3	62	11	76
(Recruitment of women begins)				
1977 to 1970	3	51	12	66
1969 to 1960	4	27	6	37
1959 to 1950		4		4
< 1949		4	1	5
Totals	27	416	98	541
				(total women)

more, placement in higher-rated skilled jobs after training, interestingly enough, did not always guarantee a higher wage than
what many of these women were already earning.[8] Because of the
job bidding system in the plant, there was also the risk of not getting placed in a high-wage skilled piecework job even after completion of the program.

In addition to the semiskilled pieceworkers, women clerical
workers and secretaries were eligible to participate in the new
training programs. However, while these office workers often
earned less than sweepers in factory jobs, a move to the shopfloor
meant a loss of benefits: they had 20 personal days leave compared
with men who had only two or three. A move also meant the probable loss of their day-shift hours and a possible disruption of family
and personal life.

Thus, despite the increased rate of training pay during the second round of courses, the lack of interest among women with seniority, pre-1978 as well as from the newer recruits from 1978–80,
may well have been the consequence of a program designed with
built-in structural disincentives to recruit women from inside the
plant. Only a few of the unskilled and semiskilled women (those
with the lowest service and the lowest wages), were motivated to
participate in the company's affirmative action program.

Most of the women in the first training cycle were hired from
outside and went directly into the MOTP course. Women in the
later courses were drawn mainly from entry level rates (R8–R14).[9]
This pattern meant that the seniority dates of the vast majority of
skilled women, in jobs that required formal training, were clustered over a seven-year period, 1978 to 1984 (see Table 2). When
the massive displacements began in 1986, few of these women
would have sufficient seniority to retain their highest skill rates or
to avoid layoffs.

If GE originally designed its affirmative action recruitment to
attract employed women with more seniority from among the semiskilled and unskilled categories (R8–R14), then when the layoffs
began skilled women would have had a wider range of service
dates. Thus, skilled women might have kept their jobs longer and/
or more often.

Women employed at GE Wilmington also had accumulated a
significant amount of seniority. However, they were contractually
restricted from even bidding for jobs in Lynn. Instead, under the
Krikorian decision, women in Wilmington were offered separate
training slots, placement, and comparable pay settlements. The

Table 2
Distribution of Seniority among Skilled Women in Metal Cutting, Fabrication, & Crafts (formal training required)
December 31, 1986

	R18–R19	R20–R22	R23–R25	TOTAL
1985	5			5
1984	12			12
1983	2	3		5
1982	3		8	11
1981	2	5		7
1980	6	4	4	14
1979	13	6	2	21
1978	12	5	2	19
(Recruitment of women begins)				
1977 to 1954	8	2	3	13
	63	33	11	107
				(total women)

company and the union refused to consider modifying the contractual relations which resulted in continued segregation of the women in Wilmington.

Ultimately, then, structural disincentives, such as excluding the women from Wilmington, and the failure to initiate training programs which encouraged recruitment from within, created serious flaws in the affirmative action program at GE. These policies made significant contributions to the exclusion of women from employment in skilled jobs and had serious effects on their layoff experience. As a group, women could not match the distribution of seniority among men. These policies led to a disproportionate loss of jobs among skilled women by 1989.

Also, GE clearly was less than sincere in its effort to publicize, recruit, and organize the various training programs. The Women's Committee of the IUE was highly critical of the company's publicity and recruitment policies. According to the committee:

> In many cases the company has done a very poor job of notifying women in the plant about the courses to be offered. This has made it difficult for women to apply for them in time, or to know what they were applying for. Individual women accepted into a course have not been notified in time to be released from work, make

child care or other family arrangements, or sometimes to know about the starting date in time. All these problems have been discouraging and upsetting for the women involved, who have sometimes felt that the company is *discouraging them from getting training* (emphasis added). Furthermore, as word of these difficulties has gotten around the shop, other women have been discouraged from applying for future courses and have gotten the impression more than ever, *that the company has very little interest in training women or in helping them obtain new skills.*[10]

Additional criticism from the Women's Committee focused on GE's rigidity in approaching the classroom portion of the training.

Before the women went into on-the-job training on the machines, they had to complete 15 weeks of after-hours classes, which many of them found were set up to be tedious, overly difficult, and not relevant to what you need to know to run a machine. In addition, people who had already completed the GE after-hours course in Blueprint, Shop Math, and Measurement were required to repeat it in the training course, instead of being exempted. As a result of these problems, only six out of the original class of 24 finished the class and have gone on to the on-the-job training. This means that, *although the company was required to train 42 women in machining overall under the settlement, it will only have graduated about half that number when this last class finishes. . . .* (emphasis added).[11]

To address these and other shortcomings, the Women's Committee initiated several grievances between 1983 and 1985 and threatened to renew legal action.[12] However, no additional programs were added to compensate for the large numbers of unfilled training slots, one of the demands of the Women's Committee.

3. Relationship Between Access and Training

GE was expanding production in the late 1970s and early 1980s, and hundreds of new workers were hired. By 1986 after completion of the company's various affirmative action training programs, women comprised about 6% of the skilled workforce, or 212 women.

Comparing my calculations of 1986 to O'Farrell's figures of 1980, skilled women increased by 72% from approximately 123 in 1980 to 212 in 1986. Although this is a significant proportional increase, the original number of women in absolute terms was rel-

Table 3
Distribution of Seniority among Skilled Women in
Inspection and Assembly/Test
(no formal training required)
December 31, 1986

	R18–R19	R20–R22	R23–R25	TOTAL
1986	1			1
1985				
1984	2			2
1983				
1982		1		1
1981	1	1		2
1980	7	3		10
1979	3	15		18
1978	3	22		25
(Recruitment of women begins)				
1977 to 1941	21	25		46
Totals	38	67		105

(total women)

atively small. Moreover, of the 212 women employed in skilled jobs
in 1986, 105 or 50%, *required only seniority, not training* to gain
access to skilled jobs.

In the GE complex, women initially were found in inspection
and support job families—these were the "clean, safe" jobs. Later
they gained access to jobs as assemblers and testers, and to piecework jobs at the lower rungs of the fabrication family. In all four
job families, lower rated semiskilled jobs (R16 and R17) enabled
women to gain experience and skill. With seniority, they then advanced up their respective career ladders getting *on-the-job training at each higher rate.* These women frequently had more seniority than those in the machining families (see Table 3). Lower
ceilings, however, within inspection, support, and assembly and
test affected how high these women would be able to rise.

Regulations imposed by the company were consistently challenged by the union, although the union signed negotiated agreements on layoff and transfer procedures. These agreements prevented women as well as men from moving across job families. The
effect of such "fences" was historically to create separate upper mobility paths for men and women, further compounding the consequences of sex discrimination.

Affirmative action training was designed to provide access to those "job families" where previous training or experience was a necessary prerequisite and where lower job rates did not exist. For women, this meant an almost total exclusion from the metal cutting job family and the crafts family—the two families that have the largest number of highest rated (R25) jobs and which comprise the basis for skilled manufacturing.

Thus, the affirmative action training programs were only responsible for placing about half of the skilled women (107) in jobs. Interestingly enough, for both men and women, such prerequisites did not enable them to move any faster up the rate scale than workers who advanced with only seniority in job families that had lower semiskilled rates. Moreover, at the same skill rate, the "untrained" skilled women (and men) earned the same rate of pay as those who were formally trained.

4. "Skilled" Female Job Ghettoes and Training

At GE it would seem that definitions of "skill" are somewhat arbitrary, as is the case in most mass production industries. On a scale of job ratings from R8 to R25, the company and the union consider any job with a rating of R18 or above to be a skilled job.[13] However, prerequisites for access to these jobs vary from one job family to another. In machining, for example, previous experience or formal training is required. By contrast, access to inspection and assembly and test jobs requires only sufficient seniority, previous experience, or having held a lower-rated job in that family.

Among the skilled jobs in 1986, the highest proportion of jobs held by women was in inspection, where they accounted for 12%, or 69, out of a total inspection workforce of 565. This was greater than in any other family. By comparison, in the assembly and test family, where no outside special training was required either, women comprised only 5%, or 39, out of 838 workers. In the three other job families, metal cutting, fabrication, and support (crafts), women represented 4%, 9%, and 1% respectively. *Thus, there seems to be no relationship between having had training, the amount of training required, and the proportion of women who have access to "skilled" jobs.*

The results suggest that while formal training through one-type training programs introduces women to rudimentary machining skills and certifies them to bid for higher-wage jobs, the requirement itself, by acting as an arbitrary determinant of "qualification," restricts job movement and even access to other jobs. The training programs thus restricted job movement by offering only narrow skill options. For example, women in MOTP were trained in a shop which has both milling machines and lathes. These are the two basic types of machining equipment. However, the trainees were only allowed to learn how to operate *either* one *or* the other machine, even though both were based on similar metal-cutting principles. Thus, those trained on milling machines found they were not "qualified" to bid for lathe jobs or vice versa. It was also virtually impossible to learn other skills once on the job.

These practices occurred despite the fact that everyone in GE is entitled to a "reasonable" period of on-the-job training. For jobs at R19 and above, a minimum of four weeks break-in is a contractual right. Had trainees been allowed to learn both milling and lathe operations, this break-in period could have allowed them to develop competence in both jobs. A woman trained on either a lathe or a milling machine and placed in an R19 rated job was effectively denied the possibility of diversifying her skill in the future. Men trained in small machine shops, where most did their apprenticeship before coming to GE, were more likely to have had experience doing a variety of jobs and thus more options to move upwards or laterally. However, the major option for women who wanted to work in metal cutting, fabrication, and crafts was only the one-type programs.

The affirmative action programs at GE provided labor power for a mass production system characterized by a highly fragmented division of labor in which only the most narrow of skills would be reproduced. At GE, as in other types of similar facilities, work is broken down into "job families," each of which has a career ladder. Within each of the five families, there may be several branches. Strict rules, including seniority and experience, govern job mobility.

Movement from family to family is typically restricted at skilled levels *even within branches of the same group*.[14] For example, a skilled worker in one job family cannot move to a skilled job in another family, or to another job in the same job family, *even if the skills required are closely related*.

In large industrial mass production facilities, the number of all-around skilled machinists is very small, while the rest of the "skilled" workforce is actually represented by workers who are largely "deskilled". A deskilled worker, once employed, requires minimal training on the shop floor. This pattern explains GE's focus on short-term one-type training to recruit women. Such regulations were consistent with the overall corporate intent of reducing training costs and maintaining a stable workforce. Inadvertently, or by intent, the regulations created a barrier to job mobility for "skilled" workers. The consequence of such fragmentation and rigidity was to restrict the development of real skill, discourage flexibility, and inhibit incentive.

Thus, the special training programs offered to promote affirmative action were designed to serve the needs of a mass production type of work organization. As already noted, most recruits were enrolled in short-term, one-type, formal training for work in particular jobs. This training was only intended to provide the minimum knowledge necessary to begin at the lowest "skilled" rates, R18 and R19. Thus, despite the stated commitment to affirmative action by GE and the IUE, very few skilled women actually made it to high levels of skilled employment rates during the late 1970s and early 1980s when training and hiring was at its peak.

In 1986, before the layoffs, women were clustered at the lower rungs of most of the skilled job categories. Aside from the special circumstances of the inspection and support families,[15] the remaining job groups reflect clear patterns of women concentrated at the lowest rungs. Most women in metal cutting, fabrication, and assembly and test were found at R18–R19 rates. While men were also highly concentrated at these job rates, they also were present in the higher ranks, but women were not. These patterns reflect the existence of skilled female job ghettoes.

The advancement of 30 women to the middle rungs in the metal-cutting family (R20–R22) demonstrates that some women, in fact, did move up in the system. However, most of these were women who received extensive training. They participated in the three-year apprenticeship programs originally designed for men and hence were eligible for R22 rates or higher upon graduation. In addition, several graduates of the six-month MOTP program who started skilled work at R18–R19, managed to move up to R20 grinding positions. These are the highest rates, however, in which these particular women can advance.

At the highest skilled rates in the plant which required training, R23–R25, the number of women increased from three in 1980 to 11 by 1986. This occurred only in the metal-cutting family and in the support crafts group, but women never approached the top rungs of fabrication (welding). These numbers are too small to be statistically significant. Yet, they do demonstrate that, for a very

few, extensive training, unavailable for most women, did provide
access to the highest-rated jobs.

Aside from sexist attitudes of personnel officers and foremen,
who often feel that women are not as qualified or experienced in
industrial environments, other factors seem to be responsible for
women's concentration at the lowest rungs of these three job
groups. The first factor is that there were relatively few job openings, especially at the higher rates, at any one time at GE. Thus,
many women were recruited and trained for jobs that never actually existed. Secondly, most women lacked the seniority to bid successfully for openings that did become available.

GE hired men in the 1980s at an average of four rates higher
than women. Before being hired at GE, men probably had opportunities unavailable to women to learn manufacturing skills. Their
previously acquired skills and experience may have allowed them
to bid on, and get a variety of jobs at higher rates than women,
whose only access to non-traditional jobs was through the one-type
training programs. Therefore, skilled women were placed at structural disadvantages compared to skilled men even before the layoffs!

5. Job Loss

By July 1989, when the bulk of the layoffs was over, 138, or
65%, women out of the original 212 lost their skilled jobs. At the
same time, only 42% of the men lost their jobs (1,648 out of 3,920).
Women lost a disproportionate share of their jobs. The union's explanation was that women have less seniority than men, because
most of them were hired during the six-year period between 1978
and 1984.

Clearly there is some merit in this explanation. However, a
closer look at the data on the job loss experience of men and women
in different job families and skill rates reveals additional explanations for this trend. Women in skilled jobs lost a greater share of
their jobs than men in *every* job family. This finding is true regardless of whether women advanced as a result of seniority or a combination of seniority and training. Only in metal-cutting is their proportional loss comparable to the proportional loss of men. Why is it
that women machinists were the only ones to hold their own during the massive layoffs? The reasons have to do with the training
program and the commitment of the company to affirmative action.

The majority of the women placed in metal-cutting jobs came to GE through one of the training programs. These programs began in 1979. Thus, when the layoffs began in 1987, most of these women had accumulated at least eight to nine years seniority. Only six skilled women were hired once the training programs stopped in 1984. Yet, from 1984 until the layoffs began in January of 1987, GE hired 244 skilled men. Ultimately then, after 1984, GE and the union leadership almost totally abandoned their commitment to the further recruitment of women, despite the availability of skilled jobs. (The Women's Committee alone urged that additional training programs be initiated.) Men were still being hired after 1984, thus, there was a large pool of men with relatively low service to lay off before the women were affected.

An explanation for the change in corporate policy might focus on a change in the political climate. By 1984, the Reagan administration had clearly abandoned its commitment to affirmative action. As a result, GE no longer felt compelled to recruit, or "train" and certify additional women for skilled, high-paid jobs. In 1984 they stopped the recruitment and training of women and, once again, hired men. At the same time, they began to employ unskilled and semiskilled women. Between 1984 and 1986, 175 more women were hired in unskilled and semiskilled jobs and only six women were hired in skilled jobs during this period; despite the ostensible commitment to affirmative action in the 1970s and the considerable funding that the company had originally committed to the creation of training programs for women.

By the mid-1980s, even women who had been given extensive training in the three-year apprenticeship program between 1983 and 1986 had a hard time getting placed. Nine women completed their two-year crafts training in 1985. However, it took until 1986 (after the filing of grievances and the threat of reopening legal action) to place them in repair mechanic jobs. Thus, those women who were finally eligible to bid for R22 and R23 skilled rates had no possibility of holding those skilled jobs very long.

To an extent, seniority protected women in the initial round of layoffs. However, as the layoffs widened and as it became apparent that the entire turbine facility would eventually be closed, eight or nine years of service and advanced training protected nothing. The end of affirmative action training interestingly enough coincided with the corporate strategy of plant consolidation and employment reduction.

III. Conclusion

After years of public discussion and legal action to establish affirmative action programs for women, GE fulfilled its legal obligations by recruiting and training a number of women in non-traditional skilled jobs. Yet, it appears that the company was not truly committed to really incorporating women into its skilled, well-paid workforce. As soon as the federal pressure was off, the training programs were dropped and men were once again hired in skilled positions while women were hired in unskilled and semiskilled jobs in greater numbers than before 1978. However, the company did not provide any training to enable them to move into skilled jobs.

The lack of a real commitment to desegregating this workforce lay behind the inadequacy of the program. Given GE's mass production system and the rigid job structure it fosters, it is not surprising that the training programs were so constructed. Perhaps neither the company nor the union can be faulted for failing to foresee the negative consequences of developing a training program which matched the mass production system. Finally, it may have been difficult for anyone in 1978 to anticipate the extent of industrial contractions seven years in the future.

It is certainly counterproductive to think of developing affirmative action programs in industries which are in decline. However, the experience with affirmative action at GE sheds light on the mistakes that were made in the context of events which could have been foreseen as well as those which could not.

One major flaw in the affirmative action strategy was the company's failure to recruit women from within the plant. Thus, many unskilled and semiskilled workers who had given years of service to GE were discouraged from training to upgrade their skills. The irony is that had they been recruited, many would have had enough seniority to remain on the job, even after the massive layoffs.

A second flaw is the failure of the affirmative action strategy to look beyond recruitment and think through the implications of the barriers for women created by the narrowly designed one-type training programs. GE established these barriers by creating spurious qualifications for employment. The company built a job structure which unnecessarily inhibited upward mobility because it artificially restricted movement between skill categories. Seniority rules reinforced these restrictions. Neither the company or the union ever developed a plan to incorporate women into the job structure after they were trained and employed at entry level jobs. The training programs helped women gain access only to the lowest rungs of "skilled" employment.

The potential progress of women was arrested by the layoffs in 1987. Future affirmative action strategies must develop programs to consider each of these issues, so that women have access to the same kinds of opportunities as men. Only then will women be able to gain entrance to greater skill training and advance to the highest levels of skilled production work.

Appendix
Skilled Job Categories Where Women are Found
December 31, 1986

I. R25   vertical boring mill
            miller

    R23   machine repair
            tester and assembler

II. R22   all-around machinist
            production machinist
            electric beam development machinist

    R21   probe machinist
            miller

    R20   internal/external grinder
            tool and cutter grinder

III. R22   inspector

     R20   inspector

     R19   assembler
            electrical assembler

IV. R19   miller
            boring mill
            vertical broach
            engine lathe
            turret lathe
            numerical control lathe

    R18   miller

V. R18   welder
              tool and cutter grinder
              babbitt
              inspector
              tester

Notes

1. This figure was computed by Susan Strauss and Ric Casilli from internal General Electric documents. See "History and Summary of Layoff and Layoff Negotiations 1986 through January 1988" IUE Local 201, January 1988.

2. In 1986 the Wilmington GE plant had approximately 950 unionized workers of whom 428 (or 45%) were women. They also experienced their own work reductions and by 1989 numbered only 550.

3. Brigid O'Farrell and Sharon Harlan, "A Report on the Hourly Workforce in Riverworks and Everett: A Response to the Company's Summary Tables," Table 2, prepared for Local 201, IUE, December 1981.

4. Sharon Harlan and Brigid O'Farrell, "After the Pioneers: Prospects for Women in Non-Traditional Blue Collar Jobs," *Work and Occupations*, vol. 9, no. 3 (August 1982): 363–386.

5. The year 1980 was the last time figures were independently collected to calculate the numbers of skilled men and women. O'Farrell's 1980 calculations, however, excluded women in R18 rates in her definition of "skilled" workers. Moreover, she did not define her criteria for which workers were included in skilled jobs. It is therefore difficult to know exactly how comparable her calculations are to mine.

6. There may have been a few other women prior to 1978 who were in the apprenticeship program and who by 1986 were working in management. However, data on this issue was not available.

7. See Mary Lindenstein Walshok, *Blue Collar Women: Pioneers on the Male Frontier* (New York: Doubleday, 1981). She argues that women who are interested in non-traditional blue collar jobs are more likely to be older than their male counterparts. They often have families or are the sole support of children.

8. This discrepancy in wages can arise because there are significant differences in piecework and daywork (hourly wages) pay rates. Such differences are found in both semiskilled and skilled jobs, and are a result of contractual pay arrangements for jobs in particular departments.

9. IUE Local 201 Women's Committee Files.

10. Women's Committee column, *IUE 201 News*, June 1984.

11. Women's Committee column, *IUE 201 News*, June 1984.

12. See Marcia Hams, "Women Taking Leadership in Male Dominated Locals," *Women's Rights Law Reporter*, vol 8, nos. 1 & 2 (Winter 1984): 71–82; Alex Brown and Laurie Sheridan, "Pioneering Women's Committee Struggles with Hard Times," *Labor Research Review*, vol. 7, no. 1 (spring 1988): 63–77; IUE Local 201, Women's Committee files.

13. My criteria for "skill" is based on three sources: *Local Understanding on Upgrading and Job Posting Agreements Between the General Electric Company and Local 201, IUE (AFL-CIO)*, for the main plant, 24 September 1974, that releases employees for promotions based on R18 and above; a maximum of four weeks' training for the "higher rated classifications," Section IV, E, under the *Supplemental Agreement between the General Electric Company and Local 201, IUE (AFL-CIO)* for the main plant, 13 May 1977; and the skilled trade pay adjustment rates that apply to R19 and above in the national contract.

14. There are two exceptions to this general rule. One is that apprentice graduates, because of their diversified training, are often moved from one branch to another or from one family to another especially during periods of industrial contraction. The other exception on mobility allows movement from daywork to piecework jobs for skilled workers based on a negotiated agreement between the union and the company. "Article XXVIII," *1988–1991 National Agreement Between the General Electric Company and the IUE*, 116–117.

15. The inspection family, with the largest percentage of women, has a collapsed rate structure, with most inspectors at the R20–R22 rate. Therefore, in these jobs men and women tend to be found in the same rates. Support/craft services also have relatively collapsed skill rates, with most of the people (overwhelmingly men) found at the R23–R25 rungs. Women in this family are almost nonexistent and so discussion of concentrations is irrelevant.

Editors' Suggested Readings

Bluestone, Barry and Bennett Harrison. *The Deindustrialization of America*. New York: Basic Books, 1982.

Brown, Clair and Joseph A. Pechman, eds. *Gender in the Workplace*. Washington, D.C.: The Brookings Institution, 1987.

Jensen, Jane, Elisabeth Hagen and Ceallaigh Reddy, eds. *Feminization of the Labor Force: Paradoxes and Promises*. New York: Oxford University Place, 1988.

Nash, June. "The Impact of Industrial Restructuring on a World Scale on a New England Industrial Community." Charles Bergquist, ed. *Labor in the Capitalist World-System*. Beverly Hills: Sage, 1984.

―――. "Deindustrialization and Economic Restructuring in a New England City," *Urban Anthropology 14*, vol. 1, no. 3 (1985): 31–82.

―――. *From Tank Town to High Tech: The Clash of Community and Industrial Cycles*. Albany: State University of New York Press, 1989.

Newman, Katherine S. "Turning Your Back on Tradition: Symbolic Analysis and Moral Critique in a Plant Shutdown," *Urban Anthropology 14*, vol. 1, no. 3 (1985): 109–150.

Rosen, Ellen Israel. *Bitter Choices: Blue Collar Women In and Out of Work*. Chicago: University of Chicago Press, 1987.

Schatz, Ronald W. *The Electrical Workers: A History of Labor at General Electric and Westinghouse, 1923–1960*. Urbana and Chicago: University of Illinois Press, 1983.

Westwood, Sallie. *All Day Every Day: Factory and Family in the Making of Women's Lives*. Urbana: University of Illinois Press, 1984.

Zipp, John F. and Katherine E. Lane. "Plant Closings and Control Over the Workplace: A Case Study," *Work and Occupations 14*, vol. 1 (1987): 62–87.

Women In Trade Union Leadership: How More Women Can Become Leaders Of Today's And Tomorrow's Unions

Susan C. Eaton*

WHEREAS, The working woman, equally with the working man, has a right to share in the control of conditions under which she works; be it

RESOLVED, That we hereby call upon the United States Government, the American Federation of Labor, and all of its constituent bodies, to guarantee to women workers adequate representation by women responsible to their organizations on all policy-making councils or bureaus, boards, or committees that deal with conditions of employment or standards of life.[1]

Resolution No. 70,
National Women's Trade Union League
Philadelphia, June 1919

I. Introduction

1. The Underrepresentation of Women

For many years women trade unionists have organized and argued for our rightful place in the labor movement. While most would agree that we are closer today than ever before to achieving equality within our unions, we are not yet where we should be. In

*I am grateful for this opportunity and I appreciate the support I have received from Victor Gotbaum, Doris Suarez and the Center. I also thank the Service Employees' International Union (SEIU) and its president, John Sweeney, for the experience itself and the support of this project. Many union sisters and brothers have given generously of their time and experience to help me understand some of the reasons for this problem, and some solutions to it. I thank them and my husband, Marshall Ganz, for support and assistance.

this chapter I present the problem of women's underrepresentation in leadership, review five key stages of a woman union leader's career using my own experience as the basis, and suggest structural, programmatic, and cultural changes which will have to occur within U.S. trade unions to support the development of women's leadership. While women will always have to take responsibility for our own growth and earn our right to lead others, labor leaders of today can also take responsibility for attacking and removing many barriers to women assuming leadership roles in unions.

In regard to the disparity between women's membership levels and the number of women leaders, a recent Bureau of National Affairs (BNA) article quoted a high-ranking male union official as saying: "At the local level, you can't do a whole lot more than exhort, but we've been exhorting for some time."[2] I argue that he, and other labor leaders, can do a great deal more! Unions with a vision for the future and a commitment to broad-based leadership and the best values of the labor movement will do more and achieve more. In fact, their own self-interest and possibly even survival depends on it.

In 1960, women were 20% of all union members. In 1990, women are 36% of union members. Two out of every three new union members is a woman, suggesting that future union membership could be majority female. At the same time that women's participation in unions has increased dramatically, union membership as a percentage of the workforce has dropped from 24% to less than 16%.

Yet, a 1979 survey found that only 8%, or 1 in 12, union leaders were female. A more recent survey finds that even in 15 major unions with the highest female membership—an average of 45%—only 9.7% of members of national governing boards are women.[3] When it comes to the highest leadership post, only four women (4.4%) are presidents or chief executives of an AFL-CIO union.[4]

Underrepresentation is a problem for women and for unions. To women, our absence in leadership roles means that our voices will not be heard, that opportunity is unequal and that unions have not transcended discrimination within society despite their long history of fighting for civil and human rights. Women's absence also assures that female members' concerns will less likely be pursued.

For unions, however, the relative lack of women in leadership is also profoundly troubling. Unions are democratic institutions which rely on elections and membership support; their credibility depends upon being able to represent effectively their membership. It is becoming increasingly difficult for some unions to succeed without enough leaders who are from the same base as their members. Further, a higher proportion of women leaders could mean that unions would be more likely to devote resources to organizing the new workforce, which is predominantly female and minority, and which must be organized if unions are to survive and grow.

A study of Canadian union women by Chaison and Andiappan summarizes the problem:

> . . . the underrepresentation of women is more than a statistical artifact. It constitutes a major embarrassment to unions that claim to be progressive representatives, and it limits the potential of unions to attract and represent women workers. One observer has suggested that the 'very future of the US labor movement depends on its ability to woo more women into its ranks'. . . . The ability to organize women workers would be enhanced if the unions had more women officers and actively encouraged women to participate in decisionmaking at all levels. The increase in the numbers and influence of female officers would lead to a greater emphasis on issues of particular concern to women in both collective bargaining and grievance handling. A substantial corps of high-level female union leaders could also be a major force in designing and pressing for legislation on issues that would help both union and non-union women. Finally, female officers increase male officers' sensitivity to the problems of female employees and the union's role in resolving them. It is difficult to see how male-dominated unions, as most North American unions are, can maintain the status quo and still entertain ideas about reversing membership declines by organizing large numbers of women. Efforts toward equality in the workplace must be matched by equal access to the union power structure.[5]

The challenge for those who work within the labor movement is to identify the barriers to developing women's leadership, and to support successful programs to remove those barriers. In this chapter, I have drawn on my own experience and those of a number of allies to learn from the successes and failures of the past decade and to focus on what unions as institutions, and union leaders as leaders, must do if we wish to reverse the decline of the labor movement: namely, drawing on the talent and strength of one-third of its current members and two-thirds of its future members!

2. The Current Social and Economic Context

There are three key social and economic factors affecting women's participation in membership and leadership roles in unions. Women's roles are changing in part because of an overall dynamic change in our economy and our culture.

The first is the transformation of the U.S. economy from an industrial to a service economy. Currently 70% of all jobs are in the service sector, and 90% of new jobs are created in the largely non-unionized service sector.

The second factor is the economic and cultural change which has occurred with women's increasing participation in the workforce. Women are now 46% of the labor force and are 66% of new entrants to the workforce. More than 56 million women work today. Yet, jobs are still very segregated and 85% of women work in only 10 job categories. According to the AFL-CIO's *The Changing Situation of Workers and Their Unions*, since women hold two-thirds of service jobs and service sector jobs are only about 10% organized, unions must organize women if we are to organize the service sector.[6]

Fifteen percent of women in the workforce, or 7.24 million women, are represented by unions. Eight unions and associations, with more than 300,000 female members each, represent nearly 60% of organized women.[7] The median weekly wage of full-time working union women was $417 in 1989 compared with $312 for non-union women workers.

Since 1940, more and more working women have also been working mothers. In 1986, nearly 63% of all women with children under 18 years old were in the workforce, including 54% of all women with children under six years old.[8] University and College Labor Education Association (UCLEA) summer school surveys show that most women activists are mothers, as well.[9] Issues affecting working families, including parental leave, child care, and pay equity, have moved to the top of women's agendas. In addition, the women's and civil rights movements have increased women's expectations of equal status and also helped to change women's perceptions of our own roles within the family and the workforce.

Third, the increase in women workers has occurred at precisely the same time as the labor movement has entered a steep and precipitous decline in membership. This suggests that unions must organize women, and also explains why some unions at least, are in a defensive posture as they struggle to protect current mem-

bers and cope with shrinking opportunities for growth in their traditional sectors. The five largest U.S. unions now include three
service sector unions, one with many service sector members and
the United Auto Workers (UAW).

II. Union Staff: The Stages of Leadership Experience

To study women in leadership roles, it is necessary to define
"leadership." I use "leader" in this study to mean anyone who
teaches, trains, supports, and encourages others; who takes responsibility for representing and advocating for others; who is elected
or appointed to a position where the well-being of other workers
depends on her; and who inspires others to action. A leader exists
only in relationship to others: her followers. In one SEIU focus
group in Chicago, women described a leader as "someone who
someone has faith in," and "someone who connects people to
others."

In unions, leadership is very dispersed and sometimes less
than clear. The elected leaders of a local or International union are
most clearly its leaders, and they play a unique role politically and
programmatically. The union staff also plays a leadership role
when organizing or representing workers, or designing programs
and determining resource priorities, though their role is less well
defined. In this paper I examine two kinds of leaders, staff leaders,
and what I will call "worksite leaders." The worksite leaders are
rank-and-file women who are often stewards. But they may be non-
steward activists or rank-and-file officers who have taken on more
responsibility than a rank-and-file member. While staff may be
elected or appointed, they share the distinction of being full-time
workers for the union. Elected full-time union women leaders are
in a key position to make changes since they have a defined base
and responsibility for policy as well as program work.

I have defined several critical stages of leadership experience
within unions. These stages are based on my own experience and
what I have learned about the experience of rank-and-filers. The
stages are: entry, orientation, training, work experience and advancement, and "passing it on."

I believe that these stages happen for all leaders, staff or
elected, whether formally or informally. Some may occur almost
simultaneously, within a short period of time or over a life's work.
I begin with my own work history and then draw out similarities

and differences for other union staff. I then summarize these issues from the perspective of rank-and-file workers and conclude with a set of recommendations for change and action.

1. Entry: Recruitment and Hiring

Most women enter their union as a member. I first encountered SEIU when I was a college student. As a campus activist with friends in the union movement, I volunteered to help in a hospital organizing campaign. I was impressed with the idealism and vision of the union staff and the multi-ethnic organizing committee, and was struck by the incredibly bad conditions of the workers. Although the organizing campaign was lost, I went away from that experience with a deep respect for SEIU based on knowing our local leaders and staff.

After writing a thesis on community organizing, I decided I wanted to work in social change and union organizing. I discovered that most unions didn't hire from outside. The unions that did, wanted to put me in their research department looking up numbers or in their communications department writing stories. I wanted to work directly with members!

I interviewed with SEIU at the time they were hiring new interns into a program established in 1972 by former president George Hardy. It was called the Research Specialist Training Program. The union hired young people with college degrees and no union experience to train for jobs as negotiators and International union staff. Hardy explained that he started it because, "the janitors were being killed at the bargaining table by these &*&* lawyers."

In 1980, the program had been in effect for eight years with a total of 35 people previously hired. Of those, only four had been women and all but one was white. In June 1980, John Sweeney was elected to be International president, and soon after, SEIU hired a "class" composed of four women. I was one of those hired. We were all about the same age: 22 years old.

The hiring process was my first introduction to the International union. First impressions are always important. I had interviewed at another International union and remembered seeing a big man behind a big desk with a big cigar. I didn't feel particularly welcome or comfortable. Although they did offer me a job, I didn't take it.

At SEIU I remember the atmosphere was one of chaos, busyness, and confusion. Everyone seemed to be working very hard, and to know everyone else. I saw white and black women as well as white men. I was given a written test and I interviewed with friendly, humorous people, including the assistant to the president. Soon after I was offered a job. I was to train in California for a year and then take an assignment wherever in the country SEIU chose. They would pay my airfare to California. I was hired!

I was happy to take the SEIU job particularly because of the strong training component and the opportunity to do a range of work directly with members. I liked the people I met and the atmosphere of the union. Even though the pay was lower, I chose it over other union jobs. I didn't mind the travel and relocation because, like the other trainees, I was young and single. It seemed like a wonderful opportunity. But for women with children or those who were more tied to their communities, the job would have been much more difficult to accept.

Unfortunately, data on the question of women's representation on union staffs is sadly incomplete. However, in the last ten years there has been remarkable progress, at least in the unions representing a largely female workforce. The Coalition of Labor Union Women's (CLUW) 1980 study, *Absent from the Agenda*, showed that only 16% of union non-clerical staff members were women. Naomi Baden's 1985 update doubled that figure to 32% for a study of 15 large unions representing 4 million women.[10] SEIU in 1985 had 35% women professional staff, and now the figure is closer to 50%. For the American Federation of Teachers (AFT) in 1985 the figure was 34%; for the Communications Workers of America (CWA) 24%; and for the Teamsters 11%. This compares to the National Education Association's (NEA) staff which was 58% female in 1985.[11] Some unions, at last, are hiring more and more women.

My experience at SEIU was unusual because the International union had made a conscious decision to hire staff from outside its ranks, and because it had a formal training program in place. More unions have turned to community and political organizations (or other unions) as a source for women staff, but many still hire only or primarily from within.

Women are more likely to be hired from within in public sector and professional unions where the members tend to have the necessary skills. In the traditional industrial and craft unions, staff are almost always hired or elected from the ranks. This makes it difficult for women and minorities who may have been hired last into an apprenticeship or training program and have less service in the union. Such unions have to develop more aggressive affirmative action plans and make revisions to the established career paths.

In addition, unions usually hire members who have been increasingly active over a period of time. Very often a member must serve not only as steward but as a committee chair, local officer, and even lost-time officer for some years before she will be eligible for hiring. This is a barrier for women who have not been able to serve in as many local offices. Again, a conscious effort to develop and promote women leaders will increase the number of women eligible to be hired.

Another route for rank-and-filers to enter staff positions is to serve as lost-time organizers. Recently, SEIU, the Hotel Employees and Restaurant Employees (HERE), Electrical, Radio and Machine Workers (UE), American Federation of State, County and Municipal Employees (AFSCME), the UAW, and the United Food and Commercial Workers (UFCW), among others, have hired rank-and-file women into temporary organizing jobs. Some of them do well and are retained for more permanent jobs. The practice does recruit talented rank-and-filers, who are more likely to resemble their coworkers in race and gender.

Unions which are both open to hiring from the outside and committed to promoting women from within will have the most women on staff. A strong recruitment incentive is an established training program and a positive atmosphere for women. Lost-time organizing jobs are another way for women to prove themselves and become eligible for hiring. But unions have to look closely at three factors which inhibit their ability to hire women staff. Apprenticeship-based promotion patterns may have a discriminatory effect by mirroring employer discrimination. Requirements for travel and relocation may effectively keep women out. And the political nature of much union hiring may exclude women. Although there has been a dramatic improvement in the representation of women on union staffs, at least in the major unions representing women, there is still further to go.

2. Orientation

Orientation to the union is critically important for new staff, especially those from the outside. A positive orientation helps to retain women staff and leaders and encourages them to succeed. The first days and weeks can easily feel like a series of tests in a complex initiation rite. Unions have to be especially conscious to avoid isolation, negative images of women's roles in the union, sexual harassment, negative reinforcement, and general alienation of women staff and leaders, particularly when they are in a minority. In a positive sense, unions can promote teamwork, good supervision, egalitarian attitudes and a sense of valuing women in the union, and a mentoring system. Current women staff and leaders should play a special role in orienting and helping new staff.

Union culture has changed greatly in the last ten years in many unions, partly because of the influx of women and minorities. My own difficult experiences would less likely be repeated today, but they still serve as a lesson on some things NOT to do.

At the SEIU local where I was assigned, there was no formal orientation. This is common, but it presents real problems. We experienced isolation. Women non-clerical staff were a rarity at the local. For the first few weeks, no one asked me or my fellow trainee out to lunch or even spoke to us outside of work. We went to lunch with the younger secretaries in the research department, and then were told it was not proper for us to go to lunch with secretaries.

We were given informal lessons about a woman's "role." For example, the senior secretary was shocked that the International would send "girls" to work as "research guys." When we asked for help with typing or copying we were told to do our own. Early on in our time there one man began to tell us stories about the other few women trainees who had preceded us. He told us about one women who had, in his words, given away a whole union organizing drive by telling some secrets about it to an organizer of a rival union with whom she had a romantic relationship. "Pillow talk," he said disgustedly. "That's why the Old Man [George Hardy] doesn't like having women on staff. Can't trust them." He told of another woman who had "failed" the drinking test she had been taken on. These stories seemed designed to let us know of the lack of success of the few previous women. They were truly discouraging, and that was their intent.

There were many instances of a pervasive anti-feminist culture. Men at the local used different language. For example, I asked about using the "he/she" in contracts—most of the workers the union represented were women but all the contracts read "he." I was told never to raise such questions again, that the policy was to use "he" and it included all women. In another example, a group of workers wanted to negotiate for child care in the contract. The petition drive leader called the union to get help in setting up a

labor-management committee. I was given her call, but told I
couldn't spend time on child-care work on worktime.[12]

The culture of the local included a weekly visit to the airport
strip joints by my male coworkers. I argued that strip joints were
exploitative of women and that they should not patronize them if
they respected women's status as equals. They hooted and made a
point of describing the strip joint experiences in even more detail.
They regularly left cards from the various strip joints on my desk
with the "try-out times" inked in. Later I was to discover that part
of what I was going through was adapting to a different class culture. The Latino staff and members I met were part of an even
more traditional culture, and at one negotiation session, I met several black Muslim men who were polygamous and explained to me
the Biblical basis for their beliefs about men's superiority.

Sexual harassment was also a problem. We learned quickly to
handle propositions from male staff and members of the union. I
followed my friend's example of using humor whenever possible to
avoid the appearance of "rejecting" someone who could then get
you into trouble. One incident in particular was deeply troubling
since a supervisor was involved; only by talking with other women
did I find out that many of them had experienced similar incidents
with this man. Together we organized to orient new staff about
this person, and began discussing his behavior with our other male
supervisors. They tended to discount it at first, but later spoke to
him.

Most of the harassment I experienced was verbal: the use of
demeaning words for women, jokes about strip joints and other
women staff, and come-ons and "off-color" jokes. At one point, some
years later, I had gained enough seniority and confidence to fight it
out at staff meetings when I objected to the language. It was a
frightening struggle but I won, and the men agreed, with support
from my director, not to use a few particular words and expres-
sions. But the men genuinely didn't think they were sexist. The
culture affected not only staff, but members. I remember a young
black woman on a bargaining committee who was constantly being
propositioned by the rep for the facility. Perhaps that is why she
did not want to become more active in the local.

In the ten years since I began work with SEIU, I believe a lot
of this verbal style has improved; it is no longer as acceptable to
make such kinds of jokes. And the union has recently issued an
employment policy on sexual harassment which makes clear that
it is unacceptable and provides a process to seek a remedy. Each

union needs to take clear, strong action to stop harassment and to make sure women are respected. In conclusion, the union worked hard to improve wages and benefits which helped its women members, yet, it did so in a way which did not challenge the sexism of society.

I believe orientation is critical for women staff (and all staff) and that it reflects the culture and values of the union. A good orientation takes effort and forethought. For women and minorities, union leaders must be especially sensitive to cultural differences and seek to ensure that their experience is not painful or isolating. This could mean setting up a conscious program of networking or mentoring for new staff women, perhaps pairing them with other women at similar or slightly more experienced levels.

Working on positive reinforcement and giving new staff a sense of "belonging" would be valuable. The leader or staff should meet with them regularly. Each union must try to insure that its staff doesn't inadvertently or consciously convey a sexist or racist message. Orientation should include the vision and goals of the union, and should emphasize contributions of women and people of color, as well as the values of social justice which the union represents.

3. Training Programs

All women, and especially minority women, request training programs more often than men.[13] Some authors speculate it is because women have less confidence in themselves and so need more certainty before undertaking new tasks. According to the women at the University of Illinois workshop, men are less worried about making a mistake, and more willing to undertake responsibility without knowing how to do it.[14] In her book, *You Just Don't Understand*, Deborah Tannen says that women are more acculturated to asking for help while men see that as a sign of weakness.[15]

I believe training is critical in developing leadership skills in women at all levels. SEIU was unique in having a year-long training program. It most resembled an "apprenticeship" in union work. The existence of such programs is one reason SEIU has done well in recruiting and training women leaders. Even within a conscious training program I experienced some of the "sink or swim" philosophy of learning. On our third day at work, the president of the local told us to prepare a stewards training program for the local. Neither of us had ever met a steward at the time. The same was true of writing contract language. When we went to negotiations, we were told that trainees, like children, should be seen and not heard. A key part of good training is giving people responsibility which is meaningful and challenging, and then providing them with support so they can succeed.

A common approach to training in unions is to learn by doing, without much help or encouragement, and with no formal training. While many labor leaders mastered their jobs and their leadership skills this way, it is certainly the hardest way to learn. It is particularly difficult for women because it places the entire burden on them and because they may not be part of the networks of support that men are.

Diverse responsibilities prepare women for handling a lot of situations and build confidence. They should be part of any training program. We had an opportunity to participate in all the nuts and bolts of the local union, from 6 am organizing leafletting to 2 am deadlines at the print shop every month. We worked with stewards and attended general membership meetings. We visited worksites with business reps and handled grievances in the complaints office. We worked in the mail room and on picket lines. We did research and worked on marathon negotiations. We raised money for politics and walked precincts and called retirees. We attended arbitrations and reclassifications and handled unemployment hearings.

Because we were trained with different locals and in different geographic locations, we encountered a variety of members and leaders. In the public sector and where the private sector unions were more secure, more women leaders were present. This suggests that there is more room to develop new leaders when the union itself is secure.

The training included exposure to a wide variety of leadership styles. I remember sitting through negotiations with my first "table-pounding" male union leader, and my reaction was one of pure fright. "I could never do that," I thought. Then I realized that seeing women leaders was important; we all needed to see leaders who we could imagine becoming! In addition, seeing women with families who were active leaders in the union was valuable. Union jobs often require many hours per week, and learning how these women juggled their many responsibilities helped us.

The most successful training experiences we had were a combination of formal and on-the-job training with good supervision. First, the International sponsored two week-long training classes, one on bargaining and one on organizing. Second, the on-the-job training was wonderful when there was real work to do and someone to supervise and give feedback. The first critical opportunity to take responsibility for important work came for me during a major strike, when suddenly there was more work to be done than anyone could do. Suddenly my help, skills and initiative were welcome. I was able to see immediately the results of my research on the company's funding, and to work with a network of others. I got immediate positive and supportive suggestions on my work. I call this "guided experience," and I believe it is more effective in the long run than any classroom training. Ideally the two should be combined.

The California locals of SEIU sponsored a women's conference at the end of our year of training. This was a grassroots conference, promoted by women at every level of leadership of each local, and each workshop was cochaired by a rank-and-file woman who had done most of the organizing work. It was a marvelously supportive experience, and the first where I felt "at home." The networking among women was remarkable, and I think it is no accident that a high percentage of women local chief executives in SEIU come from California locals.[16]

Finally, I learned a lot by undertaking a project with other union women. While this was not part of the formal training, it surely should be encouraged. Because I felt isolated at the local union, I sought out the CLUW chapter. A local SEIU member and I volunteered to work together to organize a conference on child care. We worked hard (on our evening hours) for weeks. We produced a successful conference on bargaining and organizing for child care which brought together an exciting and motivated group of union women and men from all over the area. I developed many lasting relationships working on that one conference.

In my year of training, I learned more about union culture and politics than I ever thought possible, as well as learning basic negotiation skills and strategy and a wide variety of other union skills. The range and breadth of experience was superb. Yet, this program could be improved in some ways. Although we had some formal training which was very welcome, it would have been good to have an ongoing conscious training program during the year. A reading list would have been helpful, and a monthly training class of some kind would have been great. The cultural content of the training should have been more sensitive to issues of gender, diverse cultures, and class. Going to the women's conference was a remarkable experience; training should be supplemented with such networking opportunities.

The on-the-job training worked best when there was real independent work to be done, and there was someone to give us close supervision and immediate feedback. This kind of guided experience is a model for truly effective training programs.

A thorough training program for women staff should include skills training as well as training for personal growth and development. Ongoing training programs ensure that we continue to learn, and can renew our enthusiasm when the long hours and countless problems become overwhelming. In addition, training in management and supervisory skills is essential for women in leadership roles with other staff.

4. Work Experience and Advancement

Supervisors and mentors are key to helping women perform well and qualify for increasing responsibility. In addition, getting experience in diverse aspects of union work is important. Taking responsibility for leading a meaningful activity, whether an organizing drive, contract campaign, strike, or political campaign, is essential to developing leadership skills. Finally, I believe that management roles are critical for women in demonstrating our ability to lead and in developing others to lead.

I was assigned to Georgia to represent SEIU in 10 states with 18 locals and 18,000 members. During one difficult hospital contract campaign in Texas, the International sent down a second staff person, a man named "Joe" with about ten years more experience. He was sent in to assess the negotiations and take over if needed.

Joe arrived and spent one day just observing the bargaining. Afterwards he told me I was doing a great job and that he would take charge of the strike preparations. When management turned to him the next day as if he would be taking over as spokesperson, he told them, "Oh no, I'm just here as the strike coordinator. Susan is in charge of negotiations." This support made me feel great, made the committee happy, and worried the management. Of course I relied on Joe's experience and advice but I didn't feel that the responsibility had been taken away from me. Instead, I felt more responsible and worked even harder.

When we finally settled the contract and the members ratified it overwhelmingly, Joe also insisted that I, rather than he, should call the union president and let him know. This kind of personal support and trust was great training and built confidence. Joe became a friend and an unofficial mentor in the union after that; for many years I called him for advice in tight situations. The lesson I learned is that male trade unionists can play a critically important positive role in developing women staff and leaders. At the same time, Joe was not immune to the sexist culture and assumptions within the union. One night he left me alone with a drunken mediator who took me for a long, difficult ride down a Texas highway. Joe joked about it for weeks afterward.

When I moved to Washington after four years of increasingly responsible work in the south, I took my first management position, with great trepidation. Since 94% of all managers in the U.S. are men, perhaps it is understandable that women don't easily see themselves in that role. In addition, managerial roles create a special ambivalence in union women and men since they often have a pretty negative concept of management.

My supervisors at SEIU helped me tremendously by providing management training both through my staff supervisor and through a consultant, Hal Stack from Wayne State University's labor studies program. Hal became both a teacher and a mentor in helping me develop the management staff and field programs at SEIU. He trained me and my fellow supervisors in management skills with a union focus, and soon we set up a comprehensive system for managing the staff, helping them set goals and make plans, and evaluating their performance. Hal's role was more than formal training, and I think it is worth trying to define what "mentoring" is and how it can be set up to support women with mentors both within and outside the union. As an unofficial mentor, Hal spent a lot of time on planning and goal-setting for the department and for individual staff. He provided direct training. He sent books and articles on a regular basis. He checked on my follow-up from meetings. He provided a sense of perspective and helped me figure out the politics of the union. While my supervisor also did many of these things, it helped to have someone with an outside perspective and with more time.

More and more women are seeking and earning promotions. We still do not always have the same level of experience as men seeking the same jobs, but we provide a unique perspective and set of skills as women leaders. There are few enough role models for women managers, and union leaders and staff must consciously identify potential women leaders and managers and then provide them with enough support to succeed. Concretely, this means working out "apprentice", supervisory, or "lead" roles in some cases. Providing training programs for managers is critical. Ensuring there is a conscious support system for women managers in the union is a joint responsibility of women and union leaders. Certainly the issues of time and family are critical. A recent edition of *Fortune* magazine gives the following advice to women who want to succeed: "Look like a lady; act like a man; and work like a dog."[17] This kind of advice, women can do without!

Taking leadership does require a tremendous investment of time and energy. There are two ways to go: first, help women find ways they can invest more time, and second, redefine leadership roles and jobs so they don't require sacrifices which no one should have to make. To give an example of the first approach, one woman reportedly said, "Well, maybe my teenage son could do his own laundry," when challenged to think about how she could make more time in her life for her union work. On the second approach, redefining job expectations is a tough issue which will rise to the surface as a new generation of fathers and mothers come of age in the labor movement who will demand more time at home. Part-time work, flex-time, parental leave and job-sharing are all ways to help women deal with family responsibilities. One high-placed union woman is leaving her job soon because she has small children and her new boss "doesn't believe in part-time work." This is not the way to encourage women leaders to be part of the labor movement.

III. Rank-and-File Workers: Stages of Leadership Experience

In much of this paper, I have focused on women staff leaders. Most women who are elected to full-time union office have experience as staff members, usually of a local union, first. However, some are elected to full-time posts directly from rank-and-file positions, and their situation is particularly unique.

Women who become political leaders without having staff experience usually have a difficult time with issues and roles involving managing staff. The NEA has set up its state and national affiliates so that the day-to-day operations of the union are managed by an "executive director" (often male) and the political leadership rests with the "president" (often female). While this works very well in many cases, it is important to be clear about exactly what power and authority rests with what positions.

In unions with very small locals, where the servicing, staff, and most of the financial resources are managed by a regional or district body, there are more women presidents. But there is a need to look at the positions of regional or district director and see how many women are in those jobs. Public sector associations also have a tradition of professional staff leadership and rank-and-file officers, and women are a minority among those staff directors.

It is unusual for women to be elected to a full-time union office from the rank-and-file, but when it happens it would call for special attention, orientation, and training from the other local officers and/or the International. Union leadership jobs are complex and difficult, involving a myriad of leadership and management responsibilities for which few people who achieve these roles are truly prepared at the time. If women are to earn our leadership roles, we need to ask for help and be able to count on our unions to provide it. Otherwise being elected can be a set-up for failure.

A more common path, at least within SEIU, is for women to move up the ladder from rank-and-file leadership roles to union staff and perhaps even union management, and then to run for office. These women know their locals well and the nature of the staff work to be done. However, they often need help to balance the political side of their jobs and the administrative side. Effective support groups for elected women union leaders include CLUW, local groups like Washington Union Women, and informal networks women have established in various cities. But more could be done to share knowledge and experience.

1. Entry Into Leadership

This section of the paper reviews the areas I have just explored for union staff women, paying attention to the perspective of rank-and-file or worksite leaders. Many women's experience is that of a "reluctant leader," or someone whose coworkers or union staff identify as a leader even though she may not so identify herself. In the union women's summer schools, women often talk of becoming a steward "because there was no one else who wanted it." This may be especially true in anti-union environments where becoming a steward is a sure means of attracting negative management attention. In contrast, in the auto industry or other established union workplaces, stewards often are paid, sometimes full-time, and honored as leaders of workers.

A workshop on women's leadership sponsored by the University of Illinois asked how a variety of women became involved in leadership roles. Its results confirm my own experience. There were two main reasons women became involved: concerns about wages and working conditions (and sometimes a dissatisfaction with the present leadership's role in these areas), and being requested or encouraged to become involved by a current leader of the union, usually a business rep or local president or other officer.[18] These women were both appointed and elected.

Similarly, in Wertheimer and Nelson's classic study, *Trade Union Women: A Study of Their Participation in New York City Locals*, they found that most of the women who moved from "members" to "leaders" of the union did so as a result of individual encouragement, usually from union leaders.[19] Thus, current male and female leaders at every level can make an enormous difference in our talent pool just by whom they choose to recruit and to encourage to run for office.

The steward or worksite leadership level is most likely to represent the workforce. The study by Roby and Uttal found that in three rare cases where statistics were kept the percentage of women in membership and in steward roles compared at 2% women stewards and 7% women members in one local, 55% women stewards and 68% members in another, and 86% stewards with 92% women members in a third.[20] These statistics, along with my own and other womens' experience, suggest that there are many female stewards already active in our union locals. This suggests that unions need to do very specific work to find out why the number of women leaders drops so dramatically in union-wide office and on staff.

Stewards tend to have significant longevity on the job and as a steward. The average length of work experience was 17 years for the women and 20 years for the men, while their average length of steward experience was just a few years less.[21] The study of NYC stewards found that 65% of men and 70% of women union activists were over 45 years of age. This suggests that people become active on the job early in their careers and stay active for a long time, and also that unions need to do a better job of recruiting young leaders to round out their steward ranks.

I learned about working to overcome the gap between women

in membership and activist roles and their representation in union leadership most clearly in a hospital in Texas. I was the staff person responsible for negotiating the second contract for 800 members. The workforce was overwhelmingly female and about 50% black. A number of women were stewards and active in their departments. Yet the local members had elected a white male licensed vocational nurse, or LVN, one of the few white men who worked in the bargaining unit, as their president. The executive board and bargaining committee were half male. I found this surprising and tried to analyze why so many women didn't elect a woman.

First, I think the previous union representative (also a white man) had played a role. He and the local president liked to go fishing and to the track. Because they were comfortable together and because the rep supported the male LVN as president, the members followed. Second, I think there was some sense that a white man could somehow represent them better because he was "like" the other white men who were the managers and owners of the hospital. Third, some of the members had clearly internalized the local society's view of them and their "place." I remember encouraging a black male housekeeper to run for president when the former president retired. He was a deacon in his church and highly respected by the members. "This hospital isn't ready for a black president," he told me—and refused to run. I think this was also true for many women, white and black. There were no female role models in this traditional southern town—all the other labor leaders were men.

We were able to change this state of affairs over a period of several years. First, we began an internal organizing drive and contract campaign which encouraged more leaders to emerge, take on responsibility, and be recognized. We expanded the bargaining committee, added stewards, expanded the local union executive board, and filled vacant constitutional positions like the civil rights committee and the political action committee.

In part, because they saw a woman chief negotiator and a woman organizer, more women emerged as leaders and were identified and elected or appointed to these new positions. Several women told me that our role modeling was important. This expanded the total number of leaders and identified some key women and black men as leaders in the union.

Second, we undertook consciously to confront the problem of people not seeing themselves as "qualified" or "ready" to be leaders. We established steward training classes and certified a number of stewards. I took a group of women stewards and leaders to the Southern School for Union Women which was held in Texas one summer. We drove for hours across the Texas landscape and they talked about the "ladies' school." These women had never been to an all-women event, nor spent a week with other women active in their unions. The conscious learning of skills and the spirit of union leadership and of a vibrant labor movement were very exciting. The women came back charged up and ready to run for office. They even started a CLUW chapter in the town. This, in turn, led them to meet other women in similar positions. The next president the local elected was a black woman.

For rank-and-file women workers, the union staff and existing leadership have to provide a welcoming environment, role models, and conscious support and training to overcome discrimination and their negative images of their talent and ability, and to encourage them to make the considerable investment of time and effort which every union leadership role requires. Worksite leadership development is an area with enormous potential for expansion. Unions will never achieve their potential power at the workplace and in changing workers' lives until they have a tightly organized network of members who are ready to take control of their workplaces; and stewards are the key with women stewards representing up to 180 members each. There is room for many more leaders! My own experience suggests that 1:20 is an ideal ratio of worksite leaders to members; that 1:25 is the most ambitious any union I know strives toward; and that 1:100 is a more realistic estimate of actual steward presence. Pam Roby actually found, in her study, that women stewards represented up to 180 members while men stewards represented around 100 members. To say the least, women are an underutilized resource. Young and newly hired workers need special attention. Individual effort can really make a difference in this area.

2. Orientation

Very few unions have orientation programs for new leaders. It is worth investing the time to develop materials and a process for introducing leaders to their local and to their new role. Even women from "union towns" whose fathers or brothers were in unions need to see an image of the union that includes them.

Today, high-quality videos and brochures are relatively easily produced. They could include a sense of the union's history, and a consideration of the present membership and goals of the union, both at the worksite and in the community. The future vision— where the union is going—is especially important. I would emphasize the contribution of women and people of color, and share policy resolutions of the union that especially support their unique situations. For new stewards and local leaders, I would focus on their role and importance to the local as well as ways they can get support; an orientation period ideally should be designed so that it includes some mentoring or networking component.

Experience as a steward or worksite leader is nearly always a jumping-off point for membership on the negotiating committee, for other committee appointments and chairpersonships, for membership on the local executive board, for appointment or election as a delegate to the central labor bodies, and then for election to union-wide office. Therefore, the orientation, training, and support for stewards is very important to develop their leadership abilities and to ensure that they understand the union is open to their concerns.

For women leaders in particular, I believe the union's orientation to their new role should include an acknowledgment of their family and other outside commitments. The leader who is conducting the orientation can express support for their efforts to manage diverse responsibilities, and can ask how the union can help them to be active. Even asking the question acknowledges the high stress that family commitments and union commitments can generate, and the union might get some specific suggestions.

3. Training Programs

Studies find that women value and appreciate training more than men. Most educators and academics as well as union women have identified "low self-confidence" or "women's underestimation of their own abilities" as key barriers to undertaking leadership roles. Training is an excellent remedy for this problem. It's clear that women like and appreciate training, and that it pays off in higher levels of activity. This section identifies why training is so important and suggests that it is unlikely to be improved for women if it is not improved for all workers. In addition, the section concludes with some suggestions for improving training.

The Summer Schools for Union Women, jointly sponsored by the UCLEA and the AFL-CIO, are making a positive contribution to the development of women rank-and-file leaders. In their 15 years of existence, these union women and labor educators have trained more than 4,500 women. Everyone who attends or teaches at a school comes back marvelling at the level of excitement, learning, expanded horizons, skills acquisition, and general feeling of "sisterhood."

Minority women make up one-third to one-half of the participants, and each school carefully evaluates its classes and plenaries. Most women come to the schools as first-time participants. These records are excellent documents for studying women's participation in their unions. Now 90% of the schools are sponsored by their local or International unions. While this one-week training program can only accomplish limited skills enhancement, it does make a great contribution to women's leadership development and could be expanded dramatically.

A local's approach towards its members (along with the nature of its employers) will determine how many and what quality of leaders it produces. Unions will have a hard time developing female leadership if they aren't open to developing all leaders. If the local and its leaders have a closed culture and a "service" rather than "empowerment" approach to handling worksite problems, they will be unlikely to identify, recruit, train, and sustain leaders.

Leadership development and training at the worksite level is extremely demanding and rewarding. In my experience, it requires a major time commitment on the part of the local staff and leadership and a never-ending effort to find and develop worksite leaders. This means more than sponsoring an annual steward training class, which most unions do. That class is vitally important, for it conveys the union's message and the skills the union wants in its stewards. But many stewards are appointed or elected between the classes, and many others are at a more advanced level than "one class fits all" can accommodate. In addition, stewards need the same kind of ongoing "guided experience" that I have argued staff need. The staff person or leader has to ensure that they have a key role to play, that they have the tools to succeed, and that they get feedback on their performance.

Most union education departments have developed specific materials for their members and industries. Yet steward training in most locals is not very exciting and not very well developed. I argue that improving and expanding training is one of the most valuable programmatic changes a union can make in developing leaders who are women. When done well, training gives confidence as well as skills; it can help change attitudes as well as provide knowledge. The most difficult component is not viewing it simply as an "event," but as an ongoing process which requires continuous time and effort.

To be effective, training must be based on real needs and experiences of participants, with conscious and clear objectives, which can easily be put to practical use. The program should be participatory, not lecturing, and specific about the skills, knowledge, and attitudes it develops. It should be culturally conscious and nonsexist, and strongly rooted in the values and vision of the union. The training must be followed by further work with a good trainer, supervisor, or mentor. In other words, it should be part of an ongoing program, rather than simply one event. Finally, it must be accessible, both geographically and economically. Of course not every training program can meet all these objectives at once, but the program as a whole in which worksite leaders and staff partake should have these qualities.

4. Work Development and Advancement

Rank-and-file leadership skills development is critical to the advancement of women worksite leaders within their unions. Skills needed include developing their own style of leadership, learning political skills, and developing alliances with other women. Furthermore, the rank-and-file leadership needs training to cope with massive stress and time constraints and/or personal sacrifice related to family commitments. It needs skills to create a support system, organize for change within the union, and make a plan for its political goals within the union. Not everyone can make the jump from worksite leader to union leader, but more women have to try, and staff and union leaders must provide the concrete support to make this jump a real option.

a. STYLES OF LEADERSHIP

I encountered many different styles of women's leadership in my work. Part of the role of women leaders, I believe, is to help and challenge other women to think and act as leaders. While this can be done in many different ways, union staff women differ about what styles are most effective with rank-and-file women and with men leaders.

Some hold that to succeed in the labor movement women have

to be every bit as tough as the men. They have to be as strong as the most macho male leaders so men can't stereotype us as weak and ineffective. Women who adopt this style reject any "touchy-feely" or "process-oriented" styles, and push hard on unions to deal with them just the same as with their brothers. These women leaders usually thrive in a fiercely competitive environment. Many rose to leadership in a time when there was no other option.

Other women argue for, and practice, a more inclusive and less combative or imitative style. They are more likely to believe that women's inherent style is to be more sensitive to group dynamics, to individual needs, and to issues of process as well as content. They view these as strengths and not weaknesses, and believe men should work to master these skills. Other characteristic values of these women include listening well, giving positive reinforcement, openness, and valuing shared or collective responsibility and decisionmaking more than competitive hierarchies. These women are often younger and have been influenced by the women's movement.

Some women prefer a more charismatic style of leadership. Others value supportiveness and encouragement. Some are competitive with other women while others view women as natural allies and friends. Some women seem to be more comfortable in a more traditional role, such as assisting a male leader, while others chafe if they can't blaze their own trails every day on the job. Some are superb at interoffice politics while others are impatient and just want to get the job done.

Most would agree that the goal for women leaders at any level is to develop a style with which they feel comfortable and confident. In addition, we don't sufficiently appreciate each other's strengths. A diversity of styles is needed to build a stronger labor movement. Provided that women don't undermine each other to get ahead, my view is that many styles of women's leadership should flourish and be recognized, just as men's have.

b. POLITICAL SKILLS

One serious issue related to "style" stands out in every interview or article on women in leadership. The issue is politics. Union politics. "I keep running into these union women who say, 'I don't like politics,'" said one highly successful union staffer. "I tell them they're in the wrong place. Unions are political institutions."

Lois Gray found in her article on successful women at the top of the labor movement that "mastering the rules of the game" and "being in the right place at the right time," especially winning visible successes, were critical factors in women's success to date. She also points out that "many officials, both male and female, have observed that women lack the political know-how and "stick-to-itiveness" required to line up support for themselves and other female candidates."[22]

Politics is not all a matter of skill. The playing field is not level. Teamsters leader Clara Day describes the impact of networking among men:

> I think what makes the difference is networking with the leadership of any job, who most times are male and white. There is the stopping by the bars, or the stopping by the card game, and they get to know these people, or they get to feel responsible for the ones that they stop out with or the ones they drink with or play cards with. And I guess it's deliberate, but not necessarily, working for the friends.[23]

Rank-and-file women will need to learn how to win elections in their unions to be successful, since unions are democratic institutions. And one issue which has not been addressed systematically by women or their unions is how to provide them with the skills and support they need to learn the political rules of the game and how to play it to win.

c. FAMILY ISSUES

The issues of time and family are critical for women, but earning leadership does require a real investment of time, and this is more difficult for women. As a single woman, I struggled to build a network of friends and a support system and to date when there was time. I was truly following the pattern which one male organizing director described as "married to the union." Our worksite women leaders were mostly married or single parents. The children came everywhere, and they needed time and attention all the time!

Roby and Uttal intensively interviewed 124 stewards. Their study of how men and women stewards cope differently with family responsibilities lays out the challenges women face. They found that women stewards actually had similar rates of participation as men in three out of four measured areas: union meetings attended, holding other union positions (like committee posts), and participating in other union activity. In the one significant area of difference, they did less union work outside working hours.

They discovered that women stewards had dramatically different family situations than men: 66% of men and 25% of women lived with a partner and/or children; 5% of men and 27% of women lived with only children; 11% of men and 21% of women lived with only a partner; and 18% of men and 27% of women were single. While we don't have any national statistics to compare these to, it was clear from her study that for women, the presence of a partner and/or children *lowers* their level of participation, while for men, the presence of a partner and children *raises* their level of participation.

When they began to look at the reasons, it became obvious. Most women are performing two jobs (work and home) even when both partners work and theoretically share family responsibilities. The study showed that while men tended to skip family events to attend to union business, if women skipped the family events, they didn't happen. So women either skipped union business, lost sleep, or spent a lot of time rearranging family obligations. They also found that housework responsibilities varied dramatically and that women did most of them. Finally, they found that women handled more union responsibility by cutting back on their sleep or their housework, while men usually cut back on their recreation (the Knights of Columbus or watching TV).[24] Some women even described sacrificing their marriages because their husbands wouldn't support their commitment to the union. The price for women to be leaders is higher than for men in very real personal terms. Men need to understand this.

In the absence of a domestic revolution, or at least a renegotiation of responsibilities, unions have to provide support in concrete ways for women rank-and-file leaders. Like many organizers, I learned to schedule meetings around child-care schedules, and to organize a meeting with children attending. We developed small tasks for the children to do. We met in people's homes so they could watch the children. I struggled to redefine the leader's job so I could see them on the job and reduce the outside-work commitment. While providing quality child care at meetings, conferences, and training sessions can be expensive, it also communicates to women workers that their participation is welcome, and it makes it possible for working mothers to attend.

Other suggestions made by rank-and-file women themselves include finding a way to provide hot meals at meetings, especially

evening meetings. Some successful CLUW meetings have been organized around potluck meals. Another request is to make more
union activities recreational and family oriented.[25] Getting more
paid release time is one way to make employers pay for leadership
development. Unions can implement a number of practices respect-
ing and supporting the family commitments of their members.

At the same time, unions should not be overwhelmed by the
time constraints of working women. A recent study shows that one
out of two Americans volunteers time for some activity, and looking at the large number of women active in massive volunteer organizations like Girl Scouts, League of Women Voters, and churches
and other religious groups, we can conclude that lack of time has
not been the critical reason why women haven't succeeded in union
organizations in proportion to their numbers.

d. TRAINING AND SUPPORT

Able women leaders can be found in every group of workers,
and the union must encourage them. Not every worksite leader
could easily make the transition to staff member or a union-wide
leader. A worksite leader has a base of followers, and moving on to
develop others with a base means that you have to feel secure
enough to "give up" power and encourage others to build their
power. This transformation is critical. We need more discussion
about the process of helping leaders become "leaders of leaders."

Rank-and-file women bear the most burdens in becoming
leaders. But the steps are clear. They must develop a comfortable
style of their own, learn political skills, work together with others
to break down discriminatory barriers, organize a personal support
system for their family commitments, and seek and get the training they need. Women need to be even more articulate about the
support they need, and union leaders need to listen more carefully
and act on what they hear.

Training must be simple, relevant, and able to be applied immediately. Constant support and feedback is also important. It can
be supplied by a male staffer or leader, but having women role
models is essential. The biggest problems for women in advancing
from stewards to union-wide leadership roles include not knowing
what is involved, feeling overwhelmed, not feeling they have the
skills, and time issues.

Leaders and potential leaders who are women already exist
within each worksite and we have to find them, involve them, and

encourage them to lead. There is a real risk, such as losing their jobs, and we have to be prepared to help people when that happens. Sometimes it can be a great positive opportunity in their lives.

Finally, special attention to issues of women and minority workers does make a tremendous difference. In Georgia, I worked primarily with nursing home members and janitors. The most liked leaders were women, since they were the vast majority of workers. This was especially true for many black and Latina women since they had been confined to low-wage jobs for reasons having little or nothing to do with their ability. In many cases, the union provided one of the few forums for recognition and appreciation. Many emerged quickly as leaders. I was struck by the dignity and strength of so many women living in near-poverty, working full-time, and taking incredible risks by standing up for their rights and the union. The union women's summer school was a great experience, changing the lives of some who attended. These forums will be necessary for some time to come.

5. Passing It On: Teaching Leadership Skills

In this fifth stage of leadership experience, women come to a point where we can begin to give back some of the skills and knowledge we have acquired. We are at a stage of our lives and careers where developing other leaders becomes a priority. We can also accomplish the political organizing necessary to earn our own continuing leadership roles. We need to ensure that the labor movement in general, and our own unions in particular, make the necessary changes to organize more women, take more of a lead role on women's issues, and develop more women leaders.

In this section, I briefly list the various ways I believe "passing it on" is possible within the labor movement. We have to take responsibility for our own growth and for helping other women around us. We also have to join together to organize for our rightful place in the power structure. At the same time, I believe we can do this while supporting our unions and helping make the structural, programmatic, and cultural changes that are needed to achieve our goals.

We can pass on our knowledge and skills in several ways. We need to become leaders of leaders, in the worksite and the local. Women can seek roles as chief stewards and as committee members and chairs. We can run for office in a local-wide election. We can represent our local in the community of labor or the community at large. One successful woman leader at an SEIU focus group said, "The labor movement is a great place to become a leader because there's so much work to do that there's plenty to go around! We have plenty of places to prove ourselves."

Women are becoming organizers at all ages and stages of life through the volunteer organizing programs in SEIU, UFCW, and other unions. They begin as volunteers and sometimes earn lost-time pay for training and other major assignments. What better advocate for unionism is there than a union activist from another worksite? Some people argue that women make the best organizers. Dina Beaumont of CWA says "they are people-oriented, good listeners, empathetic, and nurturing."[26] The AFL-CIO now runs organizing institutes to identify and orient potential interns, and several unions work with them to find placements for the organizer trainees.[27]

Women should be trainers. Training does not have to be a full-time job, although it can be. More and more committed union activists are teaching classes at labor studies centers, at the summer schools for union women, and at training courses in their unions. Probably people who are still doing a job are among the best people to train others how to do it, especially if there can be follow-up on the job.

A good manager is a good teacher, or she knows how to find good teachers to help her staff. Hiring, training, and supporting women staff was one of the most satisfying roles in my management experience. Working well with men staff who had never had a woman supervisor was also satisfying. Even though many women resist taking a managerial role, you truly can have a greater influence on more people than you can as a line staff person if you have the skills of managing.

Women who are ready to retire can become part of the senior leadership. Men still dominate the senior union movement, partly because men were a much greater majority of union members during their working years. However, women are coming on strong. Through orientation programs and organizing their fellow retirees women can play a much stronger role in retiree programs.

Women have been sharing leadership roles and experiences through women's organizations within unions and between unions for many years. CLUW, founded by 3,500 women in 1974, has been a strong advocate for union women, especially at the staff level, and for programs which advance women's organizing and women's concerns. Local groups like Washington Union Women play a sup-

portive role for union staff from various unions. Women's caucuses
have existed for many years. Women's departments or programs
have mushroomed from one in 1970 to 14 in 15 of the largest
unions representing women in 1985.[28]

Organizational membership, activity, and leadership is one
way to "pass on" the lessons of leadership. Women are also taking
a stronger role in central labor bodies and other labor organizations. In Oregon recently, the female directors of several large
unions got together and realized they controlled enough votes to
elect one of them to the all-male executive board of the state federation. So they did.

IV. Summary: Structural, Programmatic, and Cultural Barriers to Women's Leadership Development in Unions and Ways to Break Them Down

Women need to agitate for a variety of changes which labor
leaders need to initiate to fully support women's development as
leaders. Unions as institutions cannot be the sole determinants of
whether women succeed as leaders. Certainly U.S. corporate culture has not provided us with excellent examples of developing
leadership among women and people of color, although there are
some valuable lessons to be learned from management.[29]

Society presents formidable obstacles to women leaders, and
we must take responsibility for the ways in which we do not always seek or carry out leadership roles even when there are opportunities. To realize fully each person's potential there must be vast
social change (less discrimination, less poverty, less job segregation, more education, more child care and child development programs, and more equality between men and women within families), as well as personal change.

I don't minimize the social change, political organizing, or personal change which may be needed to help realize women's leadership potential. Rather, I focus here on the institutions of unions
because I believe that union leaders at all levels can and should
take responsibility for the change they can achieve, which will
have a dramatic impact on the future of their unions.

In looking at what union leaders who want to promote
women's leadership can do concretely, I found it useful to look at
three areas: structure, program, and content. I have used the national, or International, union as my model to reach the most

women, but the majority of these suggestions should also be carried out at the local union level.

1. Structural Changes

> I think as a woman, and as a black woman, you just have to prepare yourself to work harder at the job, to give more of yourself to the job to receive a two-thirds recognition that a man, a black or white man, would receive. . . . We must not have to rush home all the time because stopping and having a conference, a caucus, is where you really broaden your knowledge. But if you don't have child care at home, you must go home.[30]
>
> —Clara Day, Teamsters

Probably the most significant structural change unions must make is in the amount and type of resources they devote to developing women leaders. In particular, this means assigning responsibility and resources to a women's program which is broad enough to affect the whole union.

This could take the form of a separate department, as it has at about 15 unions. Women's departments offer certain advantages: an ability to focus on the issue, a ready-made networking function, and responsibility for managing the union's programs. The risk they run is the same as separate civil rights departments: being marginalized, underfunded, and not being able to influence the mainstream activities of the union because of a lack of resources and power. Unless a department has the ability and the right to influence effectively programs of other "line" departments of the union, its staff will have to rely on personal relationships and it will mainly be able to "exhort" rather than make real change.

Union leaders should create an interdepartmental work group with representative women elected leaders and at least one high-level staffer. This group can review how women's leadership development and women's concerns are reflected in all the union's programs, such as bargaining, communications, legislation, and organizing. The test of a program's seriousness is its resources, and the actual results being produced.

At SEIU, women on the executive board formed an informal group which John Sweeney soon designated as the Women's Program Advisory Committee. This group reports to the full board at regular meetings on the progress of SEIU local and International programs, and makes recommendations to the officers and staff of the union. Accountability to some leadership body is important to

avoid the two extremes of staff dominance of the program or staff
isolation from elected leaders.

The second most important structural change a union can
make is to expand the opportunities for women to earn leadership.
In some cases, this will simply mean filling vacant positions, from
the steward to committee to executive board level. In others, it will
mean expanding leadership roles. A new organizing committee
could be created with a special charge to organize in the service
sector, and a woman appointed as chair. In large organizations,
subdivisions could be headed up by women. In small organizations,
confederations could be led by women.

Fortunately, there is plenty of work to be done and many
women who can undertake it under the right conditions. This will
require unions to change their constitutional procedures in some
cases, and to exercise affirmative action in others. Even the Democratic Party has managed to ensure 50% women delegates to its
conventions; unions can certainly improve on this record. Canadian unions have created a requirement for women delegates.

Third, unions can support organizations specifically devoted to
developing women's leadership. Structurally within SEIU, this
meant an agreement between SEIU and 9 to 5, The National Association of Working Women, to create a special national local, District 925. The district remains under the control of women leaders,
and it maintains a close relationship with 9 to 5. Its programs,
organizing style, and representation are independent of SEIU, although it could always use more resources.

Other independent but affiliated organizations include the Re-
gina V. Polk Scholarship Fund for Labor Leadership, which was
set up by the Teamsters Union following the death of business representative Polk in a plane crash. This fund has sponsored many
training programs for women leaders and has sponsored many individual women as well.

Other organizations which unions should support in a system-
atic way include the UCLEA and AFL-CIO Summer Schools for
Union Women, and CLUW. Arranging yearly joint scholarships for
one or two women in each local to the summer school, and recommending that each local sponsor 20 members of CLUW every year
would vastly strengthen these important programs. CLUW is now
50% minority in its membership and leadership. There are many
other local organizations, like the Asian Immigrant Women Advocacy group in San Francisco, and also the Labor Coalition on Latin
American Advancement (LCLAA).

The fourth structural change a union can make is revising its human resources policies to fit more closely with the needs of women; it can adopt affirmative action programs with clear goals and timetables, and a variety of job-sharing, flex-time, part-time, and other positive employment practices. Unions must be able to set an example for employers on policy issues. Union jobs in particular, which often require 60- to 80-hour workweeks and extensive travel, need to be reviewed to see how they can more realistically fit the needs of working parents. Provision for child-care at conferences is now mandated by AFSCME, and there is a child-care fund at SEIU to help pay for child-care expenses on extra-long assignments.

To help women move into staff leadership positions where there is no turnover or limited opportunity at the local level, a national union should create a "job bank" of job openings at locals around the country. Perhaps unions should share this information. Hiring is still a political act, but many local union leaders have a hard time finding a range of capable staff when they do need to fill positions. It is particularly important to ensure women become managers, with real responsibility for hiring, firing, budgeting, and program development.

Fifth, the union can revise its expectations of locals to make recruiting women leaders a part of the normal routine, like raising political action funds, handling member complaints, and putting out communications. If locals and staff were evaluated on their success in recruiting women, more women leaders would be identified. The union can also create apprenticeship and intern opportunities and build them into the budget.

2. Program

A union's program encompasses its basic "business." The major programmatic change that unions should make, and women should fight for, is a dramatic expansion of training programs and opportunities for all levels from stewards to top elected leaders, including staff and managers.

Second, the union needs to identify its current and future members and leaders. Few unions have collected internal data, much less released it. While this is more easily said than done, unions should be able to make a fairly accurate estimate of their membership and leadership composition today and should try to estimate what their membership will look like in the years 2000 and 2050. Then they should set goals for leadership at all levels (including management and staff) to reflect the workforce.

Third, most unions should have an organizing program that focuses on unorganized women. It is clear that more women vote for unions than do men, and that more black women vote for unions than do white women.[31] The program must include sufficient resources to win, and a female organizing staff in which women are not mere foot-soldiers, but are the organizing leaders and managers.

Fourth, union leaders and staff also need to talk directly with their women stewards, staff, and elected leaders. What is the union environment like for them? What is working about the union's current program? What could be improved? What are particular issues for women of color? This is best done at the local level, although the national union should be the coordinator. Fifth, unions need to establish mentoring programs at a formal level. The informal mentoring which occurs now is sporadic and undependable, and people are most likely to hire and support those who "look like" them.

Sixth, it almost goes without saying that women must organize to promote issues of concern to them on the union's bargaining and political agendas such as pay equity, family leave, reproductive rights, nondiscrimination, and child care. Only a few unions have taken the lead on these issues despite a seven-million member constituency already paying dues, and millions more concerned, though unorganized, women! The current struggle within the labor movement about abortion rights finds CLUW's leadership in an unusual public advocacy position for its members to organize within each union to win support for choice. The AFL-CIO has declared neutrality.

Seventh, women should expand their efforts to win support for local, regional, and national conferences for women unionists. These are remarkable opportunities to network and to learn political and union skills as well to provide support and acknowledgment of the many extra hurdles women have to cross to win leadership. Many ideas are exchanged at conferences and long-term relationships are developed which will be critical to encouraging union leaders to support many of the needed changes. In SEIU, the California conference came into being because women leaders fought for support and resources. The statewide conference then became regional and served as the basis for the national conferences. In Massachusetts, creative women unionists have developed an annual weekend training program, the Women's Institute for Leadership Development (WILD).

Eighth, unions need to establish intern programs with lost-timers and with college students which focus on bringing in younger people. With most stewards and activists now over 45, according to both Wertheimer's and Roby's studies, unions need to attract young people as well. Finally, unions can support other women's organizations and ensure that they build links between union struggles and civil rights, women's political activities, and others. Interaction between union women and women's rights advocates is currently limited.

3. Culture

The "culture" of a union is probably the single most powerful determinant of how people act within the organization. A union's culture is the pattern of behavior, signs, and symbols which articulate its values, what's important to its leaders, and what counts as success. Culture is evident in all the tangible and intangible elements which determine how the union "feels." It is reflected in the physical location, layout, and appearance of the office; in the language that is used daily and in public statements; and in the pictures that hang on the wall and the stories that are told to new hires, new members, or anyone who will listen. A union's culture can be open or closed, flexible or rigid, informal or formal, participatory or hierarchical, multi-ethnic or homogeneous, and supportive of women or "macho."

This cultural environment is based in the history of the union and its leaders, who have the most power to shape it. It is also a result and reflection of the membership, the workplaces they come from, and the work they do. The teachers' unions, for example, place a great deal of emphasis on training and planning—skills they use in their jobs. Within SEIU, the public sector local unions are most likely to have budgets, computers, and formal administrative practices in place.

Cultures can and do change over time, but they rarely change quickly or abruptly. What is amazing in reflecting on the last 10 years is how much trade union culture has changed, and yet how traditional it still remains, and how much more change is needed before many women will feel comfortable. The problematic factor is that top leaders are the ones who can most effectively shape or change the culture, yet they are usually the ones who either created it or succeeded within it, so they have a powerful incentive not to change it. It is worth remembering that unions will continue to decline if they do not organize women members, and they can only organize women successfully into an environment where they have some level of comfort and trust. Women union leaders are key to unions' futures, however uncomfortable that makes current leaders feel.

In most unions, some more than others, the culture can be fairly described as traditional and based in working-class values and experience. In some cases there is a particular ethnic flavor to a union's culture: more likely Catholic than not, more likely based in the immigrant experience than not, more often white than not. The union leaders most often have been (and are still) white men, and the culture is largely "male." Union culture also contains traditional values about the role of women and their qualities.

Often a particular culture can inadvertently serve to exclude people even when the leaders don't intend to do so. They may not even be aware of the effect of certain habits, practices, or values. Union culture can be very intimidating to outsiders or newcomers, as women are most likely to be. One small example is the practice of signing letters, "Fraternally yours," which only in the last five years has largely given way to "In unity," which is more inclusive.

The traditionally male-dominated union culture has been changing very rapidly in some cases, especially where more women come to work for and participate in the union. But many traditions die hard. If the culture of a conference, for example, involves the male union leaders playing golf, then women union leaders miss out on the business and fun which occurs out on the course. Just as all-male country or social clubs have been held to be discriminatory, unions need to review their practices to make sure they don't have the same effect.

Sometimes women, out of necessity, or a desire for support, create their own sub-culture within an organization. This usually will create a feeling of discomfort within the dominant culture, similar to the exclusion the "sub-culturists" feel. However, there is a difference. The dominant culture is still the domain of those who are more likely to have power and resources, while the sub-culture can quickly become a place where people feel resentful at their exclusion from both. One of the challenges ahead is to master "cross-cultural communication" and to make all union cultures live up to our values of appreciating diverse experience rather than exclusively valuing one shared experience.

Culture and politics, which are closely related, can prevent or support the selection, hiring, election, training, and development of women and people of color. If the leaders at the top do not support this development, it will happen only as the result of "guerrilla warfare," with all its tremendously destructive potential.

Unions must be held accountable to create a culture which is conscious of women's worth and value, and where traditional sexist practices are discouraged or eliminated. This kind of culture already exists where the majority of workers and leaders are women; it can exist where the male majority has adopted these values. Women will have to fight the hardest battles to change the culture of our unions. But it is worth it in the end. While history plays a key role, the leaders of today are in the most powerful position to make conscious changes in the culture of their unions.

Changing culture is a complex and difficult thing. The union's culture belongs to all of us, and the leaders must do their best to make a very diverse membership and leadership feel at home. Future work is needed to review more systematically what each union is doing, how current changes have been achieved, and what a program and budget that would accomplish all these recommendations in practice would look like. If the unions we and our forebears have struggled so hard to build are to reverse their decline and grow by organizing the new workforce of women, people of color, and new immigrants, our structures, programs, and cultures will have to change so they will be more welcoming and supportive of new and excluded groups. We have tremendous opportunity for success and grave risk of failure because women need unions and unions need women leaders for each to build a more just future.

Notes

1. National Women's Trade Union League of America, *Proceedings: Seventh Biennial Convention* (Philadelphia, Pennsylvania, 2–7 June 1919), 70.

2. "More Women Gaining Positions in Union Leadership Structures," *Daily Labor Report* (Washington, D.C.: Bureau of National Affairs, 24 September 1990).

3. Naomi Baden, "Developing an Agenda: Expanding the Role of Women in Unions," *Labor Studies Journal*, vol. 10, no. 3 (Winter 1986): 229.

4. This is not a problem exclusively for unions, of course. The July 30, 1990 issue of *Fortune* magazine reports that in the top 799 industrial and service companies, less than one-half of one percent of highest-paid officers and directors are women. Yet unions fight against discrimination and seg-

regation and for equality and better conditions for women and all workers. Surely our own house should reflect the value and recognition of women's leadership skills and talent.

5. Gary Chaison and P. Andiappan, "An Analysis of the Barriers to Women Becoming Local Union Officers," *Journal of Labor Research*, vol. X, no. 2 (Spring 1989): 160.

6. AFL-CIO, *The Changing Situation of Workers and Their Unions*, (Washington, D.C.: AFL-CIO, 1985), 8–9.

7. Pamela Roby and Lynet Uttal, "Trade Union Stewards: Handling Union, Family and Employment Responsibilities," in Barbara A. Gutek, Ann H. Stromberg and Laurie Larwood, eds., *Women and Work: An Annual Review*, vol. 3, (California: Sage Publications, 1988), 217–219.

8. Ibid.

9. Ruth Needleman and Lucretia Dewey Tanner, "Women in Unions: Current Issues," in Karen Koziara, Michael Moskow, and Lucretia Dewey Tanner, eds., *Working Women: Past, Present, Future* (Washington, D.C.: BNA, 1987), 216.

10. Baden, 241.

11. Ruth Needleman and Lucretia Dewey Tanner, 210. See also Baden.

12. Eventually, our long hours of work on the child-care committee was to lead to a substantial program giving assistance to employees on child-care. The local was to be given credit in publications by the Children's Defense League and in union publications for its path-breaking efforts in child-care. This story suggests the value of "women's issues" to the union when they are pursued just as any other union issue would be!

13. Barbara Wertheimer and Anne Nelson, *Trade Union Women: A Study of Their Participation in New York City Locals* (New York: Praeger, 1975), 154.

14. Ruth Needleman and Helen Elkiss, Notes on Workshop, "Barriers to Union Participation," (University of Illinois, Unpublished, December 1988).

15. Deborah Tannen, *You Just Don't Understand: Women and Men in Conversation* (New York: William Morrow, 1990), 65.

16. In 1990 the conference expanded to a regional one. The concept has also been expanded with a Civil and Human Rights Conference.

17. Jaclyn Fierman, "Why Women Still Aren't Getting to the Top," *Fortune*, 30 July 1990, 62.

18. Needleman Workshop notes.

19. Wertheimer and Nelson, 155.

20. Roby and Uttal, 240.

21. Ibid., 224.

22. Lois Gray, "Women in Union Leadership Roles," *Interface, AFL-CIO*, vol. 17, no. 3 (August 1988): 9.

23. "Black Women in the Labor Movement: Interviews with Clara Day and Johnnie Jackson," *Labor Research Review*, vol. 11 (Spring 1988): 84.

24. Roby and Uttal, 225–235.

25. Ibid., 236–237.

26. BNA, *Daily Labor Report.*

27. Contact the AFL-CIO Organizing Institute at (202) 637–5000.

28. Baden, 241–243.

29. See Rosabeth Moss Kanter's work as well as Peter Drucker's management texts on the values of a "feminine" style of leadership.

30. *Labor Research Review*, 84–86.

31. "In Gallup Polls, for example, blacks generally (men and women) are much more favorable toward unions than whites—with nearly three out of four blacks expressing support for unions, compared to only a bare majority of whites. Black women are nearly twice as likely to be members of unions than white women, and they have higher unionization rates than the labor force as a whole—20%, compared to 12% for white women and 17% for the entire labor force in 1986." *Labor Research Review*, 79–80.

Editors' Suggested Readings

American Federation of Labor and Congress of Industrial Organizations. *The Changing Situation of Workers and Their Unions*. Washington, D.C.: AFL-CIO, 1985.

Baden, Naomi. "Developing an Agenda: Expanding the Role of Women in Unions." *Labor Studies Journal*, vol. 10, no. 3 (Winter 1986).

Balser, Diane. *Sisterhood and Solidarity*. Boston: South End Press, 1987.

Beale, Jenny. *Getting it Together: Women as Trade Unionists*. London: Pluto Press, 1982.

Bose, Christine and Glenna Spitze, eds. *Ingredients for Women's Employment Policy*. Albany: State University of New York Press, 1987.

Bureau of National Affairs. "More Women Gaining Positions in Union Leadership Structures." *Daily Labor Report*, 24 September 1990.

Chaison, Gary and P. Andiappan. "An Analysis of the Barriers to Women Becoming Local Union Officers." *Journal of Labor Research*, vol. X, no. 2 (Spring 1989).

Cook, Alice H., Val Lorwin and Arlene Daniels. *Women and Trade Unions in Eleven Industrialized Countries*. Philadelphia: Temple University Press, 1984.

Coyle, Angela and Jane Skinner, eds. *Women and Work: Positive Action for Social Change*. London: MacMillan, 1988.

Department of Professional Employees, AFL-CIO. "Conference Examines Organizing and Representing Professional Women." *Interface* (Summer 1988).

Elkiss, Helen and Ruth Needleman. Notes on Workshop, "Barriers to Union Participation," at the University of Illinois, unpublished, December 1988.

Elkiss, Helen. "A Unique Conference for Union Women: Overcoming Barriers to Union Participation and Leadership." *Labor Studies Forum*, vol. 2, no. 2 (Summer 1989).

Fierman, Jaclyn. "Why Women Still Don't Hit the Top." *Fortune*, 30 July 1990.

Geoffroy, Renee and Paule Sainte-Marie. *Attitude of Union Workers to Women in Industry*. Ottawa: Royal Commission on the Status of Women, 1971.

Glassberg, Elyse, Naomi Baden, and Karin Gerstel. *Absent from the Agenda: A Report on the Role of Women in American Unions*. Coalition of Labor Union Women, Center for Research and Education, September 1980.

Gray, Lois. "Women in Union Leadership Roles." *Interface*, AFL-CIO, vol. 17, no. 3 (August 1988).

Gutek, Barbara A., Ann H. Stromberg and Laurie Larwood, eds. *Women and Work: An Annual Review*, vol. 3 . California: Sage Publishers, 1988.

Kellner, Peter and Anna Coote. *Hear This, Brother: Women Workers and Union Power*. London: New Statesman, 1980.

Koziara, Karen and Michael Moskow and Lucretia Dewey Tanner, eds. *Working Women: Past, Present, Future*. Washington, D.C.: Bureau of National Affairs, 1987.

Melcher, Dale, Jennifer Eichstedt, Shelley Eriksen, and Dan Clawson. "Women's Participation in Local Union Leadership: The Massachusetts Experience." *Industrial & Labor Relations Review*, vol. 45, no. 2 (January 1992).

Milkman, Ruth, ed. *Women, Work and Protest: A Century of U.S. Women's Labor History*. Boston: Routledge and Kegan Paul, 1985.

National Women's Trade Union League of America. *Proceedings: Seventh Biennial Convention*, Philadelphia, 2–7 June 1919.

Needleman, Ruth. "Women Workers: A Force for Rebuilding Unionism." *Labor Research Review*, vol. 11 (Spring 1988).

Tannen, Deborah. *You Just Don't Understand: Women and Men in Conversation*. New York: William Morrow, 1990.

US Department of Labor, Women's Bureau. "Women in Labor Organizations." *Facts on Working Women*, no. 89–2 (August 1989).

Wertheimer, Barbara and Anne Nelson. *Trade Union Women: A Study of Their Participation in New York City Locals*. New York: Praeger, 1975.

Part Three

Labor and Politics: Recasting Alliances and Solidarity

The changes advocated in Part Two make good practical and principled sense: unions must organize if they are to survive, and empowering such new constituencies is in line with what unions say they are all about. But the advancement of women and the strengthening of a more democratic leadership are part of larger problems of exclusion and isolation created by a bureaucratic union structure. Inflexibility, lack of creativity, and hierarchical leadership structures within major unions has made it difficult for them to respond to the needs of new workers, which has contributed to the unions' decline. Kim Fellner's chapter examines union solidarity and organizing by exploring the fate of labor activists from the 1960s. In Fellner's words, what they found and how they fared "in the house of labor over the past 20 years says much about the current status and potential fate of American labor."

According to Fellner, sixties activists were the first generation of college-educated young people to enter the union movement since the 1930s. Many brought with them the experience and ideals of the mass social movements of the decade, and saw their participation in trade unions as a natural expression of a broader vision of democratization and worker empowerment. Concretely, they carried strategies and tactics that had proved successful in civil rights and anti-war campaigns. These approaches, when applied to union organizing, helped them win organizing drives by employing militant tactics, such as boycotts, and building coalitions between unions and community or church groups. Fellner asserts that through these campaigns, activists "fostered an organizer-centered culture, a community united in struggle, sacrifice, and solidarity."

Fellner develops a theory about organizing and its centrality to union success. Good organizing, she says, quoting Saul Alinsky, requires "breaking down of the feeling on the part of our people that they are social automatons with no stake in the future, rather than human beings in possession of all the responsibility, strength, and human dignity which constitute the heritage of free citizens of a democracy." Quoting former president of the International Asso-

ciation of Machinists (IAM), William Winpisinger, Fellner writes
that organizers "have to love people . . . (have) the ability to engender trust, an ability to create a platoon of activists in any given
workplace, (and be) recruiters of considerable skill." Finally, they
require a union culture which encourages creativity, individual
initiative, and nonconformity, and which offers tangible institutional support in the form of sizable organizing budgets, staff, job
status, and salary.

Most of the sixties activists Fellner interviewed remained on
the fringes of the labor movement, in unions which had retained a
progressive tradition and a commitment to organizing. In the hierarchies of industrial unions and particularly in the AFL-CIO itself,
Fellner says, organizing was—and remains—a low priority.
Unions have a limited financial commitment to organizing, and
the staff positions bring low salaries and even lower institutional
status. For example, a 1985 study of 7,000 full-time union staff
people in California, found only 182 organizers, less than 3% of the
total. "Organizing is like sex," Fellner quotes the organizing director of a major union, "people talk about it a lot more than they do
it."

In part, Fellner claims, this situation stems from the legacy of
the McCarthy period, when the union movement lost "its most eloquent and effective proselytizers" in the purges of left-wing activists and the expulsion of 11 unions and nearly one million members from the CIO. More important, according to the author, is that
the unions have come to resemble traditional corporate management models: hierarchical, vertical, compartmentalized, biased
against action, with a leadership largely composed of white males.
The structure encourages conformity, a service mentality as opposed to the idealistic zeal needed for organizing the unorganized,
and rewards support for a status quo in which the union role is
limited to collective bargaining.

The conditions take a heavy toll on organizers and activists.
But Fellner argues that they are ground down and eventually
defeated by recurring contradictions in their work: "between espoused democracy and internal repression, between espoused equity and institutional racism and sexism; between a commitment
to solidarity and organizing in theory, and an internal culture that
vitiates against them in practice."

In such an environment it is extremely difficult for good people
to remain in union work. For example, the SEIU employs 60 full-
time organizers, but in the last five years those positions have been
filled by more than 200 people. Unions are thus robbed of a vital

resource which is essential to the union movement's ability to survive, if not expand in the current crisis.

Ironically, Fellner finds inspiration for change in the new management literature which is itself critical of the traditional forms of corporate bureaucracy. The writings extol risk-taking, flexibility, and autonomy, values which Fellner asserts have always informed the best union organizing. These values were central to the movements which spawned the sixties' labor activists, and their broader agenda suggests an important road for the labor movement: reaching to other social groups to establish political and economic coalitions in the fight for workers' rights.

Finally, Fellner suggests an important connection between the need to democratize union culture and foreign policy. The efforts by organizers to promote attitudes and ideas which empower workers demands not only that unions become more politically involved to win progressive legislation, but that they support similar efforts abroad. Don Stillman's chapter examines the United Auto Workers' (UAW) role in an international campaign on behalf of a jailed South African trade unionist. In assessing strengths and weaknesses of the effort, his chapter highlights the problem of involving rank-and-file members in international issues, and underscores the need to develop links between trade union international policy and American workers' domestic fights for human rights and social justice.

Moses Mayekiso, general secretary of the 250,000 member National Union of Metalworkers of South Africa (NUMSA), was one of five defendants put on trial by the South African government in a marathon treason case where they faced a possible death sentence. The men were detained in June 1986, came to trial in the fall of 1987, and were eventually acquitted of all charges in April 1989. The essence of their "crime" was that they had attempted to organize grassroots democratic structures in their community, the squalid Alexandra township, near Johannesburg. Not only was his indictment a direct attack on the trade union movement, but also an attack on the efforts of unionists to link their trade union work to the broader political struggle against apartheid. A guilty verdict would not only remove a major union leader, but would criminalize the union's political work and set a precedent defining basic community organizing as treason, making the common activities of nonviolent political opposition to apartheid into capital offenses.

The UAW had long-standing solidarity links with Mayekiso's union: the UAW had provided important support for the South African metalworkers' early organizing drives, both were members of the International Metalworkers' Federation (IMF), and the UAW had intervened in Mayekiso's previous arrests. His arrest and subsequent trial prompted NUMSA and its national federation, the Congress of South African Trade Unions (COSATU) to launch an international call for support for their campaign to pressure the government to release the Alexandra Five. In consultation with those union groupings, with European unions, and with anti-apartheid groups in the U.S., the UAW helped develop a massive campaign for "Justice for Mayekiso."

The most important support came on the ground in South Africa itself. Despite the repressive conditions of a State of Emergency, workers brought attention to the trial through writing campaigns, T-shirt distribution, postering, and sporadic work stoppages. In the U.S. the campaign started with urgent telexes to senior South African officials, and soon benefitted from a personal visit to the country by UAW president, Owen Bieber, who met the Minister of Justice, and compellingly communicated the UAW message to the highest levels of the government.

The UAW also gave priority to a massive international postcard campaign. Materials were distributed at union meetings, bargaining sessions, safety seminars, civil rights gatherings, even union bowling tournaments. In the U.S. alone, more than 100,000 cards had been circulated by early 1987, partially solving the important problem of involving rank-and-file members in the campaign. The union also established a special "Mayekiso Trial Update" newsletter to communicate with the membership, and picketed the South African embassy in Washington.

The most innovative aspect of the campaign was the creation of a special oversight body, called the American Jurists' Committee Monitoring the Case of Moses Mayekiso. Inspiration for an independent ad hoc committee of 10 prominent American jurists grew out of a strategic decision by the campaign leaders that they could pressure the South African judiciary, which claims—and in many instances asserts—its independence from the South African executive branch of government. The UAW and its South African allies assessed that the pressure would be most effective if organized through a non-partisan body, interested in due process and respect for human rights. The committee was formed to make factual assessments of the testimony and evidence, and render opinions on the judge's rulings on key points of law.

Eventually, Benno Schmidt, president of Yale University and a member of the committee, made a personal trip to South Africa to hold long sessions with the defendants, observe the trial, and to meet the judge and senior members of the legal establishment. At a press conference before his departure from Johannesburg, Schmidt said the trial "is being watched closely in legal circles, in trade unions, church groups, the human rights community, and by the public." In Stillman's words, "As Schmidt flew home, no one connected to the trial could avoid the fact that the world was watching and waiting to see what the outcome would be."

In April 1989 the Alexandra Five were acquitted of all charges. While it is hard to assess the exact impact of the international campaign, Mayekiso himself, his union, and his lawyers saw it as an extremely important contribution to the result. According to Stillman, "The South African government had not confronted a union-initiated solidarity campaign of this magnitude before."

The Mayekiso campaign is an important example of the strategic value of international solidarity, illustrating that U.S. unions can generate influence to protect foreign workers, their organizations, and advance their movement for freedom. Unions can work cooperatively with their counterparts overseas to check the activities of governments and multinational corporations. In working for Mayekiso's freedom, U.S. unions strengthened their credibility in the eyes of South African unionists, in part because they intervened into an important political struggle, transcending the basic union-building support which made up the bulk of the unions' previous help to those in South Africa. These direct political experiences helped to overcome South Africans' "concern that some sectors of American labor movement have an interest in manipulating black unions as part of broader East-West ideological questions."

But significantly, these actions have direct benefits for U.S. labor. Stillman found that UAW members "related very personally to a black unionist possibly facing a hangman's noose for his efforts to improve the community where he lived." By drawing in members to learn about apartheid and repression in South Africa, the union could stimulate discussions of similar issues in the U.S.

On a broader level, the campaign yielded an important concrete result, by strengthening solidarity ties to political, church, and community groups who are the mainstays of the anti-apartheid movement in the U.S. and abroad. These practical links not only promoted the Mayekiso campaign, but established a basis for building coalitions which pursue progressive union and community politics in the U.S. itself.

In Search of the Movement:
1960s' Activists in Labor[1]

Kim Fellner

"What do you do?" the businessman sitting next to me on the plane invariably asks.

"I'm a union organizer," I reply. On good days, I gleefully anticipate his surprised response; on bad days, I brace myself for the latest malediction against unions; on terrible days, I say I'm executive director of a writers' organization, so I can spend the rest of the flight in peace.[2]

At 41, I'm one of labor's "new leftovers," one of the generation of activists who, after participating in the civil rights or anti-war movements, migrated into union work. Most of us didn't know each other in the beginning. Yet we came with a shared need somehow to hang on to the passions, however inchoate, that the sixties had kindled: for social change, for racial and gender equality, for the lifestyle and camaraderie of activism itself. We were the first substantial influx of college-educated young people to enter the labor movement since the 1930s.

What we found, and how we have fared, in the house of labor over the past 20 years says much about the current status and potential fate of American labor. Drawn by the "movement," we found ourselves in an institution more often dedicated to standing still. And on the cusp of middle age, we have become the leftovers, not merely of our own generation of activists, but of the idea of trade unionism as a vibrant force for change and for justice.

I've been a union staffer now for 15 years, first at the SEIU, then at the Screen Actors Guild (SAG) and, for the last four years, at the National Writers Union (NWU). I used to joke that each move I made took me farther from the labor establishment, and that the NWU, small, new, scruffy, and outspokenly progressive, was right on the edge of labor respectability. One more step back from the center and I'd fall off.

My vocation has, in fact, always been troublesome, not so much because of corporate management, which I always expected to be recalcitrant, if not downright immoral, but because of union management, which often seems determined to grind its organizers and activists into conformity and complacency.

Which means I've been in trouble from the start. My irreverence hasn't helped, although the red "union goon" T-shirt I sported with my black suit at an AFL-CIO convention was much admired by the ranks, if not fully appreciated by the leadership.

Much worse, I have persisted in not only having opinions, but in voicing them, from questioning election procedures at the Labor Press Association in my earliest days, to joining my ex-boss Edward Asner in challenging AFL-CIO policies toward Latin America, and those are less forgivable sins.

Along with its near-fanatic anti-communism, the AFL-CIO has embraced a classical, pre-glasnost Soviet approach to loyalty. "I'm willing to talk with you, but don't use my name," even close friends tell me when I ask about their lives in labor. "It's like China," an AFL-CIO insider half laughs, rolling her eyes.

One of my friends, an independent labor editor, was recently offered the editorship of labor's pre-eminent publication, the *AFL-CIO News*. He turned it down. "Sure, I was glad they asked," he told me, "but how could I take it? I'd have no real control, and the moment I disagreed or wanted to write a real story about real issues, I'd be out." Not long after his refusal, the job was listed in the want ads section of the *Washington Post*.

Once we coveted and aspired to such positions. Now we're no longer sure. Many of us have discovered that the very traits that make us good at movement work are impediments to union job security.

I learned early that working in unions requires a high tolerance for contradiction on many fronts. Among my disorderly files is an article I wrote more than a decade ago in praise of union work. "However," I cautioned, "it is work for believers who can survive in organizations that often mimic in style, and occasionally in substance, the corporate and management structures they were created to oppose. Those same organizations that preach dignity for workers often exploit their own. They preach equality and discriminate against women; they advocate progress and desperately fear change." All still true.

Twice a year, I vow to open a café devoted to Viennese pastry and string quartets and leave the labor movement forever. But so far I haven't, because I'm in love. Not with unions as they are, but with the labor movement as it still occasionally blooms: a dynamic community of organizers and working activists who, through collective action, struggle to achieve a redistribution of power and wealth; dignity for workers, as a class and as individuals; and an enrichment and celebration of the human spirit.

And sometimes it happens. In the crusade of the United Farm Workers (UFW), in decent locals throughout the labor landscape, in an organizing campaign where all the components miraculously come together. The knowledge that it's still possible keeps us going, but the realities of working in unions are a powerful challenge to that faith.

The contradictions between labor's principles and practices are seldom so apparent as at the ceremonial gatherings of the labor establishment, like the biennial AFL-CIO convention. "Just thinking about it makes my heart sink," says one union staffer. "All those white males over fifty. And we could fund an organizing campaign on the money it takes to host one of those receptions."

The conventions, and the meetings of the AFL-CIO executive council in Florida, are frequently the butt of mean-spirited, sarcastic commentary by the media. But sometimes it's hard to blame them. "Two young showgirls, appropriately nicknamed 'Postage Stamp Girls' by some, have provoked a fierce debate among convention-goers," *The New York Times* reported from the 1989 council meeting in Bal Harbour. "At issue is whether young women in skimpy black bikinis with sequins are beneficial to labor's drive to improve its relations with women, who account for an increasingly large chunk of the workforce.

". . . The National Association of Letter Carriers hired them to pass out small gift bags at its lavish cocktail party the other night. Men lined up to pose for photos with the women . . . 'I think it enhanced the image of labor,' said Vincent R. Sombrotto, president of the letter carriers union." The article noted that AFL-CIO president, Lane Kirkland, "who recently started an advertising campaign to bring more women and minorities into the federation, brushed off criticism, saying at a press conference 'Don't you take some things too seriously?'"[3]

If labor's commitment to solidarity is more often pro forma than proactive, the same thing can be said for organizing, the other shibboleth of the labor lexicon. No one, either in the AFL-CIO or in the national Bureau of Labor Statistics, seems to know how many labor organizers there are in the country today, although "not enough" is a common response, attested by the drop in union membership from a post-war high of 35% to a current low of less than 17% of America's workforce.

In the mid-1930s, the Steel Workers Organizing Committee, funded by CIO leaders John L. Lewis of the United Mine Workers and Sidney Hillman of the Amalgamated Clothing Workers Union, had 433 full- and part-time organizers. During the sit-down strikes, the UAW grew from 30,000 to 400,000 in one year. That intensity of effort is hard to imagine today.

A study done by two California organizers, Marshall Ganz and Scott Washburn, revealed that in 1985, out of 7,000 full-time union staff people in the state, there were just 182 organizers, less than 3% of the total. As Andrew Stern, organizing director for the SEIU wryly notes, "Organizing is like sex. People talk about it a lot more than they do it."

The definition of organizing is almost as elusive as the practice. "The clearest definition of organizing I have been able to develop is that it is about identifying and developing leadership, building a community around that leadership, and building power out of that community so it can meet its own interests," suggests Ganz. The son of a rabbi, Ganz came out of the civil rights movement, and served as organizing director for the UFW for more than 10 years. "It also requires a credible strategy and financial independence. Reduced to its most basic elements there would be just two: people and power."

That definition owes much to the work of master organizer Saul Alinsky, a friend and biographer of John L. Lewis. Alinsky first achieved recognition for his feisty community organizing in the Back-of-the-Yards neighborhood of Chicago. He based his approach on the belief that organizing should not "do for" people but, rather, enable a group of people "to do for themselves." From the late 1930s until his death in 1972, Alinsky practiced and preached the gospel of building "people's organizations." Many of the community and labor organizers of my generation were trained at his Industrial Areas Foundation, or were mentored (occasionally hectored) by those who were. His book, *Reveille for Radicals*, inspired us to regard organizing as a heroic vocation to which we should aspire.

To Alinsky, every good radical was an organizer, every good organizer a radical. The organizing rubric went beyond the conventional understanding of union campaigns to win more members (or political campaigns to win more voters), to defining an approach toward shaking up the status quo. It distinguished the educators, editors, negotiators, even the occasional attorney, who were activists and empowerers from those who were functionaries and bureaucrats.

Alinsky's systemic approach gained emotional resonance when cross-fertilized and combined with the more intuitive, but extremely powerful, movement-building culture of the civil rights movement. Organizers a shade older than I often cite SNCC, the Student Nonviolent Coordinating Committee, as their first romance with organizing. However, while the southern tradition and style differed from Alinsky's, the underlying goal of empowerment was the same.

"This is our real job," Alinsky asserted, "the breaking down of the feeling on the part of our people that they are social automatons with no stake in the future, rather than human beings in possession of all the responsibility, strength, and human dignity which constitute the heritage of free citizens of a democracy. This can only be done through the democratic organization of our people. . . . It is the job of building People's Organizations."[4]

To Madeleine Janover, an ex-union organizer who describes herself as "an upwardly mobile working-class kid from Denver, Colorado," empowerment became very tangible when she organized a small nursing home staffed by black women. "It was run by a black woman, Mrs. Albert, who was a symbol of success in this small, racist community, but treated her workers terribly," Madeleine relates. "In addition to the nursing home, she ran a small house for slightly retarded women, and one of the young women who lived there worked in the nursing home. Well, this young woman came to one of the organizing meetings. She wasn't really retarded, just a little slow, but people didn't want her to get involved because they thought if she got fired from the nursing home, she could be kicked out of her residence as well.

"I'll never forget it. She came to that meeting and told us, 'If Mrs. Albert fires me, she fires me. But it can't be as bad as the way that woman treats me, I'm not her slave.' All these women were marginal, minimum wage, bottom of the scale, and they were all scared. No one wanted to go back on welfare. And this woman, who owed her existence to the boss got up and said, 'I'm a human being, I'm not her dog, I'm in this until we win.'

"Well those women organized, and they had a tough time, and this woman did get fired, and everyone panicked, including me. But this young woman came to the next meeting after she was fired and told us, 'Don't worry about me. If I had to do it again, I would, and she won't kick me out, because I won't let her.'

"It still brings tears to my eyes, but these are good tears, because that was what it was all about. The union was something to this woman. It was her ticket to dignity, it gave meaning, a hook to what was in her already. I used to say to myself, I can't believe I have this gift, to be able to work with these people to show them the tools they already have. They became proud members of the community. And that's what I organized on. The anti-war and feminist movements were so passionate, so clear, and here I was allowed to continue that dream in a more realistic way, rooted in real struggle, and the inspiration came from very real, everyday people."

If the concept of democratic empowerment that brought us to the labor movement was inspired by the civil rights movement and grounded in the work of Alinsky, it also had roots in the labor legacy of Eugene Debs. Ask 1960s activists whom they aspire to emulate, and it's never Samuel Gompers, cigar maker, organizer turned bureaucrat, who became the first president of the American Federation of Labor. Rather, you'll hear the names of the renegades: Mother Jones, who organized in the coal fields and steel towns when she was 80; the Wobblies, who fought for "One Big Union" in the first two decades of the century; and especially Debs, leader of the Pullman Strike of 1894, pioneer of industrial unionism, Socialist candidate for president of the United States. In his heyday, the press carried columns of his aphorisms and thousands flocked to hear him speak.

It is that overarching vision, passionate and generous, that seems to have disappeared from the AFL-CIO philosophy. "Initially there were two separate streams to the labor movement," says Gus Tyler, education director emeritus of the ILGWU. "On the one hand were the pure and simple trade unionists who did not believe labor had any kind of ultimate goal and were opposed to political action, even to social legislation at the federal level. Their ideologue was Samuel Gompers.

"Then you had the radicals, deeply influenced by selfless thinking, and they were perhaps a third of the trade union movement. During the 1940s, in the Roosevelt era, there was a confluence. The pure and simple trade unionists became politicized, and the radical trade unionists became more moderate. They no longer said, 'socialism today,' but 'socialism somewhere in the back of our minds as an ultimate goal.'"

That socialist legacy was eviscerated even further in the 1950s, when most AFL-CIO unions purged left-wing activists and intellectuals during the McCarthy era. Eleven unions representing almost a million members were expelled from the CIO on charges of communist domination. That weeding out cost the labor establishment many of its most eloquent and effective proselytizers. Those who remained were often less progressive, or more circumspect, in their views.

"The McCarthy era was characterized by total surrender in the CIO, not to mention the AFL," comments Dave Livingston, president of District 65, a long-time, independent, left-leaning union now affiliated with the UAW. "It especially had an impact on the industrial unions, where leftists were concentrated, and excluded some very good organizers."

By the time I started working for a Pennsylvania social workers local of the SEIU in 1974, most AFL-CIO unions had been closed communities for more than 15 years. I knew no one active in the labor movement and few who thought well of it. The support of George Meany and the AFL-CIO for the Vietnam War, combined with labor's very white, male public face, had not endeared it to civil rights and anti-war activists; or the other way around. After all, "hippies vs. hard-hats" had been one of the media images of the decade.

"No unions were hiring in the sixties when they were strongest," says Ganz. "I first heard about unions at the Highlander Center in 1965 at a session organized by SNCC and SDS (Students for a Democratic Society). The Meatcutters and the United Electrical Workers (UE) were the only unions who came, and they were leftist, outside the mainstream. While the Peace Corps and the poverty programs were recruiting us, the unions were too afraid of communists to talk to us. The unions were so scared of young people, and an organization fearful of the young is a dying organization."

Not surprisingly then, the first real opening for sixties' activists came, not from the labor establishment, but from the fringes. The Meatcutters, UE, and Local 1199 Hospital Workers' Union had all retained a progressive tradition and remained open to new, young hires, but they were small unions with limited staffs.

It took Cesar Chavez, in search of a large cadre of organizers to build the UFW, to open up the labor movement to a new generation of idealists. Among the ranks of ex-civil rights and peace movement activists he found people, including Ganz, with the fervor to work 100 hours a week for $5 plus communal room and board. Between 1965 and 1980, mentored by one of Alinsky's co-organizers, the UFW trained several thousand activists, using as many as 500 organizers on any one campaign.

Other sixties' activists began to work at other labor causes at the peripheries of the labor establishment: in the J. P. Stevens campaign mounted by the Amalgamated Clothing and Textile Workers Union (ACTWU) against the notoriously anti-union, southern textile producer; in the efforts of renegade UMW and Teamsters to reclaim and democratize their unions; and in public employee unions winning the legal right to union representation for the first time. In these out-of-the-mainstream organizing efforts, the new generation of activists felt at home. The work was defined as part of a crusade for a more equitable society, and utilized many of the same techniques and community or church coalitions that had characterized the movements of the 1960s. In addition, they fostered an organizer-centered culture, a community united in struggle, sacrifice and solidarity.

And they were successful. Combining brilliant organizing in the California fields with a national boycott, the UFW won a contract with Gallo wine. A former VISTA volunteer, Ray Rogers, developed a corporate campaign strategy which, by applying pressure to corporate boards and financial interlocks, helped ACTWU win a contract with J. P. Stevens. The Miners for Democracy deposed the corrupt UMW president, Tony Boyle. And public employee unions became (and remain) the fastest-growing unions in the country.

These successes could not go unnoticed by other unions or the AFL-CIO. In addition, the influx of the new activists coincided with an intensified attack against unions by the New Right and a proliferation of sophisticated union-busting firms retained by companies to fight union representation. A new economic order was beginning to take form, marked by increased corporate conglomeratization and the shift from an industrial, more frequently unionized base to a mostly non-unionized, often female or minority, service workers' economy.

As labor confronted these new, perplexing problems, a few of the more traditional unions grudgingly opened their doors to some of the labor newcomers. The rhetoric of solidarity, organizing, and even struggle, slowly began to resurface alongside the more habitual 1950s' labor language of service, moderation, and cooperation.

I was lucky. When I moved from my SEIU public employee local to the union headquarters in 1976 to work on the union newspaper, I was part of the first real expansion of the professional class within the organization. But the spirit of organizing was alive and well, thanks to the union's president, George Hardy, and his organizing director, John Geagan. Hardy had started out organizing janitors in California in the 1930s and that remained the essence of his being. His trademarks were a shiny bald head and pungently bald verbiage. He was maddeningly erratic in all but his love for organizing and, until his retirement in 1980, insisted on being present at all training classes for new organizers.

No wonder then, that he should have an organizing director like Geagan. He was one of a rare breed, a staffer of the fifties' generation who unabashedly loved organizing and the people who did it. When Geagan died in 1985, all of us whom he had mentored showed up at his funeral to honor his memory and drink toasts in his name. Part bantamweight fighter (which he had been), part leprechaun, entirely impossible, with a vocabulary that knew no shame and a notorious lust for California white wine, he was one of those original characters fast disappearing from the labor movement.

When his proteges meet today, we still tell Geagan stories and laugh about how he almost landed us in jail through his high jinks on some organizing campaign or another, of the restaurants from which we got evicted because of his drunken antics. His favorite terms of exasperation were, "Christ on a crutch!" and, in moments of extreme distress, "Jesus wept!"

We were all "Hey, ace," "skeezix," "sis," "chum," but we all felt special. He was always on the lookout for fighters and talented scrappers, and many of those he identified and mentored were women like myself, who would otherwise have moldered away in some obscure corner of the organization. To the ire of the union's secretary-treasurer (a much more typical union bureaucrat), and my eternal gratitude, he spirited me out of the newspaper office and annexed me to his own department. And he bound us not only to himself, but to each other, and to an ideal of the union not as a tired, bureaucratic service organization, but as an exciting, vital, daring mission to bring light to an unorganized world.

The organizing department Geagan ran in the late seventies had fewer than 10 national organizers, two indispensable clerical workers, a host of field organizers out in the locals, no space and a perpetual air of chaos. While the rest of the office looked on in attitudes ranging from delight to horror, we noisily carried on. And we worked like maniacs. Our collective victories and defeats were recorded at the center of the office on a flip chart of campaigns. We all knew the score. And after days, or months, out on some mission or another, we would come home to the organizing department to celebrate, commiserate, and recover.

That's gone now. In the decorous, carpeted halls of SEIU today, it's hard to believe the organizing department was ever in constant motion, with the life of the union centered around it. Today, with 60 full-time national organizers, the organizing department is as large as the entire union staff used to be. But the building that houses several hundred employees is quiet, the third-floor organizing division barely distinguishable from the rest.

Ironically, those orderly offices are occupied by my very talented peers. Now in charge of this organizing department and those of several other progressive unions (the American Federation of State, County and Municipal Employees and the Communications Workers of America, among others), the activists of the sixties and seventies have moved into positions of responsibility. With them have come many of the sensibilities of my generation. The blatant language of sexism is gone, and even men can talk about parental leave without ridicule. People share progressive values, work hard, and care about winning. But underlying it all is an absence of excitement, a malaise that cannot be blamed solely on growing older.

Sandra "Sam" Luciano, a tough, funny, outspoken holdover from the Geagan era notes that some things have improved. "There is real planning and strategy. We target workplaces with real potential and then spend real money on those campaigns. And on the bigger ones, the results are better. But there's not much fun any more, no team," she adds. "I miss that flip chart we used to have. Now if you want to know what's going on, you have to pull up someone else's reports on the computer screen. There's never a time when all the people in this building do anything together anymore. There used to be a time when everyone from the president on, would pitch in on a campaign, so everyone knew it was really important. That never happens anymore. We no longer have a shared history."

Shared history is hard to achieve with high turnover. In the past five years, those 60 organizing positions have been filled by more than 200 people. "It's definitely flatter, but it's also a much bigger organization," says current SEIU organizing director, Andrew Stern, who started out at the same local as I did. The quintessential sixties' activist, Stern moved from rank-and-file agitation to become president of his local, before taking on the national organizing directorship five years ago. "It takes a real talent to have a lot of spirit in a large organization, unless you're really conscious in setting goals and getting people involved," he adds. "It's also hard to keep organizers if they have to travel all the time. Those I do keep are heavily single or divorced, or, in the case of male organizers, in traditional relationships with a wife who takes care of the kids."

Stern and his wife, also a long-time unionist, have just adopted a second child. He is a doting parent, and family pictures are the predominant personal feature of his office. "I don't know what they did before," he sighs. "It was very male and no one was ever home, sort of like Geagan. But when Geagan was dying, he talked a lot about what he'd really missed, and what he enjoyed was being home for little Johnny's soccer game, a very different message from his usual exhortation to 'organize the workers.'"

SEIU, Stern adds, has given him a lot of support. "I believe the institution still believes clearly, and in the most symbolic ways, in organizing, and has allocated resources and taken risks," he says. "But the hardest part of working in a bureaucracy isn't the work, but living in it. It's very far removed from workers, in the sense of being involved in the product."

Not long ago, Luciano claimed Geagan's ratty, old, brown vinyl couch for her office. I made a pilgrimage to see it, and we sat around and told Geagan stories. "The other day a senior staff person said I was just like Geagan," Sam relates. "He meant it as a criticism, but knew I'd take it as a compliment. What he meant is that I just go out and get things done. I do what Geagan taught me, I stay close to the people in the field. With Geagan, we never had political discussions about fomenting revolution, the way we do now, but he brought out the best in all of us, no question. It's a great couch," she adds. "When I got this new office, it looked kind of empty, so I went looking for it. I thought it should be somewhere where it would be appreciated."

The conflict between the organizer and the institution is habitual and is based, at least in part, on the nature of both the work and the people who do it. A major component is the demands of the job, in terms of skill, time, and commitment, all too often coupled with a lack of both financial and psychological recognition. "Organizers who survive have to be self-motivated. Ours are maniacs, who deny a personal life because they see themselves as building something," comments one long-time survivor.

"Most organizers have to have pure dedication and sacrifice," says IAM vice-president and organizing director, Larry Downing. "They're going to get home, at best, 24 weekends a year, and that gets worse when a campaign starts. Once, before my divorce, I come home, and I pull into the driveway. My wife's at the door, and my 10-year-old comes up to the car and tells me to stop and demands to see my driver's license. Well, we go back and forth, and finally I show her my license, and she takes a long look and turns to my wife, 'Yep, Mom, you're right, it's Pop.' I tell you, kids know when you've been gone."

Janover tells a similar story. "I had to make a choice whether to go home for my parents' 40th wedding anniversary or stay for a decertification election," she says. "We were right down to the final days, and it was in my territory. And one of my mentors said to me, 'Look, it's your choice, you just have to figure out how you're going to feel if we lose the election because you were away and didn't get to make those extra house calls, you're going to have to live with that down the road.' So I opted not to go. Well, my father died shortly after that. There was never a 45th. And I live with that instead. It was a wrong choice, and that had something to do with my eventually leaving union work, because when the commitment is so total, we just get things out of perspective."

Beyond the intense commitment, organizing requires a unique blend of personality traits not necessarily compatible with the demands of a bureaucratic organization. "A good organizer has an avid interest in people and their situation," says William Winpisinger, former president of the IAM, whom I interviewed at the end of June 1989, as he packed up boxes of books and papers in his last week before retirement. "He or she needs a willingness to work inordinately long hours day in and day out, you have to love people, and then have the kind of personality that communicates that on a one-on-one and group basis; somebody that has the ability to engender trust, an ability to create a platoon of activists in any given workplace, a recruiter of considerable skill. The rest of it anybody can learn. It's the personality traits that are important."

Or, as Si Kahn, an independent southern organizer who has worked with many unions notes, "Great organizers are gut nonconformists. They're artistic and creative and fundamentally antimanagement. Also headstrong, quirky, and profound outsiders. They don't fit well with suits and ties."

Yet labor is not even discussing, much less building, a culture in which those personalities can easily survive. Not only must union activists want to struggle and win badly enough to give up any semblance of a normal life, they must also endure situations where they have the lowest organizational status and where there are few institutional support systems for their efforts. "Organizers get little recognition," comments an AFL-CIO staffer, "and the training we give is the worst imaginable. We treat them badly, pay them poorly, and deny them a personal life."

In fact, labor frequently deals with its own employees the way inferior management deals with workers, although unionization of union staffs remains highly controversial. As one organizer explains, "Even some of my progressive friends hold that it's some kind of crime for union staff to organize. But we're also workers, and the union itself can be a miserable boss unless there's some corrective to it. I think there's some duty to practice what you preach. If you tell people they have to be willing to take some risks in their own behalf, then you have to be willing to do the same and be an example."

The eccentricity and passion that define most memorable organizers, regardless of job title, are no longer part of the institutional culture, and many organizers ultimately cannot squeeze their vivid personalities into the requisite organizational molds, raising the question of who will remain in the institution to nurture the next generation of activists. "In the old days, the organizer was a half-crazy rebel out there," one organizing director says, "but them days are gone. Them people won't exist any more. You have to be very respectable, and if the organizer cannot fit into this organization at every level, he's the wrong person."

That view has taken hold even at otherwise progressive unions. "Right now in parts of this organization, there's the culture of a backward corporation," says another organizer. "I work for a union that twice in the last six months has hired image consultants for its staff to talk about the length of men's pants and ties, and what knots are more powerful than others, and which combination for a woman makes the most forceful statement, whether you should have a dress, or a dress and jacket, and of course the suit is most forceful, and it's important for women to have stockings darker than their outfits. I thought it was disgusting. For the last speech, we were supposed to get dressed up and show we had internalized all this stuff and I came in jeans and a T-shirt and gave a speech on the evils of conformity. A lot of the staff knew I was right and had been uncomfortable, but none of them took it on; they just sort of shuffled through."

At every level, the demand is to conform, not to a level of commitment and activism, but to a bureaucratic style of organization. "The problem has to do with heaviness," says an AFL-CIO insider. "It impacts on people's individual capacities to be creative when you always have to think first, 'will I be vulnerable if I throw out this idea?' You develop a staff culture of malaise that cramps new-thinking kinds of people, the kind you need to do organizing. It's really a tragedy, the sovietization of the labor movement."

Some of these problems can be attributed to labor's adoption of the rationalist model of management that corporations are now attempting to abandon. Unions are hierarchical, vertical, compartmentalized, and biased *against* action.

"The real problem is it takes so much to organize today, you have to risk so much of the bureaucracy," says the organizing director of a large union. "With so many conflicting interests in the union, it's hard to balance risk and resources, or devote everything you have to one situation. Money isn't enough, you need tremendous commitment and vision. There aren't many Gorbys who have the courage to turn things upside down."

At all levels of union structure, iron rule by the organizational chart seems to have supplanted functional sensibilities. "It used to be that, if our organizing director needed a writer, he'd hire a person in the organizing department," says one union president. "You can't have that flexibility today and survive. It won't work from a management standpoint, it won't work from a budget standpoint, to have people with similar skills being expected to comply with different standards."

But a highly successful organizer in the same union comments, "We used to have people who worked across lines. Our researchers, for example, had to know how to organize. That's not so any more. But even though my staff are all called organizers, I try to hire people with specialties in law, writing or safety, because you'll wait a year if you go through the bureaucracy."

These are exactly the issues that Thomas J. Peters and Robert H. Waterman tackle in *In Search of Excellence*, perhaps the best known of the new business management literature. The values they espouse, risk-taking, flexibility, autonomy, shared values, respect for the individual, are exactly those qualities that have always informed the best union organizing. The absence of those qualities today in most labor organizations often makes it hard for good people to stay in union work.

Peters and Waterman are eloquent on the need to nurture and

protect champions in the business community. "The . . . champion," they assert, "is the zealot or fanatic in the ranks . . . not a typical administrative type . . . but he believes. . . . Champions are pioneers, and pioneers get shot at. The companies that get the most from champions, therefore, are those that have rich support networks. . . . No support systems, no champions. No champions, no innovations."[5]

Labor's organizers and activists are, in many instances, the same kinds of people as the inventors and innovators of the business world, the misfits of the bureaucracy who are, nonetheless, vital to the success of the organization. The special 1989 summer bonus issue of *Business Week*, boldly entitled "Innovation in America," is filled with the *In Search of Excellence* approach to organizational structure and innovation. But one would be hard-pressed to find similar union literature on nurturing organizers or proclaiming "Innovation in the Labor Movement." And the concept of an "excellent union" is likely to evince scorn from both ends of labor's ideological spectrum.

On one side are unions that mimic the worst of bad management and whose desire to change is minimal; on the other are those who believe that the new management theory is merely another corporate effort to avoid unionization. There are many reasons to reject joint labor-management schemes that provide workers the illusion of participation without the power to share equally in key decisionmaking. Unions also differ from corporations in that they are democratic organizations whose leaders must run for office; and their goals are far more complex and less quantifiable than profit. However, given those caveats, it is self-defeating for labor activists to ignore the sound psychological bases underlying new workplace configurations. The result often seems to be that management out-organizes unions for the loyalties of the workers who crave more participation and recognition on the job.

As one ex-organizer, now involved in structuring worker buyouts, puts it, "It's ludicrous to get boxed in to maintaining the old rules of the production line, when the line was an awful system to begin with. I'm not just for worker participation, but for worker ownership. Ownership and workplace democracy feed each other; workplace democracy without ownership limits the workers, and ownership without democracy is the cruelest hoax of all. But whatever happened to the concept that workers should own the means of production?"

Unquestionably, the organizational structures that inhibit innovation, the lack of institutional support or recognition for organizing, the bias for conformity and the sheer arduousness of the lifestyle, all take their toll on activists employed by unions. However, these same impediments are common to any number of work situations, from law firms to universities.

But what seems to finally grind down, and eventually defeat, union organizers and activists are the contradictions. Between espoused democracy and internal repression; between espoused equity and institutional racism and sexism; between a commitment to solidarity and organizing in theory, and an internal culture that vitiates against them in practice.

For those who can limit their vision to the small daily tasks, survival in the labor movement is possible, even rewarding: You can manage to do good organizing, if you don't concern yourself with issues of foreign policy; you can rise in the union hierarchy, if you don't defend your clerical staff; you can edit the union paper, if you don't encourage debate. Some make the compromise. For others the cost is too high. When the divide between the principles and the practice becomes too wide, people, both inside and outside the institution, lose faith. We trade incongruities like baseball cards. And we wait for the one that will finally break our heart.

1985 was the year that almost broke mine. That year, Ray Rogers and Ed Allen, independent organizers who are graduates of the J. P. Stevens campaign, were hired by Local P–9 of the United Food and Commercial Workers Union to help plan and implement a strike and corporate campaign against the Hormel meatpacking plant in Austin, Minnesota. The goal was to fend off the last in a long line of concessions demanded by the company.

While P–9 received a stunning amount of grassroots support and small contributions adding up to several hundred thousand dollars, the UFCW and its International union president, William Wynn, castigated Rogers and, together with the company, broke the strike. For more than a year, trade unionists were exhorted to take sides against each other, rather than against management. Meanwhile, the Hormel workers lost their jobs, their cars, their homes.

Then, at the 1985 AFL-CIO convention, my boss, Asner, about to finish his term as president of the SAG, took the floor to voice his opposition to the AFL-CIO's policies in Central America. "I still believe . . . that support of the Nicaraguan contras is unforgivable . . . and that labor support of brutally repressive regimes is incomprehensible," he told the delegates. "We have shared struggles together, walked picket lines together, broken bread together . . . and our work on behalf of justice, dignity, and empowerment for working people has made me proud. But it does not make me proud to see us bolstering the foreign policies of those whose stated goals include the destruction of our own labor movement, like Orrin Hatch and Ronald Reagan. *I do* know which side I'm on, and it's not theirs!"

During the four years he served as SAG president, Asner had spoken at dozens of union conventions. He had appeared at picket lines and demonstrations coast to coast, contorting his work schedule to meet the growing number of requests unions made for his time. But that devotion meant nothing to the AFL-CIO leadership in the face of his challenge on Central America. He was harshly denounced from the podium by AFL-CIO president, Kirkland.

Afterwards, Rex Hardesty, an old colleague from the AFL-CIO public relations department cornered me in the hall in front of the press room. "I'm glad Asner is quitting," he yelled. "We don't need bums like that in the labor movement. And don't you ever ask any of us to help you again." So whose side was *I* on?

"I don't think foreign policy has anything to do with being an organizer, unless you're organizing in a foreign country" scoffs Richard Bensinger, who heads up the AFL-CIO's Organizing Institute. "It's not an issue, except for people who are preoccupied with it, and they're not labor organizers. If you want to organize, you can't have a different agenda. I don't see that foreign policy has anything to do with going out and organizing workers."

But others disagree. "It's true," says organizer Kahn, "that in the process of organizing workers for the first time, you must pay careful attention to their agenda. But most workers are very much aware of the impact on their jobs of foreign imports and runaway plants, and they want to know, how the union is going to deal with it. The question is, is it business unionism or social change you're after? You can't have the latter if you preserve the old attitudes toward race, women, the environment. It's not about imposing these issues on the workers, but business unionism stifles these questions once they are raised."

Barbara Bordwell, an organizer for the National Education Association notes that her union "sometimes get criticized by members who don't understand why we have a position on Central America, on abortion, on god knows what. But there is a majority that believes there is a connection to organizing and what we produce for workers. If the work is just to get a contract, and you don't have a vision to empower masses and masses of people to change the country, then it will never occur. We'll just have better contracts. If the organizer's vision is too small, the union will be too small."

For all the years that I wrote speeches for Asner, Richard Greenwood wrote speeches for IAM president, Winpisinger. Now in his fifties, Greenwood, self-designated "flack, hack, and labor skate," looks like a caricature of a 1940s' journalist, short and wiry, with a cigarette dangling from the corner of his mouth, drink in hand and, beneath a sardonic public face, the soul of a true believer. "I'm just an old anachronism," he commented recently, contemplating Winpisinger's retirement from the IAM presidency.

"I used to think I was grooved, that I knew what I was doing here, but," he waves his hand toward the window and the AFL-CIO building on 16th Street in Washington, "as long as those people insist on a foreign policy that does more harm than good, hell, I think I'm still in the right church, but I seem to be in the wrong pew. And I'm just too tired to fight it any more. They want so badly to belong," he laughs. "They just don't want to face up to the fact that they're outcasts in this society, and that they should be proud of that role, not trying to fit in. And that makes us the outcasts among the outcasts." It takes a moment for the next laugh to come.

Meany and current AFL-CIO president, Kirkland, may have inherited labor's house but they have failed to win its soul. That belongs, as it always has, to the descendants of Debs. Even in recent years, when unions have failed to galvanize workers, the culture built by labor's rebels, the ideals, the legends, the songs, "Solidarity Forever," has the power to touch the American spirit. Hence, a film like "Norma Rae" could capture an Academy Award and a wide popular following. Its heroes were not bureaucrats, but a rank-and-file activist and an organizer.

"All the women who got involved in organizing campaigns would eventually refer to themselves as Norma Rae," Janover laughs. "And they'd do it with such pride. When I went to see the film, I thought, 'this is hokey, this isn't real.' But then I saw what an inspiration it was and how people share that desire to make a life that's better, to be proud of themselves, the work they do, and the other people who work with them."

In 1983, the AFL-CIO established a select Committee on the Evolution of Work to deal with the issues of effectively unionizing a changing workforce. Since then, it has published two reports. However, their suggestions are stolidly in the realm of the technical, not of the spirit. The committee has recommended better selection of organizing targets, an associate member program for individual workers who are not covered by a union contract, and more effective public relations. They instituted the fancy "Union, Yes" media campaign featuring Hollywood stars and credit cards for members. During the summer of 1989, they added the organizing institute that Bensinger heads, to help affiliates recruit and train new organizers, analyze strategies, and critique campaigns. All good ideas, all worth trying.

But without a sense of mission reinforced by leadership example and shared throughout the ranks, there is no capacity to inspire people to risk what little they have for some larger idea. And no amount of technological sophistication, no slick advertising campaigns, no credit cards will compensate for the absence of that culture.

We need a culture, a community in which we can grow and thrive. The farm workers were able to sustain a cadre of underpaid, overworked organizers for so long (as was Geagan at SEIU), because they built a family, a community, a culture of shared values. I often think the best thing the AFL-CIO could do for the future of organizing in New York is buy an apartment building to house its organizers, complete with communal areas and a day-care center. In a hostile and cynical world, we need each other to endure.

"People blame every goddamn thing for their organizing failures," says the Machinists' Larry Downing, "but the National Labor Relations Board isn't to blame, nor the Administration, and nothing makes me more disgusted than hearing that. I'm not saying the situation couldn't stand improvement, but those are just excuses. People only vote against the union out of uneducation. You have to educate and train, and no one comes to the union without personal contact. You've got to knock on their door. If you'd tell me I was going into servicing, I'd ask you when I could start organizing. Hell, anyone can service, but organizing . . . I could talk to you all day, because it's my life."

For Janover, the high point of her union work was the five-year campaign by the Hotel and Restaurant Employees to organize the clerical workers at Yale, which she terms an ideal union experience. "I remember this one woman who had been at Yale for 40 years. She was secretary to a dean, tall and thin, a bit like Olive Oyl. She was the sort who made the coffee, took her boss's clothes to the cleaners, stayed at the office until midnight to get the dean's call from California. After the first meeting, she comes up and says, 'Oh, I enjoyed that so much, do you mind if I come again?' And she kept coming to meetings and started getting active. One day, just before the strike, I'm walking along and she rushes up to me, just so excited, she's practically shaking from happiness.

"'Oh, I just did something, I just have to tell you,' she said. 'The dean just asked me to pickup his cleaning and, you know what I told him? I told him no. He'd have to get it himself.' This wonderful woman is now a steward. To me, that's history, that's the stuff of books. The stuff that blows you away. That's the reason you do it."

Janover recently decided to teach school in New York City, rather than return to the labor movement. "I don't know exactly why," she explains. "I'm just not ready to come back. Good team situations like Yale are very rare in the labor movement. And I wanted to be where I could use my talents and grow. For me to work in the labor movement again, I'd have to be in a situation that has a vision of the union beyond the basics of a contract, looking to involve people in their communities, politics and the arts, as whole individuals. I know that if the unorganized workforce thought that's what unions would be, there's no question they'd organize. And when they meet organizers and staff that share that vision, they want to be part of it. Who doesn't want to be part of something that's vital and growing and positive and exciting and a force for change?"

Good organizers, Kahn maintains, "have rage at the core, rage at injustice, but at the same time, are guided by great feelings of love. I think organizers can survive living in motels, the hours, the demands, so long as they have a chance to feel they are changing history. They cannot survive when they feel they no longer make a difference, when they are no longer redressing injustice. We need to make sure they're doing that, and then let them know they are heirs of a proud tradition. People who struggle for justice are the prophets of our time. It's that kind of call."

"When I started," says NEA organizer Bordwell, "I was fascinated with this vision of educated people in every single community being organized, becoming politically aware, and becoming empowered in their own right, about how powerful that could be as a force for social change in this country. And the organization itself in the 1970s when bargaining for public employees was first legalized, was a very exciting place to work. I could see very conservative people, very anti-union, transformed right before my very eyes. I'm still here because somewhere in me, I still have that vision."

Like Bordwell, I stay because somewhere in me, the vision will not die. I struggle to build the community that will sustain me. I live for those magic moments when I recognize that the work we do has the power to transform peoples' understandings and change their lives.

The office next to mine at District 65, UAW, belongs to Julie Kushner, vice president for the clerical and professional division, my friend and fellow survivor. She hardly has an evening to herself. Ever. The divorced mother of two young children, whose crayoned masterworks adorn her office walls, her life is a constant juggling of out-of-town travel, evening meetings, and child care. I've seen her negotiate all night long and come in the next morning, exhausted but still fighting.

Kushner is still passionate about the labor movement, although that's sometimes a political liability within the organization, as though strong feelings were somehow inappropriate. I've never seen her as discouraged by management, as she is by the underappreciation and non-support occasionally displayed by fellow union officers. More and more often, she wonders whether she has the stamina to ward off emotional fatigue.

A few weeks after the 1989 Labor Day parade, Kushner helped coordinate a caravan of 40 New York union staffers on a solidarity visit to the striking Pittston miners in Russell County, Virginia. The visit, which started out as a plan to participate in civil disobedience, was transformed when 100 United Mine Workers of America strikers seized one of the Pittston processing plants, the first plant take-over in the United States in 50 years.

"The plant had already been taken over when I arrived on Monday," Kushner told me. "It was night, eerie and foggy. But there were 200 supporters at the plant, and the atmosphere was charged. The plant's a huge, grey, enormous concrete structure, maybe six stories high, with chutes coming out the sides. The guys who had occupied the plant were on a balcony about four stories up. When I was allowed inside the plant, there was water dripping and coal dust everywhere, but it was so important to let them know how much we appreciated their courage, to make that contact.

"On Tuesday, the UMWA was ordered into court, and the judge ruled that unless they were out of the plant by Wednesday at 3 p.m., they would attach the union's strike fund and arrest everyone. They were planning to send in the National Guard. By then, the crowd of supporters had swelled, with contingents of miners arriving from Indiana, Kentucky, Illinois, and Indiana. It was so exciting. And by Wednesday we were all ready to take them on, anxious to defend the workers in the plant, even against the National Guard. There were close to 4,000 of us by then, so many of us we had no fear, it seemed so natural to be there. Here was a union saying no to the laws which have found all sorts of ways to restrict us.

"The union didn't leave the plant in the afternoon. It planned a rally at the plant instead. It was already getting dark when the music started. Joyful. A celebration of our power, like a victory. And then the strikers inside the plant came out on the balcony in formation, carrying an American flag. And chants rang back and forth between them and us. 'We are. Union.' 'Solidarity. Forever.' And they somehow managed to spell the letters UMWA against the wall of the plant with their flashlights, and the chants kept on, deep voices, real loud, echoing. And then the men came out of the plant and evaporated into the crowd.

"Nothing like this had every happened to me in 12 years in the labor movement," Kushner relates. "This was not a picket, but a real challenge to authority. It was like history repeated, at the same time as we were making it. We so rarely have the opportunity. And even though our contingent was only a small group, they showed us such warmth, welcomed us into the struggle, not just their struggle, but ours. When I came back to New York on Friday, I had to go to an arbitration, and I thought how mundane it was. But if you think deeply about the experience we had, it spurs you to think more creatively. You internalize it and take it with you to the next struggle. And the alliances you build are deep, people are aware, and it will not be forgotten."

"Deep in the cradle of organized labor," Alinsky wrote, "America's radicals restlessly toss in their sleep—but they sleep. There they continue to dream of labor and the world of the future . . . In spite of the parallel course of organized business and organized labor, the fault with the American radical is not that he has chosen to make his bed in the labor movement but that he is *asleep* in it."[6]

The labor movement is like the lover you can neither marry nor leave, the parent to whom you cannot be reconciled. Part prayer, part promise. A vision in the synapses of bureaucratic days. And those of us who hold it cannot sleep.

Notes

1. A version of this article appeared in *The American Prospect*, no. 2 (Summer 1990): 93–105.

2. Kim Fellner was executive director of the National Writers Union from 1986 to 1990.

3. Richard L. Berke, "Unionists Fly Eastern While Fighting Airline Chief," *The New York Times*, 23 February 1989, p. 16.

4. Saul Alinsky, *Reveille for Radicals* (Chicago: University of Chicago Press, 1946), 73.

5. Thomas J. Peters and Robert H. Waterman, *In Search of Excellence: Lessons From America's Best Run Companies* (New York: Harper & Row, 1982), 208, 211.

6. Alinsky, 32, 57.

Editors' Suggested Readings

Alinsky, Saul. *Reveille for Radicals*. Chicago: University of Chicago Press, 1946.

———. *Rules for Radicals*. New York: Random House, 1971.

Cantor, Daniel and Juliet Schor. *Tunnel Vision: Labor, the World Economy, and Central America*. Boston, MA: South End Press, 1987.

AFL-CIO. *The Changing Situation of Workers and Their Unions*. Washington, D.C.: AFL-CIO Committee on the Evolution of Work, 1985.

Bureau of National Affairs. *Unions Today: New Tactics to Tackle Tough Times*. Washington, D.C.: Bureau of National Affairs, Inc., 1985.

Davis, Mike. *Prisoners of the American Dream*. New York: Verso, 1986.

Hall, Burton H. *Autocracy and Insurgency in Organized Labor*. New Brunswick, New Jersey: Transaction Books, 1972.

Horwitt, Stanford D. *Let Them Call Me Rebel: Saul Alinsky, His Life and Legacy*. New York: Knopf, 1989.

Jenkins, J. Craig. *The Politics of Insurgency: The Farm Worker Movement in the 1960s*. New York: Columbia University Press, 1985.

Lens, Sidney. *The Crisis of American Labor*. New York: A. S. Barnes, 1961.

242 Kim Fellner

Lester, Richard A. *As Unions Mature.* New Jersey: Princeton University Press, 1958.

Matthiessen, Peter. *Sal Si Puedes.* New York: Random House, 1971.

Moody, Kim. *An Injury to All.* New York: Verso, 1988.

Peters, Thomas J. and Robert H. Waterman. *In Search of Excellence: Lessons From America's Best Run Companies.* New York: Harper & Row, 1982.

Rayback, Joseph G. *A History of American Labor.* New York: Macmillan, 1966.

Ziegler, Robert H. *American Workers, American Unions, 1920–1985.* Maryland: John Hopkins University Press, 1986.

International Labor Solidarity:
The Campaign for Justice for Moses Mayekiso

Don Stillman*

I. Introduction: The Summer of '89

For the South African security forces assigned to monitor the comings and goings of Moses Mayekiso, trade unionist and anti-apartheid activist, the summer of 1989 seemed to last forever.

As co-chair of the newly formed Mass Democratic Movement (MDM), Mayekiso could be found in townships, factories, and cities from Johannesburg to Port Elizabeth urging massive defiance to protest the general election in September that excluded blacks from any role in choosing the country's leadership.

As general secretary of one of the largest black trade unions in South Africa, the National Union of Metalworkers of South Africa (NUMSA), he called out thousands of autoworkers at Toyota, Nissan, Samcor, and other companies who struck successfully in July and August for wage and benefit increases.

As chair of the Alexandra Action Committee (AAC), he returned to the squalor of the black township in which he lives and reactivated community organizing efforts with a cleanup campaign involving more than 3,000 residents who had boycotted a similar effort organized by authorities two weeks earlier.

As an anti-apartheid leader, he barnstormed the U.S., Britain, Scandinavia, West Germany, and Australia speaking out at gatherings ranging from the United Auto Workers (UAW) convention to the Commonwealth Council on the need for the apartheid gov-

*I wish to acknowledge a number of individuals who were of great help, in one way or another, in the preparation of this paper. Among them are: Glenn Adler, Steve Beckman, John Bell, Halton Cheadle, John Christensen, John Duray, Beverly Jones, Denis MacShane, Norman Manoim, Kate Pfordresher, Judy Scott, and Pat Walsh. Any conclusions and errors of fact or judgment are those of the author alone.

243

ernment to free political prisoners, end the State of Emergency and begin negotiations that would lead to a democratic South Africa.

Such activities resulted in a middle-of-the-night police raid on his home in Alexandra, the arrests of two brothers and two colleagues, and several weeks of waiting in London and Stockholm in September before Mayekiso's attorneys were given assurances he would not be arrested upon his return to Johannesburg. That harassment came at the same time the newly elected government of F. W. de Klerk was proclaiming its own version of a kinder, gentler nation by allowing some previously outlawed protest marches to occur.

What is extraordinary is not the breadth and depth of Moses Mayekiso's many roles in the black struggle in South Africa—because the cauldron of hate that is apartheid has turned out a number of courageous and brilliant leaders. Rather, it is that he was out on the street, free to fight on behalf of his union, his township, and his people. A year earlier, languishing in the filth of his jail cell in a Johannesburg prison, few including Mayekiso himself thought his future held much other than many years or a lifetime behind the bars of apartheid's jails.

That Moses Mayekiso is a free man today is a tribute to many factors: his own courage and that of his family, the support of his trade union brothers and sisters in NUMSA and the Congress of South African Trade Unions (COSATU), the residents of Alexandra (the township where he lived), his attorneys and advocates, and many others on the front-line of his country's struggle.

But when asked, Mayekiso himself singles out an additional element as the key to winning his freedom: the international campaign of labor solidarity waged by unionists in many countries on his behalf. This paper is an attempt to look at that solidarity campaign, particularly the actions waged by unions here in the U.S., to see which components worked and which did not, with the hope future efforts could benefit from what has been learned.

When the Center for Labor-Management Policy Studies selected my proposal to examine the solidarity campaign on behalf of Moses Mayekiso, the outcome of his trial on treason, subversion, and sedition was very much in doubt. Most of those following the trial closely believed it would end with convictions and prison sentences; the debate tended not to be over the verdict, but rather on how long a jail term Mayekiso and his four co-accused would have to serve.

The Mayekiso case was an important one for a number of key reasons, among them:

-his imprisonment, indictment, and trial represented a direct attack on the black trade union movement; he was the highest-ranking labor leader to be tried for treason in many years, with the clear intent to have a chilling effect on other unionists;

-he had taken the organizing skills and democratic structures of the union movement and applied them in an effort to improve the conditions of the 100,000 residents of Alexandra township where he lived; in doing so, he linked the challenge of union activism with community activism with the result being that union-community solidarity was on trial;

-he and his four colleagues were the defendants, but also on trial were the full array of tactics of the anti-apartheid struggle, ranging from rent and consumer boycotts to township organizing and political demonstrations; and

-his case ultimately was one around which developed the largest union-initiated solidarity campaign in South Africa in many years, if not ever.

South African unionists and anti-apartheid leaders rallied around the Mayekiso trial in part because of fears that guilty verdicts would have meant that any act of non-violent political opposition could have been potentially considered treasonous. Because the activities of Mayekiso and his co-accused fit the pattern of political struggle used by many other unionists and community activists fighting the apartheid system, a conviction could have opened the door for the jailing of many other people.

The Mayekiso trial emerged from the shadows of other high-profile prosecutions of anti-apartheid activists—members of the United Democratic Front (UDF) and others—because the outcome would serve to define the line in South Africa between acceptable political dissent and criminal activity in the eyes of the apartheid government. If non-violent opposition is treason, where would that leave South Africa's black majority, which is denied the right to participate in the political and legislative process?

For all those who care about lofty ideals, such as justice and freedom and unionism and solidarity, the campaign on behalf of Moses Mayekiso provided an opportunity to take concrete actions. The repression was real, the stakes were high, the need for outside help was pressing. In the end, unusual in such circumstances, a major victory was won.

Our task must be to learn from this experience, because today there are many other workers and unionists facing repression from governments and employers throughout the world. As we mobilize on their behalf, we also recognize that international solidarity is a commodity which American trade unionists will increasingly seek as the world economy becomes more and more internationalized.

1. June 1986: Flying Home to Arrest

The flight from Stockholm to Johannesburg takes 14 hours, providing Moses Mayekiso with plenty of time to reflect on the weeks he had just spent talking with unionists in Great Britain and Sweden about the struggle of workers in the factories and black townships of South Africa.

In small meetings with shop stewards and large, more boisterous rallies of anti-apartheid activists, Mayekiso described a country in which a white minority government dictated where blacks could live and work, where blacks have no political rights, where blacks who resist the virtual domination of their lives by whites are jailed or banned, and where repression of basic freedoms is a rule, rather than an exception.

He talked, too, about the efforts of the emerging black trade unions to win a voice in the workplace, where blacks were stuck in the lowest paying jobs with limited rights and benefits compared to their white counterparts. As general secretary of the Metal and Allied Workers Union (MAWU), an aggressive and independent black union in the metalworking sector, it was a subject he knew well.

And he told of his own efforts to apply the skills and techniques of organizing learned in the union movement to the struggles for a better life in the black townships, particularly Alexandra where he lived with his wife and seven children. In the face of government and employer resistance, black workers employed tactics that had yielded gains in the workplace and Mayekiso believed the lessons of those experiences could be adapted to attack the squalor of the townships as well.

As the DC-10 made its way south over Africa, Mayekiso reflected on the events that had occurred while he was out of the country. In particular, he focused on the new State of Emergency that had been declared by the apartheid government some two weeks earlier, on June 12, 1986. Massive unrest in black townships and a nationwide "stayaway," a general strike by black workers, had led South African president, P.W. Botha, to proclaim a State of Emergency which gives the government the cloak of law to take actions that would otherwise be illegal even under the apartheid statutes.

It was a further tightening of what seemed to be a permanent condition in which the government contended that it faced an ongoing "emergency" because of black unrest which could not be coped with under the "ordinary" laws of the state. Among the broader powers provided were the ability to make an arbitrary arrest and hold a detainee without charging him or her with an offense or conducting a trial in a court of law. Police and security forces had the right to enter, search, and seize property without warrants and had broad indemnity for their actions, unless they could be shown to have acted maliciously—an almost impossible requirement to prove in a South African court.

Mayekiso believed the extreme measures of the Botha government had been imposed because it saw clearly the relationship between black protest in the workplace and in the townships. Each separately posed a threat to the minority government and the comfortable lives led by many white South Africans, but together they meant insurrection.

Although there are far fewer whites than blacks in South Africa, whites have far more guns and tanks, and they control the jails. What's more, they have the will to use them, early and often, and use them they did in June of 1986. Thousands of blacks from Transvaal to the Cape, from Natal to the Orange Free State were detained. Church and community activists, workers, and union leaders, children and the elderly packed apartheid's jails.

It was a massive exercise in repression. Many of the detentions seemed to make little sense. In some cases, rank-and-file workers were picked up and held despite not having played any role in strikes or union actions, while some top union leaders remained free. The same was true of church leaders and community activists, yet enough of the key figures in the opposition movement were jailed to have an intimidating result.

As the long flight from Stockholm ended for Moses Mayekiso on June 28, 1986, he looked forward to seeing his wife, Kola, and his children, and to getting back to see what could be done to free jailed members of his union and his township. He knew his leadership was needed now, more than ever.

So did the South African police force, which was at Jan Smuts Airport to meet Mayekiso as he left the plane. He was arrested and placed in solitary confinement at John Vorster Square prison without charge or access to attorneys and family. Jail was not a new experience for Mayekiso, who had been detained twice earlier. But this time would prove to be different. This time, he would face the possibility of death by the hangman's noose.

2. *From Autoworker to MAWU General Secretary*

Moses Mayekiso began to make a name for himself in 1977 as a shop steward at a Toyota warehouse near Alexandra. Quiet yet tough, his fellow workers elected him secretary of the shop stewards' committee of MAWU.

MAWU members struggled for recognition at Toyota, which resisted the union's efforts. Mayekiso's organizing approach centered on a steady, meticulous set of contacts from the bottom up. He conducted general meetings of rank-and-file members weekly or even more frequently with emphasis on the importance of members controlling decisions and leaders obeying the wishes of the workers they represented.

By 1979, Toyota management had had enough of Mayekiso's innovative tactics and fired him. He worked as a voluntary organizer for MAWU until he was named to organize in Wadeville, a large factory area on the Witwatersrand, the industrial heartland of the country which includes Johannesburg. The union then had members in only one Wadeville plant.

He held meetings in the hostels in the black township of Katlehong where he could reach workers from many different factories at once. A number of them joined MAWU, but membership soared after Moses faced down the police who tried to disperse one of the meetings. He continued on, touting the need for a democratic structure with which to counter the power of the employers, while taking breaks for negotiations with the police.

Mayekiso's effectiveness came in part from his own early days during which he faced poverty and limits much like those of the workers he sought to organize. Born in Cala in the Transkei, he could not finish school because of the financial problems suffered by his father, a migrant laborer in Cape Town, nearly 1,000 miles away. The oldest of seven children, Moses initially worked in the mines to help support the family. Like most other rural workers, he had few options other than the mines because he did not possess the travel documents needed to leave the Transkei and seek work in the urban factories.

In 1973, hating the miners' working conditions, he went to the Johannesburg area and settled in Alexandra. Initially, both his residence and employment were illegal, because he had not registered in terms of the influx control laws. Eventually, an employer registered him and he was able to live and work there legally.

Mayekiso's success in the Wadeville organizing campaign won him the respect of many black unionists who were helping to build unions that made up the Federation of South African Trade Unions (FOSATU), a forerunner of what is today called the Congress of South African Trade Unions (COSATU).

"Moses had phenomenal ability to persuade workers and great personal bravery," recalls Bernie Fanaroff, an official of the metalworkers' union who knows Mayekiso well. "He avoided rabble-rousing tactics. He always explained things to workers and made sure they understood. He does not believe in promising things which he cannot deliver, or in 'triumphalism'—unrealistic optimism."

Fanaroff cites an example, a walkout of about 2,000 workers at McKechnie Brothers in Wadeville. A personnel officer had just addressed the strikers and the mood was tense as Mayekiso sought to convince them they could best achieve their goals by joining MAWU. A pro-company clerk grabbed the floor and suggested that Mayekiso must be a spy, since no one knew him. Moses slipped back into the crowd until the clerk departed, recaptured the strikers' attention and then led the entire group across Wadeville on a march to the MAWU office where they joined the union.

During this period, Mayekiso helped to lead an action that presaged the community activism he would later pursue in Alexandra. At his urging, the shop stewards' council took up a campaign to stop the authorities from bulldozing squatters' shacks in the township of Katelia. The rallying of township residents and pressuring employers and local officials paid off. The bulldozing stopped. It was one of the earliest "interventions" of black unionists, themselves focused on strengthening their base in the workplace following adoption of new labor laws, in community resistance.

Mayekiso's effectiveness in confronting managers accustomed to exploiting the black workforce with impunity propelled him into the top leadership of MAWU. He helped lead a major "stayaway" strike in 1984 that resulted in his arrest and solitary confinement at John Vorster Square prison until charges against him were dropped when his co-accused fled the country.

In late 1985, he helped draft the constitution of COSATU, to

which most of the progressive unions affiliated. COSATU's formation consolidated much of the progress made by the "emerging"
independent unions and began a process of unifying those unions
into a single entity per industry in many cases.

At this same time, conditions in Moses' own township continued to deteriorate and government authorities planned to destroy
the homes of Alexandra residents and forcibly move them further
away from nearby Johannesburg. Earlier discussions with
MAWU's shop stewards' council in Johannesburg had led to the
idea of attempting to build a community organization based on
trade union principles.

The activities of that organization, the Alexandra Action Committee, led to Mayekiso's indictment on treason, subversion, and
sedition charges by the apartheid government.

3. From the Golden City to the Dark City

> Alexandra is one of the oldest townships in South Africa. It is
> closely related to Johannesburg. From the centre of the Golden
> City to the centre of the Dark City is a mere nine miles. Where
> one starts the other ends and, where one ends, the other begins.
> The difference between the two is like day and night. Everything
> that says anything about the progress of man, the distance which
> man has made in terms of technology, efficiency, and comfort: the
> Golden City says it well; the Dark City, by contrast, is dirty and
> deathly. The Golden City belongs to the white people of South
> Africa, and the Dark City to the black people. The Saturdays and
> Sundays of Alexandra roar, groan, and rumble, like a troubled
> stomach. The same days in Johannesburg are as silent as the
> stomach of a dead person. The weekdays of Alexandra are those of
> a place which has been erased; in Johannesburg, weekdays are
> like a time when thousands of people arrive in the place at the
> end of their pilgrimage. Nothing is still, the streets buzz.[1]

The overpowering stench remains in one's memory longer than
anything else after a visit to Alexandra township, which is almost
completely surrounded by the affluent white suburbs of Johannesburg. No water-borne sewage disposal system existed for its
100,000 residents, so waste was removed in buckets.

In the absence of storm drains, open ditches following the terrain carried the run-off water and its dumped contents down and
eastward to the Jukskei River. The only potable water consisted of
stand pipes with one tap for every four to six dwellings. Because no

refuse disposal system existed, garbage piled up with putrefying effect along the untarred roads of the township. Young children played in the trash and waded in the repellent run-off waters.

Many residents lived in corrugated sheetmetal shacks or shanties made of cardboard and plastic sheeting. A few lived inside the shells of old buses long ago abandoned. Those fortunate enough to have real concrete-block houses often lived with other families in hopelessly overcrowded conditions. Often, in a yard intended for a single-family house, up to 15 families occupied the space in rooms, outbuildings, and squatter shacks. Much of the housing was old and in disrepair. As the judge in the Mayekiso treason trial was to note with some understatement in his final verdict, "the physical features and lack of amenities were only too apparent to me when, with counsel, I drove through Alexandra during the course of the trial."

A great many of those living in Alexandra were unemployed. Joblessness and overcrowding combined with the absence of any effective crime control and judicial system result in serious crime problems throughout the township.

From its founding in the early 1900s until 1958, Alexandra was not directly controlled by any municipality. As a result, there was no funding for municipal services and township infrastructure, while at the same time, the absence of governmental control caused an influx of blacks who could not live elsewhere under South Africa's laws.

By 1963, the government decided that Alex, as it is popularly known, would become a hostel township in which single workers would be housed to be near the factories, mines, and shops in the area. Some relocation occurred, but opposition to the "death sentence" given to family life slowed it down and by the mid-70s, the plan was scrapped.

The grievances of Alex residents seethed on, as they did in other black townships, and finally erupted in the aftermath of the Soweto uprising in June 1976. Blacks burned stores and set fire to buses belonging to the Public Utility Corporation. Alexandra High School was torched, as were other schools throughout the country, because it was a symbol of the hated "Bantu Education" system. The actions yielded a wave of repression by the government and hundreds of deaths.

By 1980, a new "master plan" for Alex was announced, with redevelopment to lead to what one government official described as a "Little Switzerland." Residents had hopes that the plan would result in improvements in housing and living conditions, but five years later only about 10% of the redevelopment had occurred.

During this same period, the South African government sought to cope with unrest and an economic recession by essentially abandoning direct responsibility for the townships. Alexandra was established as a black local authority, with an elected town council. Lacking an industrial tax base, that council turned to the residents for income, which came mainly from rent on the shacks and houses there.

Sharp increases in rent and service charges, the failure of the redevelopment plan, the worsening of sanitation conditions, the prolonged lack of job opportunities, and the increased incidence of crime all made Alexandra a tinderbox by 1986.

Lacking popular support and under attack from township residents, the members of the Alexandra town council, like those of many other black townships, eventually resigned. The collapse of administrative structures at a time of growing unrest led to a predictable response: the Botha government sent massive numbers of police and troops into the townships, including Alexandra. Confronted with this crisis, Alexandra residents turned to a trade union leader who lived on 7th Avenue. His name was Moses Mayekiso.

4. From the 'Six Day War' To the Alexandra Boycotts

The anger and despair felt by blacks in Alexandra ignited in February 1986, when a security guard at the Jazz Stores in nearby Wynburg shot and killed Michael Diradeng, a youth leader and former member of the students' representative council at Alexandra High School.

Because the Botha government prohibited political demonstrations by blacks, funerals played a dual role in South Africa of commemorating the dead and protesting the repression under apartheid. About 13,000 residents of Alex gathered at the township stadium to pay tribute to Diradeng and to express outrage at the cause of his death. Mayekiso served as "master of ceremonies" at the request of the dead student's family and friends.

The funeral itself occurred without interruption by South African police and defense forces, but as mourners walked from the graveyard to the Diradeng home, tear gas canisters were fired into the crowd. People ran in all directions to escape as the confrontation escalated. Mayekiso looked on as troops shot down unarmed mourners.

Youths barricaded streets with burning tires until finally the troops pulled back. Left behind was the body of 14-year-old Mono Lucy Ledwaba, a student at Minerva High School, shot while standing at the gate of her home.

The next day, as clouds of thick smoke from the burning rubber hung over Alex, angry residents attacked homes and businesses owned by blacks who had served on the town council as well as those of local police. They were seen as collaborators—agents of apartheid.

The "Six Day War" had begun. When the violence finally abated, at least 19 people were dead, and 30 or more wounded.

In the midst of the "Six Day War," a group of Alex residents, which had been meeting since January to talk about the township's problems, chose Mayekiso to lead what was to be called the AAC. The AAC's acting executive committee would coordinate "all activities and problems in the township, such as education, unemployment, welfare, cultural unity, comradeship, and solidarity-political and social."

It was to represent the views of the residents to the authorities and other "outside bodies." Part of the AAC's role was to heighten residents' understanding of their problems and ways to solve them. One element of that process was to educate people about the "bad way of apartheid and the way people can stop this apartheid."

Mayekiso's wife, Kola, had been in Queenstown in the Cape Province over the Christmas holidays and urged the AAC to adopt a system of street committees, which had helped residents of the township in Queenstown cope with crime and problems similar to those of Alex. Moses, whose trade union work was based on a system of accountability starting with mass meetings of workers up through shop stewards' councils and finally to the union executive committee, liked the idea.

The AAC adopted a system of yard, block, and street committees as the ideal method of organizing the community. The residents of a yard appointed someone to liaise with the block committee, which in turn chose a representative to the street committee. The street committee reported to the executive committee. Decisions were not to be taken without thorough and lengthy discussion and consensus building from the yard committees on up.

The first order of business for the AAC was an effort to get the South African Council of Churches and other prominent religious figures to intervene to stop the violence of the "Six Day War." The Right Reverend Desmond Tutu, then Anglican Bishop of Johannesburg, and others addressed a meeting of about 40,000 Alex residents at the soccer stadium.

Tutu appealed to the crowd not to confront the police and asked that workers return to their jobs. He promised to take their demands to high government authorities. The tensions diffused somewhat and the crowd dispersed peacefully.

A mass funeral for 17 of the dead followed on March 5 with about 60,000 mourners attending, including representatives from foreign embassies of the U.S., Great Britain and other countries. Coffins were draped in the banned African National Congress' (ANC) black, green, and gold colors and the victims were laid to rest.

Mayekiso had been arrested on February 18 under the regulations of the State of Emergency that allowed detention without charge. Jailed until March 7, he missed the mass funeral on March 5. (In the treason trial that followed nearly 18 months later, Mayekiso was cited for rousing mourners in a speech at the funeral; an act that did not occur because he remained in detention until two days later.)

The AAC continued to hold meetings of Alex residents in the weeks that followed. Discussions focused on removing police and South African defense force patrols from the township, as well as more basic problems such as the inadequate sewage and rubbish disposal, poor housing, rampant crime, and lack of electricity.

On April 19, a consumer boycott of local businesses, particularly those owned by town councilors and policemen, and by whites, began. Called by the Alexandra Consumer Boycott Committee, the residents demanded:

1. Troops should be withdrawn from the township;

2. The missing corpses of those killed in earlier confrontations should be returned;

3. All political prisoners should be released;

4. All political organizations should be unbanned;

5. Better housing and adequate electricity should be installed in the township;

6. All members of the Alexandra Town Council should resign; and

7. Rents should be lowered to a level everyone could afford.

Three days later, on the evening of April 22, large groups of armed men entered Alex and attacked the homes of activists, burning some to the ground and destroying cars and other property. Dressed in powder blue shirts and blue trousers, typical clothing worn by members of the South African police, the vigilantes moved ahead of the heavily armored police vehicles called "casspirs."

The police did not intervene as the rampage continued. Many Alex residents were beaten. Some were shot. At least three died from the attacks.

Upon returning home from a shop stewards' meeting, Mayekiso found an unexploded gasoline bomb had been thrown through his window. Neighbors told him that "suspicious" people had come to his house earlier, asking about his whereabouts. From that evening on, he and his wife no longer slept at home for fear of their lives.

South African police invited reporters into Alex the next day and told them the vigilante attacks occurred because the collapse of authority and governance in the township had led to anarchy. They cited alleged "cruel acts" inflicted by so-called people's courts.

In response, Mayekiso called a press conference to deal with the charges and to draw attention to the role of the police in the vigilante attacks. With the town council having resigned, he received numerous questions about whether or not the AAC was in de facto control of the township. Needing to project legitimacy and to protect the group's political leadership role, Mayekiso refused to deny that the group was in control of Alex.

Mayekiso and the AAC also faced pressures from angry young people in the township, especially the young "comrades" who had seen a number of their own killed by the troops and who talked openly about the need to make Alex "ungovernable." The AAC shunned this approach because of the anarchy it implied and instead continued to pursue its bottom-up organizing. It emphasized its role as a negotiating force on behalf of Alex residents, rather than taking on functions of government directly.

In the weeks that followed, Mayekiso and his fellow AAC leaders met with the administrator appointed to oversee Alex in the aftermath of the collapse of the town council structure. They also met with officials of neighboring white communities. Mayekiso repeatedly stressed the AAC's desire to restore "normalcy" by having troops withdraw and restoring and upgrading the minimal services in the township.

After those sessions, Moses left for meetings with unionists and anti-apartheid activists in Europe. Knowing the importance of international pressure, he wanted to describe firsthand what had been occurring in the townships and workplaces and enlist the support of those who heard his message. Those days were his last as a free man for nearly two-and-a-half years.

5. *From the Indictment to the Verdict*

When Mayekiso learned he was being held under Section 29 of the Internal Security Act, rather than under the State of Emergency regulations, he knew his arrest was more serious than those he had experienced earlier. The use of Section 29, which gave police powers of indefinite detention, implied the State was preparing major charges against him.

Under Section 29, he sat in solitary confinement for months without access to his attorneys. Nor could he receive visitors, not even Kola or his children. The food was almost inedible. The only book allowed him was the Bible.

More than six months later, on January 26, 1987, Moses appeared in court for the first time. Joining him were his brother, Mzwanele, and three other activists he had worked with in the Alexandra Action Committee: Obed Bapela, Paul Tshabalala, and Richard Mdakane. A prosecutor informed the judge that the five were to be charged with sedition and subversion, but the indictment was not then ready.

The five co-accused were denied bail. Under South African law, the attorney general can prevent a judge from hearing an application for bail if the attorney general believes release on bail would prejudice the safety of the State. The prosecution thus can ensure that defendants, particularly in political trials, remain imprisoned throughout what usually are very lengthy trials. The judge hearing the case may believe bail is justified, but only if the attorney general assents can the judge even hear the bail application.

More bad news came on April 15, 1987, when the indictment was handed down. In addition to alternative counts of sedition and subversion, the State charged Mayekiso and the four others with a main count of treason.

Treason in South Africa is a capital offense for which death by hanging can be imposed if a conviction occurs. With someone hanged approximately every three days in that country, no one doubted the intent or severity of the apartheid government's charges against the Alexandra Five.

The 160-page indictment charged them with an unlawful and "hostile intent to coerce and/or overthrow and/or usurp and/or to endanger the authority of the State" by conspiring to "seize control of the residential area of Alexandra and/or to render the area ungovernable by the State."

The "so-called organs of people's power" and the "so-called popular organizational structures" of the AAC formed the basis of the charges. The State alleged that the five co-accused campaigned against the town council and that they urged removal of security forces from the township as part of the conspiracy. The indictment cited support for rent and consumer boycotts and actions of the so-called people's courts as elements of the treason conspiracy. Under subversion, the State charged the defendants with seeking to achieve or promote political, social or economic change. Under sedition, the accused allegedly jointly planned and participated in gatherings with "seditious intent" to defy or subvert the authority of the government.

COSATU, the labor federation to which Mayekiso's union was affiliated, was named as a co-conspirator in the indictment. It also named the ANC and the South African Communist Party (SACP) as co-conspirators.

Since South African law contains no obligation to provide a prompt and speedy trial—the Alexandra Five languished in prison until October 19, 1987, some 16 months after Moses Mayekiso's arrest—before the case commenced. During the long delay, his union colleagues made clear their strong support for him by electing him general secretary of the National Union of Metalworkers of South Africa, a new union created by merging several large metalworkers' unions including MAWU, as part of COSATU's "one-industry, one union" drive.

At the launch of NUMSA, union activists said they believed Mayekiso's arrest and treason indictment were intended to serve as a warning to other unionists to stick to "bread-and-butter" issues and not attempt to extend their organizing from the workplace into the community. Strikes had taken place timed to his court appearances to underscore the view of workers that the attack on Mayekiso was an attack on the black trade unions.

The opening of the trial brought the first good news in many months. Judge P. J. van der Walt, an Afrikaner with a reputation for being tough and competent, announced that, having examined the charges, he did not intend to have assessors hear the case with him. That decision effectively ruled out the possibility of death sentences should the defendants have been found guilty of the treason charge. In South Africa, which does not have jury trials, two assessors hear the case along with the presiding judge if the death penalty is potentially to be imposed upon conviction.

The trial progressed slowly. The state prosecutors frequently came to court unprepared and sought numerous postponements that were granted by Judge van der Walt. The delays, which some attributed to the State's inability to produce witnesses to substantiate their charges, had two results. Because the State prevented a bail hearing, the accused waited out the long recesses in the confines of prison. And, the longer the trial, the greater the legal costs required to mount the defense.

The first round of witnesses called by the prosecution testified in closed court because most lived or worked in Alexandra and the judge agreed to *in camera* proceedings to reduce fear of intimidation. Their testimony focused primarily on events in Alex during the first sixth months of 1986, including the rent and consumer boycotts and the efforts to get troops withdrawn from the township.

The problem for the prosecution was that none of their witnesses could provide direct evidence against Mayekiso. They described what occurred in Alex, but had no firsthand testimony linking Mayekiso to those events. The only potentially damaging evidence offered came from a witness who described an inflammatory speech given by Mayekiso at the mass funeral on March 5. On cross-examination, defense attorneys brought out that Moses was already jailed in John Vorster Square prison on that date, making it impossible for him to have incited the mourners as claimed.

Many of the State's witnesses were hostile to the prosecution. Having offered up whatever evidence they had, defense counsel then was able to query them about conditions in the township, attacks by police and troops on residents, and other facts favorable to the defendants.

The other half of the prosecution case rested on documents found in possession of the accused, particularly Mayekiso. When he returned from his trip to Britain and Sweden in 1986, he brought back a large quantity of materials that were seized when authorities arrested him at the airport in Johannesburg. Two raids on his house in Alex yielded additional documents, including notes in Mayekiso's own handwriting.

Some of the publications brought back from his European trip covered a range of ideologies, reflecting the diversity of the groups and individuals he had met during his stay. The prosecutor would read various paragraphs out of the publications which had been underlined and ask Mayekiso to comment on their meaning and describe why he underlined them. This approach was soon jettisoned when the judge pointed out that, on many of the documents in question, the underlining had been done not on the originals seized from Mayekiso, but instead on the photocopies being used by the prosecution.

Many of the documents dealt with various trade union issues. The prosecutor singled out a set of letters from different organizations indicating support for a major strike by the metalworkers at BTR's Sarmcol operations. He read one which stated that "The CPSA has encouraged its members to support the BTR Sarmcol strike and to give money to MAWU (the union)." He suggested to Mayekiso that the abbreviation CPSA stood for the Communist Party of South Africa.

The judge asked for the letter and, after having examined it, noted for the record that the first page spelled out the full name of the CPSA as the Civil and Public Services Association.

The lengthy probing of the publications provided Mayekiso an opportunity to outline at length the history of the trade union movement including the formation of FOSATU and the evolution that led to the launch of COSATU. He laid out the impact on the emerging black unions of the reforms coming out of the Wiehahn Commission (appointed by the government in the late 1970s to recommend changes in labor laws) and described the unions' growth in the early 1980s under new labor statutes.

Attempts to link Moses to the then-outlawed ANC, which could have strengthened greatly the treason charge, fell flat. All evidence linking the accused to the ANC was indirect. Several of them had ANC literature in their homes and had used slogans similar to those of the ANC in speeches, but no evidence emerged of the defendants plotting a conspiracy with the ANC. Indeed, what came strongly through in the trial was evidence that the accused themselves, rather than outside forces, were the architects of the political strategy in Alexandra.

The remainder of Mayekiso's testimony dealt with the events in Alexandra, such as his refusal to respond negatively to reporters when asked if the AAC controlled the township de facto after the town council resigned. Prosecutors also pressed extensively on a speech made by Moses at a night vigil after the killing of Michael

Diradeng, the 19-year-old youth leader whose death set off events leading to the "Six Day War."

When the State concluded its case, the defense moved to have the treason charges dismissed on the grounds that, under South African law, an element of violence is necessary to prove treason. It was the first time this point had been argued in a South African court.

Judge van der Walt, in a major setback for the defense, ruled that violence need not to have occurred for treason still to have been committed. That decision raised the stakes in the case, setting up the clear possibility that the outcome could set a precedent substantially broadening what constituted treasonous activity.

Could involvement (particularly during politically disturbed times) in consumer and rent boycotts and the organizing of community residents dissatisfied with living conditions constitute treason? If such activity could be treasonous, then what room would remain for the expression of peaceful opposition by persons excluded from political participation in the governmental system?

The defense team clearly outclassed the prosecution. Norman Manoim and Amanda Armstrong of the Johannesburg law firm of Cheadle, Thompson & Haysom charted the legal strategy, while David Soggot and Nick de Vos argued the case before Judge van der Walt. The defense was far better prepared and rebutted allegation after allegation made in the indictment. As the weeks went on, the more outlandish claims of the State appeared to collapse under the weight of contrary evidence. Still, the breadth of South African law and the nature of its system caused few hopes to be raised in supporters of the Alexandra Five.

When the case adjourned for the Christmas holidays in late 1988, the defense again sought approval from the attorney general for a bail hearing. To the amazement both of attorneys and defendants, he agreed and the judge promptly ordered the release of the accused on bail.

Although imposing stiff conditions that included the five defendants reporting daily to a police station and barring them from attending gatherings of 10 or more people, the decision not only gave Mayekiso and his colleagues their first taste of freedom in 901 days, but also indicated for the first time that even the apartheid government was wondering about its own case.

The trial resumed in February 1989, and by late March, just as final arguments were to be made, a bombshell hit.

Prosecutors announced the State intended to drop the treason charges against all five accused. Obviously chagrined, they argued that sufficient evidence existed to prove treason, but they had been unable to bring it forward for various reasons, such as witnesses' fear of intimidation.

That left sedition and subversion. Sedition, like treason, is a common law crime, while subversion is a statutory crime under the far-reaching Internal Security Act of 1982. Under the Act, subversion is defined as any attempt to bring about social, economic, or political change. It is also subversion to commit any act that "demoralizes" the public or that seeks to force the government to act or to refrain from acting.

Such definitions seem ludicrous to Americans, who are taught that an essential element of democracy is the people organizing to pressure the government they elect to act. But in South Africa, that's subversion.

Hoping for the best and fearing the worst, Mayekiso and his four co-accused passed the days waiting for Judge van der Walt's verdict. When it finally came, on April 24, 1989, courtroom 2C in Rand Supreme Court in Johannesburg was packed, primarily with NUMSA and COSATU members and Alex residents.

The white-haired judge began reading his 57-page decision to the tense crowd. Twenty minutes or so into the presentation, which to that point had consisted of a history and description of Alexandra, the defendants' hopes rose. The Afrikaner jurist surprised those in the courtroom by noting that "while white South African citizens may have a democracy, black South African citizens certainly have no share in it," a fact he called "notorious." He noted that "the black trade unions have served to a great degree to organize black workers and also to give expression to their demands in the workplace as well as their political aspirations."

When the judge had entered the courtroom that morning, nearly all blacks there had refused to heed the summons to "rise in court." By the lunch break, it was clear where the decision was headed and when court reconvened most blacks rose to their feet when the judge reentered and took the bench.

Van der Walt went on to rule that the forming of the AAC's yard, block, and street committees, people's courts, and the staging of rent and consumer boycotts during the unrest in the township were a reasonable response to primarily justifiable grievances and aspirations. Such activities, he said, were intended not to make the country ungovernable, but to improve township conditions. The judge blasted the government for having brought treason charges and said Mayekiso and the four co-accused "are just striving for a better South Africa."

Shouts of "Amandla" (power) echoed in the courtroom as the judge ended by announcing all defendants had been acquitted on all counts and were free to go. Black unionists and other supporters danced on the courthouse steps and hoisted Mayekiso to their shoulders as riot police with guns and truncheons ordered them to disperse.

At a victory rally at a Methodist church hall, Mayekiso said, "It is a big victory for the working class of South Africa because the aim of the working class is to end apartheid. We built democratic structures that can assure accountability, democracy, and that the leaders can't go loose from the masses."

Later, he said, "As far as we are concerned—myself, my family, the co-accused, the workers generally, the NUMSA members, and COSATU in particular—we believe that if it was not for the international solidarity, we would have faced serious convictions. The judge was aware of the international focus on the case, so the judge and the white community had to look for justice and had to acquit us." He added, "Today, we are partly free, a little more free."

Then Mayekiso joined the others in hopping into waiting vans for a symbolic trip back to Alexandra township, where the struggle remained far from over.

II. The International Solidarity Campaign

1. Early Solidarity

The first act of solidarity on behalf of Mayekiso by American unions occurred in late 1984, when South African authorities jailed him for his role in the Transvaal stayaway strike. At the request of the IMF, the Geneva-based trade union secretariat to which both the UAW and Mayekiso's union belonged, UAW president, Owen Bieber, sent an angry telex to South African president, P. W. Botha, urging Mayekiso's release. I followed with a letter to the South African ambassador in Washington, D.C., on his behalf.

Several of those involved in the stayaway whom police failed to apprehend fled the country while Mayekiso remained detained, and shortly afterward he was freed. His own union, then called the Metal and Allied Workers Union, had rallied support within South

Africa and had asked the IMF, through its South Africa council of which MAWU was a part, to seek international pressure.

Again, when Mayekiso was detained in February 1986, this time as the result of the turmoil in Alexandra township, the UAW and other unions moved quickly with telexes and letters to South African authorities protesting his jailing and demanding his release. Although there was little awareness at that point of Mayekiso's efforts to apply trade union techniques to organize his community, he was a union brother in an apartheid jail and needed what help could be provided from afar.

I met Mayekiso for the first time two months later, in April 1986, when I went to South Africa, along with representatives of the United Steelworkers and International Association of Machinists, to attend the Congress of the IMF South Africa council in Johannesburg. Groggy from jet lag, I joined a small group that included IMF general secretary, Herman Rebhan, a UAW member, that hoped to attend a funeral of a member of MAWU who had been killed by police in Tembisa township several days earlier.

As our modest caravan of vans approached the township, we confronted a phalanx of armored vehicles blocking the road. Stopped by the security forces armed with automatic weapons and truncheons, our group was detained for an hour or so as instructions were sought from higher authorities once our passports had identified us as foreigners.

While waiting I joked with Mayekiso that "we could paper the walls of my office with all the telexes and letters sent to Botha demanding he let you out of jail." He had a good laugh, and then said, "Don't get rusty, man, I may need some more of them before long." It was a light, but in retrospect, prophetic comment.

All of us were denied entry into Tembisa to attend the funeral, including Mayekiso, who was to preside. As we left to return to Johannesburg, an ABC correspondent named Jim Hickey showed up on the scene and began filming until security forces moved in. Hickey had covered the UAW negotiations with General Motors and Ford in 1982 and, as the union's public relations director, he and I had logged many tedious hours in bargaining press rooms and even a few in various watering holes near the GM Building and Ford World Headquarters.

I steered him to Mayekiso and, after moving down the road a half-mile or so, he shot an interview with Mayekiso framed in the backdrop of the armored military vehicles called "hippos" and "casspirs." Wanting a U.S. tie-in, he began asking me questions on-camera about what the UAW was doing to aid the black unions in South Africa. On the ground less than 24 hours, I began a spirited denunciation of apartheid, the jailing of Mayekiso two months before, and the killing of the MAWU member in Tembisa.

Just as I was hitting stride, Hickey noticed two of the "hippos" loaded with troops coming full speed down the road, obviously intent on interrupting the filming. All of us beat a hasty retreat, not wanting to test the security forces' patience any further.

South Africa was a hot story in 1986 and the government had not yet imposed tight media restrictions. While hardly big news, Hickey's report did air on ABC, albeit on one of the overnight and early morning shows. A friend called my wife to say he'd seen me under attack by South African soldiers, a development that necessitated several trans-Atlantic phone calls before some calm could be restored in my household.

Some days later, Mayekiso took several of us into Alexandra to see the conditions there for ourselves. Technically, we required permission from the authorities to enter the township, but Mayekiso knew Alex so well we had no problems as we moved covertly from the clinic to his home to the sites of various killings during the "Six Day War." Having learned a great deal about the state of the unions during the IMF council meetings earlier, we now got an education on township life and what the AAC was doing to organize residents there.

Shortly after our visit, the vigilante raids assisted by police occurred resulting in killings and burnings of a number of homes. The firebomb thrown through Mayekiso's bedroom window and the "suspicious" people asking about his whereabouts made it clear he was a marked man.

A May Day stayaway that shut down the entire country followed. So, too, did the continuing unrest in townships across South Africa. Momentum began building toward another stayaway timed to commemorate the 10th anniversary of the Soweto massacre of 1976. The Botha government responded in June by declaring a new and far more draconian State of Emergency. Some two weeks later, Mayekiso was arrested at Jan Smuts Airport and hauled off to John Vorster Square prison.

2. Bieber's South Africa Trip

The solidarity campaign on Mayekiso's behalf began slowly. This was so in large part because South African authorities had arrested so many workers and union leaders in the aftermath of the new State of Emergency. Many people thought the detentions had occurred primarily as a show of massive force by a government nervous about the extent and duration of the township unrest and about the muscle-flexing of the unions embarking on their second nationwide stayaway in five weeks.

As the summer of 1986 went on, a substantial number of releases occurred, although the pattern of who got released was quite erratic. While the decisions about mass detentions came from the highest levels of government, the local authorities carrying out the jailings seemed to have a high degree of discretion to decide who the "troublemakers" were in their areas. Mayekiso's arrest differed from most of the others. He had been detained under Section 29 of the Internal Security Act, rather than under the regulations of the State of Emergency. This clearly signalled that the State regarded his actions more severely than those of other detainees.

In mid-August, UAW president, Bieber, and I flew to Johannesburg at the invitation of the National Automobile and Allied Workers Union (NAAWU), which later merged with MAWU and a third union, the Motor Industry Combined Workers Union (MICWU), to form the National Union of Metalworkers of South Africa.

The UAW had a long history of support for NAAWU and its predecessor unions in the auto sector, in part because both General Motors and Ford had major auto-producing operations in South Africa. So, too, did a range of U.S. companies in the parts industry. The black unions sought and received UAW intervention on numerous occasions with the U.S. firms. Such interventions succeeded in some cases and failed in others, but we always tried.

The success of the IMF in bringing together a broad range of metalworkers' unions, mostly led by blacks, but including others run by whites, helped widen the UAW's contacts and relationships as well as increase the understanding of the broader range of debate on union strategy and political views of labor there.

Because Bieber served on the Secretary of State's Advisory Committee on South Africa—a group appointed by President Reagan that was later, after much debate, to reject the Administration's "constructive engagement" policy and urge tougher sanctions against South Africa—he could not be denied a visa. And a number of high ranking government officials agreed to see him during the visit.

Bieber met with leaders and members of a wide range of

unions. He went to auto plants and talked with shop stewards and workers. One of the most moving sessions occurred at the MAWU offices in Johannesburg, where Kola Mayekiso described her husband's plight and asked for help.

The UAW president immediately fired off a telex to the commissioner of police in Pretoria, protesting Mayekiso's detention and demanding a visit so that he could make an independent assessment of his condition [see Appendix 1].

Many such interventions do not receive any response. This one did. Three days later, a Brigadier Gloy telexed Bieber to deny his request to visit Mayekiso in detention. The decision came as no surprise, but MAWU officials thanked Bieber, telling him that the demand to see Mayekiso could only help because authorities had great sensitivity to foreign pressure.

Bieber went on to Cape Town, where he met with the Minister of Justice, Kobie Coetsee, who among other responsibilities directed the country's prison system. Having interviewed a number of union detainees, the UAW president outlined some of their stories, which included accounts of torture and inhumane treatment while jailed.

The minister, a crusty Afrikaner, angrily denied the mistreatment and claimed South Africa's prisons were a model to the world that met and exceeded the Geneva protocols and other international standards. Having been briefed on Bieber's full schedule in the days ahead, he issued a challenge: "Come with me tomorrow morning and we'll visit any prison you choose in the entire country unannounced and you'll be able to see that conditions are more than adequate."

A veteran of rough-and-tumble union politics and of the give-and-take across the bargaining table, Bieber immediately grabbed the opportunity. "I accept," he said. "We'll go to John Vorster Square prison where I want to see my good friend Moses Mayekiso from MAWU, who's been held there since June without being able to see his lawyers or his family. What time shall we leave?"

Coetsee turned ashen. It was a response he had not expected. Immediately, he began sputtering about how that could not be done; it would be out of order and would require other approvals he could not give. After some heated discussion, the meeting ended. Bieber's message had been communicated at the highest levels of the Botha government.

Just a few hours before Bieber's departure from South Africa, Kola Mayekiso arranged for him to visit Alexandra. The trip had been planned at the beginning of his stay, but canceled after shooting had broken out in the township. As he walked through the squalor and saw children playing a few feet from raw sewage and garbage, Bieber choked up. "On the farms around Grand Rapids where I grew up, the animals lived in better condition than this," he said. "I can see why Moses wants to do something about it. I would too if I lived here."

3. Activating the Campaign

In the months that followed, we talked with Mayekiso's colleagues in South Africa frequently. They had printed posters, T-shirts and other "Free Moses" material, and MAWU members at some workplaces had engaged in sporadic work stoppages to protest his continued detention.

Discussions with Herman Rebhan and Denis MacShane at the IMF led to a decision to launch a postcard campaign. The cards on one side had a photo of Mayekiso surrounded by a group of laughing children. On the other was the demand that Mayekiso and other political prisoners be freed by the apartheid government immediately.

The IMF cards were addressed to President Botha. We decided to address those printed by the UAW to the South African ambassador in Washington, D.C., because we felt many rank-and-file members might fill out the cards but never mail them, given the difficulty of determining what sort of postage a card to South Africa requires.

We launched the campaign at the UAW community action program's (CAP) annual conference in Washington in February 1987. The meeting was attended by more than 2,000 local union political activists from throughout the country. Most are seasoned political pros, adept at the nuts and bolts of motivating their members. Former UAW president, Walter Reuther's vision for CAP had been to create a political apparatus that extended beyond the election cycle. He called it the community action program, because he saw its mission to carry far beyond phone banks and get-out-the-vote efforts.

Every delegate got a letter from Bieber describing Mayekiso's plight, a copy of his telex demanding to be able to visit Moses, the rejection in reply and a batch of postcards to take back to the local union. In his keynote address, Bieber made it clear that the campaign for Mayekiso's freedom had great importance. He described in passionate terms his talks with unionists who had been detained and tortured, his meeting with Kola and the horrible conditions he saw in Alexandra.

All those in attendance left knowing that the postcard campaign was a top UAW priority. Soon orders for bulk shipments began flooding in and, by the time of Mayekiso's treason indictment in April 1987, more than 100,000 had been circulated. Some, no doubt, never got filled out or mailed, but many did. Cards would be passed out at a wide variety of union meetings: bargaining council sessions, health and safety seminars, civil rights committee gatherings, and union bowling tournaments. In order to ensure a steady flow to the South African embassy, we would collect all the cards filled out at a particular meeting or occasion, and mail 30 or so each day from our Washington office. With the name, address, and local union number all signed in different handwriting, we felt the D.C. postmarks did not undermine the legitimacy of the effort (and, of course, many other cards flooded in with postmarks from around the country as well).

The postcard campaign helped to answer one of the key questions any labor solidarity effort faces: how do you involve rank-and-file members and what do you ask them to do? Passionate speeches about jailed unionists in faraway countries can arouse members' interest, but to really build momentum, vehicles must be found for them to take action even if it is, as in this case, relatively modest and easy.

With activists urging members to fill out the cards, we quickly realized that a broader range of literature was needed. Workers had questions about who Mayekiso was and why he was jailed. Most were sympathetic to the effort, but wanted more information.

With the treason indictment handed down, Mayekiso faced a possible death sentence. The stakes had gone up. We decided to produce a brochure describing the case. The cover had a photo of Moses and headline type that stated: *Don't Let South Africa Hang This Labor Leader*. Above his picture was a die-cut through to an inside page that showed a hangman's noose. When the brochure was opened, one could see the noose was set in white over a map of South Africa.

Although somewhat graphic, we concluded that our main goal had to be to hook the reader, to get the brochure picked up and read. Another polemic about the evils of apartheid wouldn't do the job. This time, the focus was on the human story of one man, a black trade union leader in South Africa, facing the gallows because he tried to make his township a better place to live.

The publication made it clear that the South African government targeted Mayekiso as an attempt to weaken the black trade unions, which had emerged as the leading force in the anti-apartheid struggle, particularly after the repression against church and UDF activists. It described who Mayekiso was, including his background as an autoworker and union organizer, and laid out the charges against him. And it outlined what could be done to help, with a focus on the postcard campaign. In addition, to place the case in broader context, the brochure described what apartheid is and how blacks in South Africa are treated.

We made a decision at this point to spend the money necessary to have the brochure be a first-rate professional job. The goal, because we also intended to circulate it to officials of the South African government, was to communicate the idea to them that this solidarity campaign was well-financed and professionally run. We wanted the people in the embassy in Washington and in the government offices in Pretoria to understand that this was not being run by a couple of ideologues in a garage with a mimeo machine.

The French philosopher Sorel once argued that what is important is not whether a myth is true, but whether it is believed. While this campaign was firmly rooted in truth, we sought to have the apartheid government believe its parameters were much larger than, at least initially, they were. The South African government had not confronted a union-initiated solidarity campaign of this magnitude before. We wanted them to know they were in for a real fight.

During this period, we pumped out a range of stories in union publications, some in those with national circulation and others prepared for reproduction in local union papers. In different ways, they told the Mayekiso story and noted he faced the possibility of death by hanging. These stories again urged individual involvement through the postcard campaign. Blessed with UAW labor editors and writers with terrific skills, Moses' plight began to become widely known within the union and with it came an expanded awareness of what South Africa and apartheid were about. The case became a component in union education classes as well. Workers attending sessions at the UAW's Walter and May Reuther Family Education Center in Black Lake, Michigan, where some thousands go each year, heard about and discussed the case. So, too, did those at regional summer schools around the country.

As more and more UAW members learned about Mayekiso, we began looking for opportunities for action. For example, when about 400 health and safety representatives came to Washington for a conference, we decided to hold a demonstration in front of the South African embassy.

Our director of occupational safety and health, Dr. Frank Mirer, had spent two weeks in South Africa some months earlier running training classes for the metalworkers' unions as part of an IMF health and safety program. He kept urging me to charter enough buses to transport 300 people. I finally yielded, although privately I expected only 100 or so to actually show up. To my surprise, every bus was packed and some 350 safety reps spent an hour-and-a-half carrying signs up and down the sidewalk near the embassy demanding freedom for Moses Mayekiso.

With a good internal base of support created, we began to turn our attention outside the UAW.

4. The American Jurists' Committee

In the summer of 1987, Halton Cheadle, whose Johannesburg law firm represented Mayekiso as well as a number of black trade unions, spent a few days with me in Washington after a two-semester sabbatical of sorts at Yale Law School. A brilliant and combative lawyer, Cheadle had been banned for prolonged periods by the apartheid government.

During lengthy discussions on my back porch in the humidity of a brutal Washington summer he helped to educate me on the nature of the South African system, particularly on the role of the judiciary. Like most people, I had until then made little distinction between the branches of government there, assuming pretty much that the judicial branch was about as repugnant as the executive and legislative branches were.

But as I listened to Cheadle describe various legal initiatives and strategies taken by labor and human rights attorneys, I began to see that some degree of independence existed in the judicial community. Not frequently, but on occasion, a judge would find on behalf of unions or detainees or others who had fought the system. Often, the Parliament or State President would immediately pass laws or promulgate regulations to negate a positive court judgment, but the decisions occurred nevertheless.

This suggested a possibility of a two-tiered element to the solidarity campaign: continuing our effort to pressure the government, while looking for ways to focus on the judiciary as well. Virtually all judges in all countries will claim to be independent of political forces, assessing facts and applying laws with fairness and impar-

Photo 1. UAW members demonstrate in front of the South African Embassy in Washington, D.C. (photo by Bill Burke/ PAGE ONE).

tiality. This, of course, is seldom true. Even where honesty and integrity reign, politics is the mother's milk of justice.

A grave danger can be posed by actions perceived to cross an invisible, shifting line beyond which one is interfering with judicial independence by attempting outside the courtroom to influence the administration of justice. To do so in the Mayekiso trial in South Africa would result in a backlash much as it would in this country.

Cheadle talked about the positive effect several U.S. judges had had when they went to South Africa to observe some of the major political trials of anti-apartheid activists. As those judges observed proceedings, a sort of peer pressure developed. A climate was created in which it was harder for the South African judges presiding to rule on points of fact and law that flew in the face of international law. Some did, of course, but knowing the outside world was watching seemed to make it more difficult.

He also carried on at length about the relative lack of attention trials of unionists such as Mayekiso received compared to those of other opposition activists. While totally supportive of the worldwide focus on trials of political leaders, Cheadle argued that the key role unions play in organizing and exercising what power blacks have in South Africa should entitle labor leaders like Mayekiso to comparable international concern and help. Coming out of those discussions, we made a decision to develop a component of the solidarity campaign around the judiciary: to shine the spotlight of international opinion on the judge and the conduct of the trial itself. UAW president, Bieber, sent out letters to 13 prominent American jurists, asking that they serve on an independent, ad hoc committee to monitor the Mayekiso treason trial. Incredibly, 10 of the 13 accepted.

The media at the time carried frequent stories about so-called black-on-black violence and South African authorities promoted wide distribution for film of blacks "necklacing" other blacks with tires doused in gasoline placed around their necks and set on fire. Those who agreed to serve on what was called the American Jurists' Committee Monitoring the Case of Moses Mayekiso did so basically on faith, trusting the UAW's good reputation. With allegations of "people's court" activity included in the indictment, one could see why such prestigious individuals might have shied away from any association from the case. But they didn't [see Appendix 2 for a list of participants].

During discussions over whom to invite to serve, some had argued for a group of lesser stature but greater "political reliability." We rejected that approach for two reasons. First, the impact of the monitoring committee in South Africa depended upon its members being perceived to be major establishment legal figures. The group we had chosen clearly was of a stature to ensure against claims it was a "puppet" of the UAW. Second, we thought that, whatever political disagreements might occur, every member of the committee had a clear record of abhorrence of the apartheid system.

A well-attended press conference in Washington launched the jurists' committee. Standing in front of a large illustration of the Alexandra Five behind bars, Bieber and Eleanor Holmes Norton (a law professor who later was elected to the U.S. House of Representatives) outlined the group's mandate.

The New York Times carried a long story on the committee and the UAW's campaign along with photos of Mayekiso and Bieber. Other stories appeared in major newspapers around the country. The announcement made headlines in the South African press as well. As with the independence of some judges, some of the newspapers there cover stories adverse to the government. With the press censorship regulations that followed during the Emergency, such coverage declined, but greater freedom of the press exists than most Americans would expect. That is not true, however, of the South African Broadcasting Corporation, the government-controlled television system, which is a propaganda arm of the State.

A glossy brochure was produced containing photos and bios of each of the members of the jurists' committee, along with a description of their mission of monitoring the Mayekiso trial and the facts of the case. We circulated it to a wide range of opinion-maker groups in the U.S., particularly organizations of lawyers involved in human rights work.

Before forming the committee, we had met with the Lawyers Committee for Civil Rights, which has a Southern Africa project that has done excellent legal assistance work in South Africa. We asked their advice and support and made clear that our committee was an ad hoc group that had formed around a particular case and would pose no competitive threat.

We also talked through our strategy with others doing legal work around human rights issues, both to get their ideas and to ensure we would not be seen as cutting into their substantive or fundraising "turf." Some gave us more help than others, but most importantly, none undercut us.

Photo 2. Owen Bieber and Eleanor Holmes Norton at a press conference launching the American Jurists' Committee monitoring the case of Moses Mayekiso, Washington, D.C. (photo by Earl Dotter).

Word came back from South Africa from both the unions and from Mayekiso's attorneys, and their response to the committee was upbeat. Discussions had been held at length at that end, including with Mayekiso and his co-accused, before the decision to convene the committee had been made. Now that it was launched and the trial had begun, there was general agreement that the profile of the case had been raised substantially and that a sense existed in South Africa that the trial was attracting high-level international interest.

The long delays sought and won by the prosecution drained some of the intensity, however. By April 1988, we decided on another effort to put South African authorities on notice that the committee was continuing to monitor the treason trial.

Full page ads, paid for by the UAW, ran in the major commercial papers such as the *The Star*, a Johanneburg-based newspaper, and the Cape Town-based *Cape Times*. Both papers initially rejected the ads, which described who the committee members were and why they were following the trial. Some toning down of the already relatively objective copy enabled us to convince the papers that the ads did not violate the legal restrictions under the State of Emergency. One paper, *Business Day*, did refuse to carry the ad.

"The [Mayekiso] case is an unparalleled test for South Africa's legal system beneath the spotlight of international opinion," the ad stated. "The Committee believes the trial of Mayekiso and his four co-defendants raises critical questions about the fundamental issues of justice and due process under law." The ads generated a new round of publicity in South Africa for the monitoring effort. They also reached a broader audience there and helped strengthen the country-wide profile of the case.

As the trial progressed, we received regular reports from Norman Manoim and Amanda Armstrong, Mayekiso's lawyers, which were passed on to committee members and also circulated within the UAW and to other U.S. unions and groups concerned about the case. The reports were factual and objective accounts of the testimony and evidence presented and of the judge's rulings on key points of law. Originally, we hired an American attorney living in South Africa to observe the trial and report back to us, but it soon became clear that the cost for a lengthy trial would be prohibitive.

Based on the information received from Manoim and Armstrong, we produced a newsletter, *Mayekiso Trial Update*, which we sent to UAW local union leaders, and to those in other unions. Because of our close relationships with U.S. anti-apartheid organizations such as TransAfrica and the American Committee on Africa, we got mailing lists of their supporters and sent the newsletter to them as well. Each copy contained a postcard that could be torn out and sent to the South African embassy urging justice for Mayekiso.

Although the committee had achieved the goal of directing greater international attention to the trial, we knew it could not fulfill its mandate without sending at least one of its members to South Africa to observe the proceedings firsthand. That was the next step.

5. Observing the Trial

In November 1988, Yale University president, Benno Schmidt Jr., one of those who had accepted Bieber's invitation to serve on the jurists' committee, agreed to go to South Africa to observe the trial on behalf of the group. But the trial adjourned several weeks earlier than expected. His trip was postponed until the trial reconvened in February 1989.

Schmidt's credentials for the task were excellent. A legal scholar specializing in constitutional law, he had served as Dean of the Columbia University Law School before becoming the 20th president of Yale in 1986. Shrewd and personable, Schmidt could think fast on his feet as he proved repeatedly as moderator of public television programs on the U.S. constitution.

As Yale president, Schmidt had not supported the total divestment of the university's investment portfolio, a fact that bothered at least one member of the committee. Yet his stand also served to enhance his credibility with the South Africans we sought to influence.

The first step, getting visas, proved difficult. A common tactic then of the apartheid government was to delay issuing a visa until after the event you had hoped to attend had ended, or to withhold issuance so late that you had to cancel the trip or had great difficulty with appointments and travel arrangements.

Having had this problem on two previous occasions, I applied, as did Schmidt, listing a departure date two weeks earlier than we actually hoped to go. After a month of waiting, and some negative rumblings from the embassy, we sought and got letters to the South African ambassador from George Mitchell, Senate majority leader; Paul Simon, chair of the Senate Africa sub-committee; Nancy Kassebaum, the ranking Republican on that sub-committee;

and Howard Wolpe, then chair of the House Africa sub-committee. All urged that South Africa grant the visas.

Their interventions not only helped pressure the South African government to grant the visas, but also sent a message to Pretoria that key members of Congress with the power to shape sanctions legislation had a strong interest in the Mayekiso case. This was underscored by the fact that Republican Kassebaum had written, as well as the more liberal Democrats who might be expected to take such action.

At 6 p.m. on February 3, Ambassador Piet Koornhof sent word the visas had been approved and, in a letter to Schmidt and myself, said he wished us well on our journey. He also expressed his "extreme displeasure" about remarks by Bieber that Mayekiso was on trial so as "to weaken the anti-apartheid system" or because black trade unions "have emerged as the key force opposing apartheid."

Some weeks before our departure, I had asked Manoim at Cheadle, Thompson & Haysom if lawyers there could prepare briefing materials for Schmidt on relevant legal issues, particularly South African law on treason, subversion and sedition, as well as on other subjects, such as facts about Alexandra township that were not available in the U.S.

I also had sought help from the human rights project at Harvard Law School run by Henry Steiner. He had put me in touch with Professor Jack Tobin and a law student named Carl Landauer, himself a former history professor at Stanford before enrolling at Harvard Law. Landauer had prepared an excellent paper on the laws on treason in the U.S. and other nations.

One of our basic contentions about the Mayekiso indictment continued to be that, even if the defendants had committed the acts with which they were charged, those acts would hardly constitute the crime of treason by the standards of international law. How could rent and consumer boycotts in one black township of 100,000 residents be treason? Although a strong argument, we needed the legal underpinnings for it.

Landauer's research provided that in great detail. The paradigm of treason "involves either a direct attack on the State or an act which in some way aids an external enemy" and must be linked "to a violent attack on the State from within or without." Having examined the treason laws of various nations, he concluded that "the acts of Mayekiso and the others in the present South African case do not fall under the definition of treason elsewhere."

On the long set of flights to Johannesburg, which included a nine-hour delay in London, Schmidt devoured the briefing materials and hit the ground running. He immediately went into meetings with the advocates and attorneys representing the five accused.

In the days that followed, he met with the attorney general, Klaus von Lieres, who was responsible for prosecuting the case, and with those actually arguing the prosecution case in the courtroom. In addition he held long sessions with the five defendants, hearing their views on the trial as well as the history of their actions in Alexandra that led to the indictment. He also spent an afternoon in Alexandra, where residents continued to live in deplorable conditions despite an influx of government funds aimed at improvement.

Schmidt also met with officials of the U.S. embassy, as Ambassador Edward Perkins had attended the trial on two occasions to show U.S. interest in the case. The Yale president also spent two hours with Kobus Meiring, the deputy minister for foreign affairs, hearing Pretoria's official position on the case.

After having conducted his observation of the trial itself in Courtroom 2C of the Witwatersrand Supreme Court in Johannesburg, Schmidt had his most important meeting: a private, one-hour session with presiding Judge van der Walt. Careful to avoid any statement that could be construed in any way as an attempt to influence the judge, Schmidt described the members of the jurists' committee and outlined why they had an interest in the issues raised by the trial.

Van der Walt wanted to know how the committee planned to follow the trial from America. Schmidt responded that appeals court judges are not physically present for a trial, but they pass judgment based on the court record. With the ability to do likewise, Schmidt said he was confident the committee would be fair and objective.

Shortly before departure, Schmidt held a press conference. "There is great concern in America about the seemingly widespread use of treason indictments against opponents of the government and its apartheid policies," he said. "That concern is particularly sharp in those cases in which defendants were engaged in peaceful, non-violent activity."

"Our jurists' committee is asking, as I did in meetings here, where the line is between acceptable political dissent and treasonous activity," Schmidt noted. "That is an extremely important question in a country where some 70% of the population is excluded from the political and legislative process, lacking voting rights and other rights taken for granted in democratic countries. Is the South African government, through these treason prosecutions and convictions, criminalizing what would be considered legitimate political dissent in the context of international legal norms?"

Schmidt also raised the subversion and sedition charges, noting that subversion as defined in the statute "seems to be capable of being interpreted in an extraordinarily broad manner and could make unlawful conduct that would be considered clearly legitimate political action in my country and elsewhere." And he took note of due process questions, such as the lengthy detention without charge or access to attorneys and the denial of the bail application from being heard for nearly two years.

Citing Mayekiso's role as a key trade union leader, Schmidt told reporters that there was great interest in the trial in America and many other countries. "It is being watched closely in legal circles, in trade unions, church groups, the human rights community and by the public," he said.

The message had been delivered. As Schmidt flew home, no one connected to the trial could avoid the fact that the world was watching and waiting to see what the outcome would be.

6. The International Campaign

Throughout Mayekiso's detention and trial, the solidarity campaign on his behalf in the U.S. occurred against the backdrop of a much broader international effort. In countries such as Britain, Sweden, and West Germany, metalworkers' unions were joined by other labor groups, anti-apartheid organizations, churches and others concerned about the case. As in the U.S., the campaigns functioned autonomously with unionists in each country deciding what forms of activity were possible and desirable.

The IMF in Geneva, however, continued to play a key role. The IMF kept union activists in different countries up to date on developments in the trial and served as an informal clearinghouse, passing on leaflets, newspaper ads, and other materials, and suggesting ideas for op-ed newspaper articles. It coordinated fundraising for legal and other expenses and maintained liaison with other international supporters of the campaign, such as the International Confederation of Free Trade Unions (ICFTU).

In an op-ed of his own in the *International Herald Tribune*,

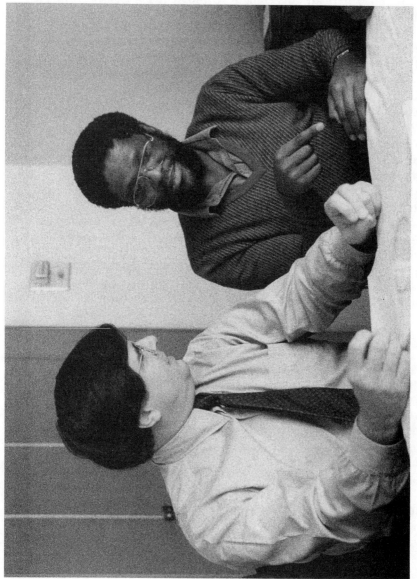

Photo 3. Yale University President Benno Schmidt, Jr. meeting with Moses Mayekiso, Johannesburg, South Africa (photo by Don Stillman).

then IMF General Secretary Herman Rebhan spread word of the trial. He closed by stating, "The man on trial in Johannesburg represents part of the future of his country. I only hope that when Moses Mayekiso is sitting in some ministry in a majority-ruled South Africa, he will be as merciful toward his former guards and judges as they are likely to be pitiless toward him."

The article drew blood. J. B. Shearer, permanent representative of South Africa to the United Nations, responded in a letter to the *Herald Tribune* on the Mayekiso case that described "the notorious, arbitrary executions of black by black by 'necklacing,' stabbing, stoning to death or setting alight with gasoline."

The South African official's letter continued: "It is hard to see how Mr. Rebhan can describe anyone involved in this activity as 'merciful.' One can understand that the general secretary of the IMF is anxious to come to the defense of a fellow trade unionist and friend. But in so doing he should not mislead readers as to the nature of the allegations, nor impugn the impartiality of South African courts, whose international reputation stands extremely high."

Shearer himself, of course, committed the act of misleading readers as to the nature of the allegations. Mayekiso had not been accused of any act of violence, let alone 'necklacing,' stabbing or stoning anyone to death. But as the international publicity on the trial, virtually all of it unsympathetic to the apartheid government, continued to mount, South African officials such as Shearer made it clear they, too, could play hardball.

The IMF printed postcards urging Mayekiso's release in seven languages and distributed nearly 200,000 of them. It produced a special "Hello Moses! May Day Greetings From the Metalworkers of the World" postcard that could be sent to Mayekiso in prison and later a similar Christmas greeting timed to the holidays.

Denis MacShane, the IMF's press officer and a former president of the National Union of Journalists in Britain, arranged for a prominent British jurist, Lord Hooson Q.C., to go to South Africa to observe the trial shortly after it began. Hooson arrived only to find the trial had adjourned unexpectedly for one of its many prosecution-sought postponements.

He was able to meet Judge van der Walt as well as defense and prosecution lawyers, much as Schmidt did later. Lord Hooson also had held meetings with key officials of the British foreign office and had been in contact with Sir Geoffrey Howe (an old friend of his) before his South African trip. Hooson continued to follow the trial throughout, forming a one-person U.K. version of the American jurists' group.

MacShane attended the trial on behalf of the IMF in February 1988. He then wrote an excellent article on the case that was reprinted in a number of union publications in the U.S. and Britain. The British Trades Union Congress (TUC) also sent a member of its international department, Tony Shaw, to monitor the case on three separate occasions. There were observers who attended the trial from the ICFTU and the International Federation of Journalists as well.

In West Germany, one of South Africa's largest trading partners, the German metalworkers' union, I. G. Metall, took out full page ads in German papers on the case. One was an open letter to President Botha from the union president, Franz Steinkuehler, demanding Mayekiso's freedom. Steinkuehler later convinced top officials of West Germany's conservative government to raise Mayekiso's plight during their contacts with South African officials. Given the huge German investment in that country, the impact had to be felt at the highest levels in Pretoria. Steinkuehler also travelled to South Africa and visited Mayekiso in prison.

One of the most active support efforts came from the Swedish Metalworkers, led by its president, Leif Blomberg. That union, with a long history of support for the anti-apartheid movement and for the black unions in South Africa, felt a special responsibility since Mayekiso had been arrested after getting off his flight from Stockholm in 1986.

Blomberg took out full-page ads addressed to Mayekiso. One of them, on May Day 1988, said: "When I talk at (union) meetings, few will understand why after your visit you had to go to prison and even less why, after two years, you have not been released. Your demands are our demands. Your words are our words. Your goal is our goal. We celebrate May Day in freedom. You do not. Why?"

As an example of the cross-fertilization of the international effort, the Swedish metalworkers took the UAW brochure with the noose and the headline *Don't Let Them Hang This South African Labor Leader* and reprinted it in Swedish for distribution throughout that country.)

Other countries developed campaigns as well, such as the Netherlands and France, with the metalworkers' unions leading the way. One country that could have added a great deal to the international pressure on South Africa in the Mayekiso case was

Japan. Like West Germany, Japan has extensive investments in South Africa, primarily through licensing and other arrangements aimed at allowing Japanese companies full access to that market without concurrent acceptance of responsibility.

At a meeting between North American metalworkers and our Japanese counterparts in April 1987, I drafted a resolution condemning the government of South Africa for Mayekiso's indictment, which occurred the week of the conference. It urged the dismissal of the indictment and expressed solidarity with Mayekiso and his co-accused.

Because the meeting was in Tokyo, the resolution noted that Mayekiso had been a Toyota worker and had helped to organize a union at Toyota. This seemed relevant for dissemination in Japan, where the case had received almost no attention. The hope was the Toyota link would perhaps elicit coverage and greater interest there. To my chagrin (but not surprise), several key leaders of the Japanese delegation took me aside and politely, but firmly said the resolution was unacceptable without the deletion of the reference to Toyota. It would be "an unfortunate embarrassment" to mention the Japanese automaker, they said. The reference was deleted.

As time went on, some Japanese unions including the autoworkers did take up the case. Leaflets were distributed by the IMF Japan council that attempted to explain apartheid and that described Mayekiso's plight. But unlike the efforts in Europe and America, Japan lagged far, far behind. The case provided an excellent opportunity for educating union members on race and apartheid issues, but most Japanese unions missed it, perhaps out of their usual reluctance to act independently of the Japanese companies.

Probably the most intensive solidarity effort of any country occurred in Britain where the campaign was coordinated by Terry Bell, an exiled South African and former member of the ANC. The "Friends of Moses Mayekiso" organized by Bell, a journalist, had the support of most British unions, including the TUC.

The British effort had a stronger grassroots base than in any other country. A steady barrage of meetings, rallies, marches and fund-raisers occurred over the entire period of Moses' jailing and trial. The group published a regular newsletter to keep supporters up-to-date on developments in the trial and the union movement in South Africa. They also took out frequent ads in newspapers such as *The Guardian* and *The Independent* to put the issues before the broader public.

Their solidarity effort got off to a rocky start, however, when the campaign was attacked by the South African Congress of Trade Unions (SACTU), the federation smashed by the repression of the early 1960s. Its leaders for the most part went into exile then, but maintained liaison with the ANC. The expansion of black unions inside South Africa which have developed their own direct contacts with unions in other countries had diminished SACTU's role, but it continued to have ties to labor, particularly in the U.K. and Canada.

SACTU sent letters to all general secretaries of British trade unions in August 1988, demanding that "there should be no support for, nor affiliation to" the Friends of Mayekiso campaign in Britain. The letters complained of a lack of consultation and opposed the singling out of Mayekiso for a campaign.

"The reason for discouraging the adoption of individual trade unionists is because it is difficult to know what criteria has been used in selecting an individual detainee over and above thousands of other detained trade unionists, workers and activits (sic). Concentration on individuals can cause adverse reaction in the union. Other members see that all attention is being focused on only one of the detained members. This can lead to rivalry, bitterness and other forms of unpleasantness," the letter stated.

The attack ignored the fact that Mayekiso was more than a detainee, he was the only trade unionist at the time who faced treason charges and a possible death sentence. It also ignored the call that had been made by the black unions in South Africa for international campaigns on his behalf. And it ignored the fact that Mayekiso had been made a symbol in the labor fields, albeit one sector of a broader community, much as Nelson Mandela was for the wider political movement in a far more prominent but similar manner.

What could have been a divisive and unfortunate sectarian debate soon ended, however, when top ANC officials rejected the SACTU criticisms and urged full support for the Mayekiso solidarity effort in Britain and everywhere else. On numerous occasions throughout the Mayekiso campaign, including at meetings with unionists in the U.S., top ANC leaders such as Oliver Tambo and Thabo Mbeki repeatedly backed the actions and urged even more vigorous efforts on Moses' behalf.

Given the range of ideologies and nationalities involved, what is surprising is not that there were incidents such as the SACTU intervention, but that there weren't more of them. While many of those who participated in the Mayekiso campaign had different views on politics, disinvestment and other issues, all seemed to see the basic questions of repression and injustice as most central to this specific effort.

7. The Labor Committees Against Apartheid

In a number of U.S. cities, informal coalitions of local unions and district councils have formed to work on anti-apartheid issues, particularly those dealing with labor. These committees played an extremely important role in moving the Mayekiso solidarity effort beyond the core group of metalworkers' unions such as the UAW, Steelworkers and Machinists. Those unions were active in the local committees, of course, and as a result carried the Mayekiso story to a broader network of union activists.

Two of the best examples were the New York Labor Committee Against Apartheid and the Illinois Labor Network Against Apartheid. In each case, local and regional union activists had come together around the desire and need to organize and support the black union movement in South Africa.

The Mayekiso campaign came at a time when the New York committee had been through a dormant period. But in 1987, a core group of union officers and staff decided to reactivate the group around two issues: the Mayekiso trial and the Royal Dutch/Shell boycott campaign. Funds were raised to hire Kate Pfordresher, a talented organizer, to staff the committee, and Communications Workers of America (CWA) Local 1180 agreed to provide office space.

They kicked off their efforts with a breakfast meeting in January 1988, at which I described the status of the Mayekiso trial and the broader context of union and community activism in which it was occurring. Ken Zinn of the United Mine Workers laid out the history of the National Union of Mineworkers call for solidarity action against Shell after it fired a group of miners at Rietspruit who had protested unsafe working conditions.

Soon some 30 locals and district councils in the greater New York area took up both campaigns. AFSCME's District Council 37, UAW Local 259 and District 65, Amalgamated Clothing and Textile Workers Union (ACTWU) joint boards and locals and many others soon had literature circulating among their members.

"The Mayekiso case really motivated people at the local level," Pfordresher recalls. "A lot of the anti-apartheid work is not directly about labor, but this was something rank-and-file members could relate to—it was a clear example about the nature of the

South African movement and what it's up against." The New York committee publicized the trial in its newsletter, which is a well-written and professional publication. It produced a "Free Mayekiso" button that was sold to raise funds. And it widely distributed the UAW postcards to its more than 30 locals and district councils.

The Illinois Labor Network Against Apartheid carried out similar work. Based in Chicago and coordinated with great skill by Kathy Devine, the labor network involved some 20 labor groups in anti-apartheid work around labor issues in South Africa. In addition to the postcard campaign, the group organized a series of demonstrations as part of the effort to publicize the Mayekiso trial. One of them occurred at the South African consulate in Chicago, where Jack Parton, a regional director of the Steelworkers, and Bill Stewart, a regional director for the UAW, were arrested at a "Free Mayekiso" rally.

Other committees around the country took up the Mayekiso campaign as well. In Philadelphia, the Labor Committee Against Apartheid led by ACTWU and SEIU officials distributed literature and postcards to local unions, for example. In San Francisco, a group called the "Committee to Free Moses Mayekiso" formed and conducted a number of demonstrations as well as a petition drive that sought signatures of Bay area unionists. This group appeared to have a slightly younger base, as evidenced by a flyer they sent us for a benefit at the Ashkenaz Music and Dance Cafe in Berkeley featuring the "Looters" and the "Beat Freaks!"

In March 1989, Kola Mayekiso set out on a month-long speaking tour in Britain organized by Terry Bell of the "Friends of Moses Mayekiso." She agreed to an invitation from Bieber to spend a week in the U.S. following the British tour.

The grassroots groups formed an easily mobilized base for Kola's visit. Bieber and UAW official Bob King kicked it off with a rally at Local 600 in Detroit which was packed with union members who donated more than $8,000 to the Mayekiso defense and to support for the families of the accused. From there, she went to Chicago to address a meeting of the Illinois Labor Network and then on to Washington, D.C., for a fund-raiser at the UAW office which raised more than $10,000.

While in Washington, we arranged for meetings between Kola and Senator Paul Simon, who chairs the Senate Africa sub-committee, and Representative Howard Wolpe, who then chaired the House Africa sub-committee. Both heard firsthand the story of

Mayekiso applying union organizing techniques in Alexandra and the indictment and trial that followed. Photos of her with Simon and Wolpe were sent back to South Africa with the hope that word would spread that key players in the Congress were watching the trial carefully. She also met with the acting assistant secretary for African affairs at the State Department to urge further pressures be brought to bear by the Bush Administration on the case.

The speaking tour helped to focus a flurry of activity just as the trial drew to a close. Earlier in the campaign we had learned the value small victories could have in strengthening the resolve of those participating in the campaign. Just two days before the trial began in 1988, we had received word that the treason indictment had been dropped; unionists participating in the rallies had a sense that the solidarity effort was paying off because some progress was being made in a case that seemed destined to end in lengthy jail terms for Mayekiso and his colleagues.

Just three weeks later, after Kola Mayekiso's speaking tour, those hopes turned to elation as word spread of Judge van der Walt's acquittal of all defendants on all counts.

III. The Lessons Learned

As his fellow union members carried Mayekiso on their shoulders down the courthouse steps, no one could doubt that a tremendous victory had been won. Convictions, even on the subversion count alone, would have effectively criminalized virtually all forms of non-violent, peaceful dissent. They also would have had a chilling effect on both the black union movement and the effort to organize township residents for a better life.

Instead, the judge rebuked the apartheid government for having brought the treason indictment in the first place, and even for the very nature of the country's lack of democracy for the majority population. It was a set-back for those in the government who envisioned immobilizing opposition forces by even more widespread use of treason charges. And it was a victory for the concept of structures such as those set up by the AAC and the use of boycotts and other non-violent protest strategies.

After the acquittal, Mayekiso briefly visited the U.S. and attended the UAW convention in June 1989. I asked him about the victory.

"Our acquittals strengthened the ties between the trade

unions and the community organizations," he said. "Some people had felt that community issues are different from labor issues. But in South Africa you can't differentiate between political issues, community issues and trade union issues. All those are interlinked because the economy rests on politics and politics rests on social issues. For example, you get better wage increases at the factories. But those increases will be swallowed by increases in fares from the bus companies that transport the workers and also by rent increases, electricity increases and the like in the townships."

Probably the most tangible result of the international solidarity campaign on Mayekiso's behalf is that today he is back as leader of his union calling strikes and winning gains for the members and back in Alexandra revitalizing the structures through which residents can put forth their grievances and aspirations. Freedom for an activist like Moses is never a guaranteed condition, but for now he's once again in action instead of inside a jail cell. It should be noted here that Obed Bapela and Paul Tshabalala, two of the Alexandra Five, were jailed again for about two weeks in September 1989. Police attempted to search the homes of all five of those tried in the Mayekiso case as well. During this period, Moses once again was in Europe and remained there until the solidarity network created during the trial had deluged the newly re-elected government of South Africa with protests. He returned after Bapela and Tshabalala had been freed and the authorities had given assurances he would not be arrested.

The old line about victory having a thousand fathers while defeat is an orphan might apply here. It is impossible to single out any one factor or component as the "cause" of the victory. Most of the credit surely must go to those in South Africa who fought on the front-lines of this battle, and will do so again, no doubt. But the international effort on Mayekiso's behalf, as he himself says, clearly played an extremely important role.

What are some of the lessons learned from the campaign? They are many, but a few stand out both on the positive and the negative side. Among the pluses, beyond the most important which was that the campaign ended in a victory:

1. Tighter links have been created between American unions and their counterparts in South Africa. That's certainly true in the case of the UAW and NUMSA and of the Steelworkers and Machinists unions as well. Much of the earlier support and contact laid the base, but the Mayekiso campaign strengthened these relationships. This was true in part because of the inherently political

nature of the case, which transcended basic union-building support which possibly made up the bulk of the U.S. unions' help to those in South Africa.

For a variety of reasons, there was a concern during this period that some sectors of the American labor movement had an interest in manipulating the black unions as part of broader East-West ideological questions. The Mayekiso campaign helped to build further credibility for those unions involved in it because they supported unionists involved in the broader political struggle.

Out of the tighter links forged as a result of the solidarity campaign has come far better communication between American and South African unions. The New York Labor Committee Against Apartheid, for example, has created close ties to both NUMSA and the Chemical Workers Industrial Union (CWIU). Those ties helped the committee mobilize support here for NUMSA demands to Goodyear and the CWIU demands to Mobil that the terms of their disinvestment from South Africa be negotiated with the workers they represent.

2. In a similar way, the Mayekiso campaign helped to build linkages elsewhere. The labor committees that took up the case succeeded in broadening their coalitions to involve more unions and more individual members concerned about South African issues. A base exists today on which further support work can be done, whether that be in the union-to-union help around bargaining and workplace issues or in the political arena.

Likewise, linkages were created in the campaign between union activists here and church and anti-apartheid activists. The church community has long been in the forefront of this struggle as have groups such as the American Committee on Africa, Trans-Africa, Washington Office on Africa, Amnesty International (AI), and others. The effort on the Mayekiso campaign strengthened labor's credibility with many of these groups and created new relationships that can be used in future struggles. Such relationships helped improve the efforts to lobby for sanctions, against the rollover of South Africa's international debts and other forms of pressure in the struggle against apartheid.

3. The Mayekiso campaign provided an excellent vehicle for basic trade union education around South African issues. It is often difficult to organize solidarity around conditions for workers in a country far away that gets covered infrequently and inadequately by the media. The case provided a compelling human story that proved to be an excellent "hook" to get union members involved.

People related very personally to a black unionist facing a possible hangman's noose for his efforts to improve the community where he lived. Drawn in, they learned about the broader issues of apartheid and about the repression black unionists and others face in South Africa.

What was particularly important was the interest that built in the U.S. among both black and white workers. At the onset, there was a strong base of black support around the case. As time went on, the issues involved in the campaign sparked broad interest. I think, for example, of the demonstration of UAW health and safety reps from local unions at the South African embassy, made up overwhelmingly of white members motivated strongly by the Mayekiso story.

In education classes and at local union meetings, the solidarity effort reminded members that, while they face tough problems in their own communities and workplaces, so too do workers in other countries. It provided a starting point for discussions of the international trade union movement operating in an increasingly complex world economy.

4. The tactic of formation of a committee of prominent judges and lawyers to monitor the trial helped give the campaign an impact it would otherwise have lacked. By understanding that there was a difference in how pressure was brought to bear on the government on the one hand and the judiciary on the other, we were able to pursue a more effective strategy. The South African government is extremely sensitive to international opinion. The numerous ads and op-eds appearing here and in other countries no doubt ended up being faxed back to Pretoria, as were accounts of various demonstrations and rallies on Moses' behalf. The government clearly knew, as the campaign mounted, that there was great international interest in the case.

But the judiciary, with its proclaimed independence, created a different problem. Blatant efforts to affect the judge could only have backfired. But the formation of a monitoring group including a former U.S. Supreme Court justice, former attorney general, three sitting Courts of Appeal judges, the Brooklyn district attorney and the Yale University president created an acceptable form of scrutiny.

Only the judge himself knows exactly what the impact really was of the jurists' committee and its observation mission to South Africa. He may have come to exactly the same decision he made regardless of any outside factor. At a social occasion following the long trial, however, the judge did inquire of one of the defense attorneys as to what the jurists' committees reaction was to his verdict.

Observation missions to political trials have been going on since the Dreyfus case nearly a century ago. What was slightly different in this case was that it was labor that convened the monitors in a trial involving a union leader. There is no reason why this tactic could not be applied in other situations. Union leaders in COSATU and their attorneys have talked, for example, about convening a group of prominent jurists to examine the circumstances surrounding the horrible violence being inflicted upon unionists and their families by Inkatha vigilantes in Natal and throughout South Africa.

Moving out of the realm of legal observation missions, one could envision spinoffs of the tactic along the lines of the old "blue-ribbon" commissions employed in earlier labor struggles. In the United Mineworkers strike against the Pittston Coal Group, for example, the company attempted to slough off its obligations for health and retirement benefits. A committee of carefully selected, progressive business leaders and business school deans might well conclude, as *Business Week* did, that Pittston's demands and conduct were irresponsible.

5. The high quality of the literature and materials was important. It established to everyone involved in the campaign that it was a serious effort. This is not to say that such campaigns cannot be won without such quality, rather that a helpful momentum is created by first-rate publications and paraphernalia. In addition to communicating more effectively the story and the issues of the campaign, they also signal that it is important enough that serious resources are being employed. That was a message we hoped the South African government would get as well.

6. The campaign had the right mix of support from above and below. There was a strong grassroots component in the field and unequivocal backing from top union leadership. In the UAW's case, there is no question that Bieber's commitment to the Mayekiso effort made a huge difference. His own trip to South Africa where he intervened on Mayekiso's behalf, met with union leaders and saw the conditions in Alexandra helped make this a priority issue. To mount a campaign such as this one, there is no substitute for the kind of personal support Bieber provided. The leadership of the UAW knew the Mayekiso campaign was a priority and they pursued it as such.

But the efforts of regional and district officials and local union activists gave the campaign a real base of support as well. In any such effort, there is always the danger it will be perceived as a Potemkin village: a facade with nothing behind it. The grassroots work at the local level, by individual unions and the various labor committees, ensured this was not the case.

What were some of the minuses, the things that could have been done better?

1. Press coverage, while adequate, should have been more extensive. Given the potential impact of convictions, the Mayekiso case should have been the subject of far more news stories. In retrospect, the story seemed to fall in between "beats" or assignment areas. What few labor reporters there are today looked at the story as one for the foreign desk, while the South African correspondents viewed it as less important (until the verdict) than the comings and goings of Archbishop Tutu.

As Steven Friedman notes in his excellent book, *Building Tomorrow Today—African Workers in Trade Unions, 1970–1984*, the black unions may well have done more to bring political change nearer than any other black organization in South Africa's history, yet news coverage of them has been minimal.

> Because the unions have played so important a role, we would expect their story to have been told again and again in books, newspapers, and other media . . . But few of those who talk or write about South African politics could name many of the leading unions, let alone discuss their policies, achievements or defeats. Still less would they be able to name more than half a dozen leading unionists, some of whom represent thousands of people.[2]

The lack of press coverage in South Africa, due perhaps to the long, drawn out nature of the trial, meant that the international solidarity campaign had to sustain itself without depending on dramatic developments coming out of the courtroom in Johannesburg.

Friedman's observations about the media are even more true of American coverage. With some notable exceptions, attention to the black unions' pivotal role in the South African struggle has been minimal. Why, for example, were we unable to get either major newspaper in Detroit, a city with a majority of African Americans, to cover the Mayekiso story? Was it a marketing problem? Or, insufficient time and personal energy devoted to shopping for the right reporter? In the end, the lack of coverage may have come from the fact that too few people had too much to do: organizing rallies and writing leaflets. Perhaps someone or some group should have been given the public relations assignment as a sole responsibility. Or maybe we should have sought out *pro bono* help from a public relations firm with ties to labor.

2. The monitoring effort faced a difficult task given the distances and costs involved. It was difficult to sustain the credibility of the monitoring over the two-and-a-half years of the trial because the jurists' committee lacked a tangible presence in South Africa. One possible option might have been to have the committee issue an "interim" report which could have focused on the issues not immediately before the judge. The report could have criticized some of the due process questions, such as the lengthy detentions without charge and the denial of bail, without being seen as interfering with the progress of the trial.

3. The campaign suffered somewhat from the lack of central coordination. While some of its strength derived from the autonomy and spontaneity of the various support groups that emerged, all might have benefitted from better information flow and the cross-fertilization that such coordination might have provided. Although a tremendous number of hours and a great many union resources were devoted to the campaign, there were no full-time staff. All of us who worked on it had other responsibilities and work obligations. A perennial problem of trade unionism, too much to do and too little time to do it in, clearly was a culprit here. Had we been able to hire one person to work as a full-time coordinator, the campaign's effectiveness might have been greater. Absent that, we nevertheless could have done a better job of communication. Sometimes, a report on the status of the trial got circulated to key people in various cities. Other times it did not. We needed a better system, but failed to develop it.

I should note here that the fax machine has made a huge contribution to the process of communicating both to supporters of the campaign in the U.S. and, far more importantly, to and from South Africa. Before the fax, mail to and from South African unionists often never arrived. A reluctance to talk candidly over phones and the difficulty of getting visas to travel made communications difficult. Telexes worked, but that was a cumbersome process and few union offices had machines. Today, most of the unions in South Africa have fax machines that enable their statements, reports, legal documents and other communications to be sent to us with ease. Conversely, the fax made it possible for us to send down drafts of our publications and statements to NUMSA and to the attorneys on the Mayekiso case to ensure we were accurate and within political and legal bounds. Communications to and from South Africa also were made easier by the fact that we have the English language in common. Where language difficulties exist, they can seriously complicate a campaign like this one.

4. The campaign's outreach effort could have been better in getting those outside the union movement involved. Although excellent church and anti-apartheid ties were developed as noted earlier, they tended to be with those forces already deeply involved in South African issues. Much more could have been done with civil rights groups, for example. The Mayekiso campaign should have developed a deeper base of active support with the NAACP, the Southern Christian Leadership Conference and other organizations. The same is true of certain church groups. In retrospect, we should have targeted the Methodist church and sought its assistance, given that Mayekiso was raised in that faith. In a number of key cities where the campaign was active, we could have reached out more extensively to the black churches, which can be very potent politically.

Our efforts to get the interest of the Human Rights Division of the American Bar Association, while vigorous, did not get very far. Nor did attempts to enlist the help of the National Bar Association, which is made up of African American lawyers. Even the approaches to Amnesty International to get Mayekiso declared a "prisoner of conscience" lagged. It was never clear why AI hesitated, although eventually they did accord him that status, which put its many groups of letter writers behind the effort.

5. We did not realize the fund-raising potential for the campaign until it was nearly over. While the IMF, UAW, and other international unions carried the bulk of the expenses, there clearly was an excellent fund-raising base out there.

Many of us looked on in awe at UAW Local 600 after Kola Mayekiso's speech in April 1989 when members of the audience stood up and pledged donations that totaled more than $8,000. That money and other funds raised during her trip went to support the families of the accused and to help pay legal bills. Given the nearly three-year duration of the case, we missed opportunities to raise more money at the grassroots level.

6. The campaign could have benefitted from coming up with ideas, in addition to filling out the postcards, which would have given union members something they could do to help. Once the card had been filled out, there was a sense of involvement, but we

needed to develop more options for individual activity in the campaign. People want to feel they are making a difference, and while we built a good base of interest, we were light on activities the rank-and-file could embrace.

7. A potential danger in a campaign such as this one is relying too much on lawyers. Happily, the pitfalls were avoided, in large part due to the fact that Mayekiso's attorneys were extremely respectful of their clients decisionmaking roles and the democratic structure of the union. In addition to being extremely competent, they also understood the importance of the international campaign.

Given NUMSA's scarce resources, it would have been unrealistic to expect the union to have someone in court each day monitoring the developments and communicating them to the U.S. and the other centers of solidarity activity. The Cheadle, Thompson & Haysom lawyers played this role and did so with great sensitivity.

Within the South African context, a number of the functions that might be done in-house by an American union are often performed by people outside the direct employ of the union: legal assistance, research help, etc. Those individuals and groups have been an important force in the building of strong unions. But there are potential dangers, avoided in this case, that can come from relying too heavily on outside forces, rather than the unions themselves for communications, analysis and strategy.

8. Another danger, again avoided for the most part, but worth noting, is that in devoting great energy to a campaign such as this one, we ignore other developments and issues worthy of our support.

The hunger strikes by detainees that swept the prisons of South Africa beginning in late February 1989 are an example. They were an important set of protests, and while we continued our work on the Mayekiso campaign, the UAW also began a series of rolling, 48-hour fasts to show our support for the detainees' hunger strikes. Bieber kicked off the fast, and two days later it was picked up by another UAW officer and so on from February through to the union's convention in June.

During this period, we helped teach health and safety seminars (with one occurring in neighboring Swaziland because of visa problems getting into South Africa). We carried on the Shell boycott. We fought for a tougher, more comprehensive sanctions bill in the Congress. And so on.

The lesson must be that a solidarity campaign, no matter how important, should not overwhelm to the point where it causes other important aspects of an international struggle to be totally ignored. Priorities must be set, and we must be able to handle a number of activities at the same time.

9. Conclusion

The campaign for justice for Moses Mayekiso is over. This paper has attempted to describe some elements of that campaign. No doubt there are many parts of the story still to be told by others who saw it from their own vantage points. Others may draw different lessons from the experience. That is as it should be.

In the end, though, all can agree about one thing: five black South African activists are free today to pursue their struggle, instead of rotting in apartheid's jails. Others, however, are not free and they need our help whether they be in South Africa or South Korea, El Salvador or Indonesia, Czechoslovakia, or Chile. Some are not free because they are in prison; others because they are exploited by employers which place profit before justice.

In the end, we take on campaigns of international labor solidarity because we believe the chant we shouted so often in front of the South African embassy in Washington: "None of us is free, until all of us are free."

Epilogue

Since this paper was written in 1989, massive changes have occurred in South Africa, including the release of Nelson Mandela and the repeal of a number of apartheid laws. Some, including President George Bush, rushed to declare apartheid dead.

Yet in 1992, black South Africans still do not have the basic political freedoms such as the right to vote. Nor do they have the economic empowerment that a post-apartheid society must bring.

And while President De Klerk has managed to project through the news media an essentially false image of a so-called "new South Africa," the reality is far different. For example, his government recently was found to have funded an Inkatha-controlled union federation, the United Workers Union of South Africa, which has sought to undermine COSATU and its affiliates and has fomented violence in factories and hostels.

Unionists have borne the brunt of violent attacks often initiated by Inkatha, the political vehicle of Chief Gatsha Buthelezi.

The apartheid government also provided covert funding for Inkatha in a now admitted attempt to weaken the ANC as negotiations over a new constitution for South Africa began.

Despite some 2,000 deaths in township violence in the last year, the De Klerk government has failed to bring indictments in all but a handful of cases.

Mayekiso, free to continue his union work, was re-elected as general secretary of NUMSA in June 1991.

Appendix 1

The following is the text of UAW President Owen Bieber's telex to the South African Commissioner of Police:

Moses Mayekiso, general secretary of the Metal and Allied Workers Union, is currently being held in John Vorster Square in JHB. He is detained under Section 29 of the Internal Security Act in solitary confinement. I am informed that he has not been allowed to be seen by his attorneys or family and that no reasons have been given for his detention.

He is kept in a cell with lights on 24 hours a day and TV cameras monitoring him at all times, and has been denied basic necessities such as reading material other than the Bible. The food given to him is not, in our opinion, adequate.

I am communicating my strong demand that I be allowed to visit Moses Mayekiso to make an independent assessment of his condition.

As president of the United Auto Workers union representing over 1.1 million members in the USA, I am deeply concerned over Mayekiso's detention. He is a top official of a union we regard as our counterpart. Both UAW and MAWU are affiliated to the International Metalworkers' Federation, and I serve as the president of the IMF World Auto Council.

We strongly urge his immediate release and intend to support the broad international campaign to bring Mayekiso's case—and those of other union detainees including Jerry Moropa and Petrus Tom and others I have previously communicated about to the State President—to the widest possible public attention.

I am in South Africa all week and can be reached through Mayekiso's lawyers, Cheadle, Thompson & Haysom Tel. 011–724–0221, so that appropriate arrangements can be made for me to see Mayekiso promptly and to take him reading material and food.

OWEN BIEBER
PRESIDENT, UNITED AUTO WORKERS

Appendix 2

Those who accepted UAW President Owen Bieber's invitation to serve on the American Jurists' Committee Monitoring the Case of Moses Mayekiso were:

–Griffin Bell, former U.S. Attorney General, who for 15 years served as federal judge on the U.S. Circuit Court of Appeals for the Fifth Circuit;

–William Coleman, a lawyer and Chair of the NAACP Legal Defense and Education Fund, who had been U.S. Transportation Secretary;

–Marvin Frankel, a New York City attorney, who for 13 years served on the U.S. District Court for the Southern District of New York;

–Arthur J. Goldberg, who served on the U.S. Supreme Court from 1962–65 following two years as Secretary of Labor—now deceased;

–Elizabeth Holtzman, then District Attorney for Brooklyn, N.Y., who served previously as a Member of the U.S. Congress;

–Damon Keith, a federal judge on the U.S. Circuit Court of Appeals for the Sixth Circuit, who formerly was Chair of the Michigan Civil Rights Commission;

–Abner Mikva, a federal judge on the U.S. Circuit Court of Appeals for D.C., who previously served five terms as a Member of the U.S. Congress;

–Eleanor Holmes Norton, a law professor at Georgetown University, who is the former Chair of the Equal Employment Opportunity Commission;

–Stephen Reinhardt, a federal judge on the U.S. Circuit Court of Appeals for the Ninth Circuit, who had been President of the Los Angeles Police Commission; and,

–Benno Schmidt, Jr., the President of Yale University, who formerly was the Dean of Columbia University Law School.

Notes

1. Mongane Wally Serote, *To Every Birth Its Blood* (1981), quoted in M. Sarakinsky, *From 'Freehold Township' To 'Model Township'—A Politi-*

cal History of Alexandra: 1905–1983 (Dissertation, University of the Witwatersrand, 1984).

2. Steven Friedman, *Building Tomorrow Today—African Workers in Trade Unions, 1970–1984* (Johannesburg: Raven Press, 1987), 5.

Editors' Suggested Readings

Adler, Glenn. *Withdrawal Pains: General Motors and Ford Disinvest from South Africa.* The Graduate School and University Center of the City University of New York, Center for Labor-Management Policy Studies, Occasional Paper no. 6 (November 1989).

Baskin, Jeremy. *Striking Back: A History of COSATU.* Johannesburg: Ravan Press, 1991. Ravan Press books can be obtained in the U.S. through Ohio University Press, Scott Quadrangle, Athens OH 45701.

Bendiner, Burton. "Trade Unions and the Multinational Corporations in South Africa and some Developing Countries." Burton Bendiner, *International Labour Affairs: The World Trade Unions and the Multinational Companies.* Oxford: Clarendon Press, 1987.

Danaher, Kevin. *The Political Economy of U.S. Policy Toward South Africa.* Boulder, CO: Westview, 1985.

———. *In Whose Interest?: A Guide to U.S.-South Africa Relations.* Washington, D.C.: Institute for Policy Studies, 1984.

Friedman, Stephen. *Building Tomorrow Today: African Workers in Trade Unions, 1970–1984.* Johannesburg: Ravan Press, 1987.

Labor Research Review, vol. 13 (Spring 1989).

Lambert, Rob and Eddie Webster. "The Re-emergence of Political Unionism in Contemporary South Africa?" William Cobbett and Robin Cohen, eds., *Popular Struggles in South Africa.* Trenton, NJ: Africa World Press, 1988.

MacShane, Denis, Martin Plaut, and David Ward. *POWER! Black Workers and the Struggle for Freedom in South Africa.* Nottingham, England: Spokesman, 1984.

Mufson, Steven. *Fighting Years—Black Resistance and the Struggle for a New South Africa.* Boston: Beacon Press, 1990.

Ray, Ellen. *Dirty Work 2: the CIA in Africa.* Secaucus, NJ: Lyle Stuart, 1979.

Seidman, Ann and Neva Seidman. *South Africa and U.S. Multinational Corporations.* Westport, CT: Lawrence Hill, 1978.

South African Labor Bulletin. 8 issues per subscription. P.O. Box 3851, Johannesburg, South Africa, 2000.

Part Four

Conclusion

The eight chapters in this volume reflect a wide range of union programs and activities, and tell a varied story about labor's experiences in the changing international and national political economy. Some of the chapters report on joint labor-management programs promoted in the 1980s, and touted by management and international unions. But the authors tell the side of the story as experienced by rank-and-file members and staff members responsible for carrying them out. They present problems which they and their unions find difficult to address, especially management's retention of unilateral control over investment and production. In these chapters, management too frequently could ultimately ignore labor's demands for improved health and safety and affirmative action. Some of the chapters advance strategies for overcoming these setbacks.

In other chapters, the authors' unions achieved modest successes, whether organizing new workers, or constructing principled foreign policies. Together the chapters present hopeful union initiatives to reverse the long-term trend of declining union membership, influence, and power.

Above all, these chapters raise the issue of control, and the limited extent of worker participation in companies' central decisionmaking processes. It cannot simply be assumed that workers will benefit from the changes in production techniques, new technologies, and corporate reorganization. Indeed, these accounts emphasize that deskilling—as much as enhancement of skills—results from such changes. Furthermore, labor's descent is connected to the decline of regional economies, especially northeastern cities with an industrial economic base. Management control over relocation, production and investment has signalled an increase in runaway shops to non-union regions in the U.S. or across our southern borders and overseas, and the subcontracting of work to non-union shops. Unions in the meatpacking, auto, garment, machine, bakery, confectionery, and tobacco industries have been challenged and wounded by the downsizing of plants and the loss of jobs. Robbins, Rosen, Chen, Strauss and Scannell relate their union's struggles in the changing industrial economy, and put forth programs and/or strategies to find ways to ensure not only that restructuring avoids degradation on the job, but that it also empowers workers.

Collectively, they ask the questions: restructuring on whose terms, and how must unions change to challenge management? Their inquiries confront the system of labor-management relations that has been largely sanctioned by both sides from the 1930s until the present. The social contract accepted collective bargaining over certain well-defined issues, and sharply confined workers' activities. The passage of the 1947 Taft-Hartley Act which banned wildcat strikes and outlawed secondary actions such as boycotts and sitdown strikes, the 1959 Landrum-Griffin Act which obligated unions to open their books to the government, and the anti-labor policies of the Reagan and Bush administrations, have further limited the scope and power of unions and workers. The employer's obligation to bargain has largely been limited to matters of wages, benefits, and working conditions. Unions have deferred to management on decisions concerning the company's economic position including investment strategies, profits, relocation, technology, and production. Thus, labor is not in a position, legally or structurally, to bargain over the terms of new forms of international competition and workplace restructuring which began in the 1970s and which will escalate in the nineties. The social contract worked to provide workers with bread-and-butter benefits in times of industrial growth. However, the imbalance of power favors the employer during a period of crisis and restructuring.[1]

The chapters all point to the detrimental effects on unions and their members by the narrow limits of the old social contract and they urge that the contract be expanded beyond the traditional terms of collective bargaining. An expanded social contract must include at least three components: a redefinition of relations between capital and labor at the point of production with workers gaining rights beyond the limited agenda of traditional collective bargaining; a broad agenda for the working class which closely meshes workplace rights with broader social and political rights, and which implies an alliance between labor and other social movements; and a closer linking of domestic and international workers movements.

At the first level, the papers show how workers' ability to bargain over health and safety, job security, and retrenchment are drastically curtailed by their lack of participation in key investment decisions and technology choices, which remain the almost exclusive prerogative of management. The steel workers at A. O. Smith, as Rosen showed, constructed an elaborate health and safety system in a plant which, unbeknownst to them, was undergoing drastic downsizing resulting from transfer of work to non-union satellites. Scannell's essay calls for new contract language which expands negotiable issues to the point of production, especially the design, introduction, and operation of new technologies. The advancement of collective bargaining into the sphere now reserved for capital should give labor not only the power to upgrade workers skills, but also the leverage to protect workers health and safety and job security, and promote the hiring and training of new groups of workers. This certainly implies better programs than those tried in the 1980s and whose failure is so vividly described by Robbins, Rosen and Strauss. Meaningful health and safety and affirmative action programs and other approaches designed to improve the quality of worklife are doomed unless unions too can exert economic control.

The second element of the social contract demands that workers and their unions develop new strategies which link workers' rights at the point of production to a broader social and political vision. In fact, a progressive economic role for unions cannot be achieved without addressing issues such as discrimination, civil rights and democracy. Current attitudes and practices sometimes undermine labor's ability to develop new organizing strategies even as its numbers are declining. The labor movement needs to work for political reform and social change both in its' own formal structures and in the national and international society. The significance of this broader political commitment is clearly illustrated in the essays by Chen, Eaton, Fellner, and Stillman. Chen, for example, discusses the intertwined social and economic exploitation, exacerbated by the shrinking of New York City's industrial economy, endured by new immigrant Asian workers. The potential to organize these workers in large numbers can be realized if the city's unions develop programs sensitive to their needs, culture, and experiences. Strauss, too, shows how the commitment to reform in the workplace is shaped by prevailing practices and attitudes in the society as a whole. The impetus for affirmative action in her company came neither from the union nor the company, but from a caucus of women workers who were able to appeal to the EEOC. The effectiveness of the intervention, however, was blunted by the shortsighted vision of the union and company, and eventually reversed as the Reagan Administration hostility towards affirmative action mortally wounded the EEOC. Perhaps Barbara Bordwell of the NEA, interviewed by Fellner, expresses this nexus best. "(Our union) sometimes get(s) criticized by members who don't understand why we have a position on Central America, on abortion, on god knows what. But there is a majority who believe there is a connection to organizing and what we produce for workers. If the work is just to get a contract, and you don't have a vision to empower masses and masses of people to change the country, then it will never occur. We'll just have better contracts. If the organizer's vision is too small, the union will be too small."

At the third level, the new social contract demands a recasting of unions' international alliances and politics. Business unionism has also stifled the formation of transcontinental alliances between unions even in an era of global economic interdependence. Yet, present developments in the world economy demand international labor solidarity more than ever. For example, "Europe 1992," the creation of a European common market, will establish greater mobility of workers, goods, services, and capital across the borders of the 12 member-states of the European community. The unions in these countries are concerned about "social dumping,"[2] and other management moves which would impair workers' interests. The U.S. - Mexico Free Trade Agreement, now being debated in Congress, is opposed by American trade unions who are alarmed that it will mean the erosion of income levels or even the loss of many jobs for workers in the textile, apparel, auto, steel and electronic manufacturing industries. Companies will increase their movement across the border into Mexico where they set up *maquiladoras*: unsafe, unregulated, U.S. owned plants, where Mexican workers (often including children) earn on average less than $1.50 per hour.[3] For many of the same reasons, Canadian labor unions opposed the 1989 U.S. - Canada Free Trade Agreement, and Western European unions fear the influx of Eastern European immigrants into their job markets. Labor needs to have a voice in determining solutions that will prevent workers from being played off against one another, solutions which can protect and link workers' rights in different countries. Without a united stance by labor, such international agreements and laws will erode workers' rights and benefits in the U.S. and advanced European countries. The dismantling of these standards will ensure the continued exploitation of workers in less economically advanced European countries and the Third World. Fellner's and Stillman's chapters recognize the need to build international labor solidarity and they suggest strategies to establish these bonds.

Finally, the authors are all too painfully aware of the economic pressures on firms: foreign competition, the need to invest in expensive technologies, and the imperative to pursue increased productivity and profit, and try to factor these considerations into their strategies. Rosen, for example, reports on how A. O. Smith workers tried to weigh off benefits and losses resulting from the introduction of new, less dangerous presses which were more efficient and could contribute to job loss. In another example, Chen describes how her union had to balance their drive to organize new members in the burgeoning sector of marginal family-owned garment firms, where unionization could threaten the viability of the enterprise. Not only do the unionists address these issues, but unlike the bulk of popular commentators and academic accounts of economic restructuring, they do so from the perspective of workers' interests in employment stabilization, enskilling, and empowerment. They show that if workers are to take such economic concerns seriously, they must participate in crucial investment and production decisions as well as profit sharing. The seriousness of their accounts indicates that their ideas deserve to be engaged in debates over restructuring. It also suggests the importance of vesting far more responsibility for governing the economy in unions, rather than in an increasingly footloose management.

The authors' goals demand, at a minimum, a strong commitment to organizing, to expanding the union movement into the most dynamic sectors of the economy, and into those constituencies most degraded by the economic transformations of the 1980s. They also require a political vision which can promote the agendas of such a movement at state and national levels, a movement which above all directly embraces workers' concerns at the workplace and beyond.

The work by the Gompers' fellows is the product of on-going efforts by rank-and-file members, as well as local and national staff to come to terms with immediate problems confronting them in their daily lives. But they go well beyond a concern for the routine issues of union work, and begin to define the groundwork of a new social contract for labor. These chapters, however, do not purport to provide a blueprint for labor's resuscitation, nor to construct a program for achieving a new social contract. At the end of the day, such an ambitious task will be worked out through struggle and not through arguments in books. Rather, the chapters have a much more modest goal of providing a rough guide to the broad issues unions will need to consider. Their valuable experience and inside perspective ought to be brought into debates on the future of the labor movement in the changing political economy of the 1990s and beyond.

Notes

1. For a discussion of the post-war labor relations system, the "industrial pluralist paradigm," and its legacy, see Katherine Van Wezel Stone, "The Post-War Paradigm in American Labor Law," *Yale Law Review* 90 (June 1981): 1509–80.

2. "Social dumping occurs if regional disparities in wages and working conditions drive down standards in high standard countries, or cause them to lose market share." Seamus O'Cleireacain, *The Emerging Social Dimension of Europe 1992*, The Graduate School and University Center of the City University of New York, Center for Labor-Management Policy Studies, Occasional Paper no. 4 (14 April 1989): 11.

3. Ann Lowrey and David Corn, "Mexican Trade Bill: Fast Track to Unemployment," *The Nation*, vol. 252, no. 21 (June 3, 1991): 735–738; "Free Trade's 'Competitive Edge'," *UAW Solidarity* (May 1991): 15–19; Ernesto Mora, "Worker Solidarity Across the Border," *Labor Unity*, vol. 77, no. 2 (March - April 1991): 12–13; and "Bahr: Social Charter Needed Before U.S.-Mexico Reach Free Trade Agreement," *CWA News*, vol. 51, no. 2 (March 1991): 10.

Glossary

AAC	Alexandra Action Committee
ACTWU	Amalgamated Clothing and Textile Workers Union
AFL-CIO	American Federation of Labor-Congress of Industrial Organizations
AFSCME	American Federation of State, County and Municipal Employees
AFT	American Federation of Teachers
AI	Amnesty International
ANC	African National Congress
BC&T	Bakery, Confectionery, and Tobacco Workers' International Union
BCTWIU	Bakery, Confectionery, and Tobacco Workers' International Union
BEST	Bringing Employee Skills Together
BLS	Bureau of Labor Statistics
BNA	Bureau of National Affairs
CAP	community action program
CIM	computer-integrated manufacturing
CLUW	Coalition of Labor Union Women
COLA	Cost of Living Allowance
COSATU	Congress of South African Trade Unions
CPSA	Civil and Public Services Association
CSWA	Chinese Staff and Workers' Association
CTR	Carpal Tunnel Release
CTS	Carpal Tunnel Syndrome
CUNY	City University of New York
CWA	Communications Workers of America
CWIU	Chemical Workers Industrial Union
EEOC	Equal Employment Opportunity Commission
ESL	English as a Second Language
FOSATU	Federation of South African Trade Unions
GE	General Electric

307

HERE	Hotel Employees and Restaurant Employees International Union
IAM	International Association of Machinists
IBP	Iowa Beef Packers
ICFTU	International Confederation of Free Trade Unions
ILGWU	International Ladies' Garment Workers' Union
IMF	International Metalworkers' Federation
IUE	International Union of Electronic, Electrical, Technical, Salaried and Machine Workers
LCLAA	Labor Coalition on Latin American Advancement
MAWU	Metal and Allied Workers Union
MDM	Mass Democratic Movement
MICWU	Motor Industry Combined Workers Union
MIT	Massachusetts Institute of Technology
MOTP	one-type training program
NAACP	National Association for the Advancement of Colored People
NAAWU	National Automobile and Allied Workers Union
NEA	National Education Association
NLRB	National Labor Relations Board
NSAIDs	non-steroidal anti-inflammatory drugs
NUMSA	National Union of Metalworkers of South Africa
NWU	National Writers Union
OSHA	Occupational Safety and Health Administration
PATCO	Professional Air Traffic Controllers Organization
PLC	programmed logic controller
PSI	Participative Systems Inc.
QPP	Quality Participation Program
QWL	Quality of Work Life
RTDs	repetitive trauma disorders
SACP	South African Communist Party
SACTU	South African Congress of Trade Unions
SAG	Screen Actors Guild
SDS	Students for a Democratic Society
SEIU	Service Employees' International Union
SNCC	Student Nonviolent Coordinating Committee
SPC	Statistical Process Control

TUC	British Trades Union Congress
TWIU	Tobacco Workers International Union
UAW	United Automobile Workers
UCLA	University of California at Los Angeles
UCLEA	University and College Labor Education Association
UDF	United Democratic Front
UE	United Electrical, Radio and Machine Workers of America
UFCW	United Food and Commercial Workers
UFW	United Farm Workers of America
UMWA	United Mine Workers of America
UPWA	United Packing Workers of America
VISTA	U.S. Volunteers in Service to America
VWFS	Vibration white finger syndrome
WILD	Women's Institute for Leadership Development
WISCOSH	Wisconsin Committee on Occupational Safety and Health

Contributors

GLENN ADLER is completing his Ph.D. in Political Science from Columbia University, on trade union organization by black workers in the South African automobile industry. He is a lecturer in Sociology at the University of the Witwatersrand, in Johannesburg, where he is also a member of the Sociology of Work Program, and is a former Styskal fellow at the Center for Labor-Management Policy Studies.

MAY YING CHEN is the Assistant Education Director for Local 23–25 in New York City of the International Ladies' Garment Workers Union. Before joining the ILGWU, she was an organizer for the Restaurant Workers. Currently she sits on the Executive Board of the Coalition of Labor Union Women, and is active in her community working on voter registration, political education, and parent-teacher organizations.

SUSAN C. EATON has served as Assistant to the President for Programs and Services at the Service Employees International Union as well as Western Regional Coordinator during her eleven years with the union. Since receiving the Gompers Award, she has taken a leave from the SEIU to study women's leadership in social change movements as a Fellow at Radcliffe College's Bunting Institute in Cambridge, Massachusetts.

KIM FELLNER was Executive Director of the National Writers' Union for the last four years. She has been a union staffer for fifteen years, first with the Service Employees' International Union, and then at the Screen Actors' Guild, where she was the speechwriter for then-president, Ed Asner.

VICTOR GOTBAUM is Samuel Gompers Professor of Labor and Management Relations at the City University Graduate School, and is Director of the Center for Labor-Management Policy Studies. From 1965–1987 he was Executive Director of District Council 37 of the American Federation of State, County and Municipal Employees.

TOM L. ROBBINS became fascinated with the union movement at his first union job in the meatpacking industry. He served in several offices including Chief Steward of the United Food and Commercial Workers Locals 191 and 179, subsequently becoming Business Agent for UFCW Local 230 in Ottumwa, Iowa. Since receiving the Gompers Award, he has completed a Legal Assistant program and enjoys working with local unions and labor oriented attorneys.

JONATHAN D. ROSEN served as safety officer for The Smith Steelworkers DALU #19806, Milwaukee, Wisconsin. He worked for the A. O. Smith company for 17 years as a welder, press operator, stock hanger, and assembler. Throughout that time he was an active member of the union, a steward, and chairman of the Union Safety Committee for eight years. Since receiving the Gompers Award, he is coordinating the Health and Safety Program for the New York State Public Employees Federation, AFL-CIO.

RAYMOND F. SCANNELL is Director of Research for the Bakery, Confectionery, and Tobacco Workers International Union (BC&T). He came to the BC&T in the fall of 1980 from Cornell University's School for Industrial and Labor Relations where he earned an MS in Organizational Behavior. He served as Assistant Director of Public Relations and Research & Education, as well as Assistant Editor of the *BCT News* prior to assuming his current position.

DON STILLMAN is the Director of Governmental and International Affairs for the United Auto Workers. He formerly served as the Director of Public Relations and Publications for the UAW. Prior to joining the Autoworkers, he edited the United Mine Workers' *Journal*, and was active in the Miners for Democracy movement.

SUSAN R. STRAUSS was a Shop Steward for Local 201 of the International Union of Electrical Workers. She has been a machinist since 1979 for the General Electric Co., in Lynn, Massachusetts. Since 1987 she has been an elected member of Local 201's Women's Committee and Legislative Committee. Before becoming a machinist, she was a doctoral candidate in Sociology and an Instructor in Sociology at the State University of New York, Binghamton.

DORIS SUAREZ is a doctoral candidate in Political Science at the Graduate School of the City University of New York. She is writing her dissertation on the new technology and its impact on the printing union in New York City. She is Special Assistant to the Deputy Director and a Styskal fellow at the Center for Labor-Management Policy Studies.

Index